THE LAW OF THE SEA

The role of the Irish delegation at the Third UN Conference

THE
LAW
OF THE
SEA

The role of the Irish delegation at the Third UN Conference

Mahon Hayes

RIA

The Law of the Sea: the role of the Irish delegation at the Third UN Conference

First published 2011

by Royal Irish Academy
19 Dawson St
Dublin 2

www.ria.ie

Copyright © 2011 Royal Irish Academy

This publication has received support from the Marine Law and Ocean Policy Centre, NUI Galway

NUI Galway
OÉ Gaillimh

ISBN 978-1-904890-72-0

British Library Cataloguing in Publication Data. A CIP catalogue record for this book is available from the British Library.

Printed in Ireland by Turner Print Group

10 9 8 7 6 5 4 3 2 1

CONTENTS

ACKNOWLEDGMENTS

Since venturing to write this memoir on the role of the Irish delegation at the Third United Nations Conference on the Law of the Sea I have enjoyed encouragement and assistance from many sources, and I would like to acknowledge at least some of them.

I deeply appreciate that I was given access to the relevant Department of Foreign Affairs archives, without which I could not have undertaken the task. In this respect, Patricia O'Brien, then Legal Adviser in the Department (now Legal Counsel to the United Nations), was immediately enthusiastic about my suggestion regarding the memoir. She then pursued on my behalf the granting, not only of the necessary permission in regard to the archives, but also the use of office space to facilitate their perusal. The then Secretary-General of the Department graciously acceded to these requests.

Several other officers of the legal division were extremely helpful in different ways (not least, in some cases, in providing patient assistance in regard to information technology, on which I was, and am, a novice). These included James Kingston, Declan Smyth (who was particularly generous with his time), Naomi Burke, Nuala Ní Mhuircheartaigh, Lisa Walshe, Paul Johnson and Ann Spollen.

A special word of thanks is due to Maureen Sweeney (formerly Keane). It was a huge advantage to me that she was in charge of the relevant files in the archives when I undertook my researches. As an official in the legal division at the time of the Conference and administrative assistant to the Irish delegation at most of the sessions, she was fully familiar with the subject and the documentation and ensured that all the relevant files were identified and made available.

Several of my colleagues in the Irish delegation encouraged the venture and were most helpful both in their advice and in filling gaps in my knowledge and recollections. These included Brendan Finucane (formerly of the Department of Finance and the National Board of Science and Technology), Piers Gardiner (formerly of the Geological Survey of Ireland), Geraldine Skinner and Paul Dempsey (both formerly of the Department of Foreign Affairs), and Agnes Aylward (formerly Breathnach and of the Taoiseach's Department). They all read early drafts, on which their comments were most useful, and continued to offer helpful observations. Time and mortality deprived me of the opportunity of seeking similar assistance from Con Cremin, James Kirwan, Raphael Siev and Aidan Mulloy (all from the Department of Foreign Affairs), Seamus Mallon (from Fisheries) and Colm Ó hEocha (from University College Galway and the National Science Council). All were valued friends whose absence I deeply regret for more important and personal reasons than that I could not avail of their help. I consulted some other delegates on specific details but was unable to reach several others for various reasons.

I appreciate the granting of access to the UCD Library and the helpfulness of the Library Staff, including my niece Karen Hayes. My first draft was read by my daughter Loraine Hayes, who has experience of writing and publishing articles on legal subjects. I valued her comments and suggestions and reassuring assessment that the work was both readable and interesting.

When I first envisaged this undertaking I did not have publication in mind. In fact my reaction was just that when Patricia O'Brien raised the question, and it was only when she pressed the point that I responded that consideration of publication was at least premature at that stage. I was subsequently persuaded to a more positive reaction by her urging and that of several of my colleagues, but particularly by Professor Ronan Long of the National University of Ireland, Galway (NUIG) and Micheál Ó Cinnéide of the Marine Institute (formerly of the Department of Foreign Affairs and briefly a member of the delegation at the Conference). I met both at a seminar on the law of the sea in Dublin and was invited to address the students at the Institute. Since then Ronan Long has been a tower of support, furnishing most useful comments on my draft, steering me through the maze of procedures leading to publication, persuading NUIG to grant the necessary funding and constantly encouraging me. I am most grateful to the Royal Irish Academy for its decision to undertake publication, as suggested by Ronan Long and on the basis of its own assessment; and to NUIG for providing the necessary funding. I thank also Ruth Hegarty, Helena King and Roisín Jones of the Academy's publications staff, for their considerate and helpful attitude during this process. Again I thank the Department of Foreign Affairs, more specifically the Minister, for permitting publication, and the Secretary-General, David Cooney, for his role in the lead-up to this decision. I greatly appreciate that Satya Nandan, a very significant personality at the Conference and in his subsequent United Nations appointments, acceded so kindly to my request to write the Foreword to this document.

ACKNOWLEDGEMENTS

Last but not least my family, my wife Kathleen and our children
Carolyn, Fiona, Loraine and Frank. In the 1970s when the Conference
was in full spate our children were teenagers and younger. My long
absences from home to attend the Conference sessions and other events
were presumably a burden on them all, if in different ways. Kathleen
was left to cope alone for lengthy periods with all the household
demands and the children's needs. I perhaps flatter myself that the children were conscious of neglect by their father. While my absence must
have had some impact, I am glad to be able to say that their later development did not suggest any long-term damage. More recently Kathleen
had to tolerate my preoccupation with the task of preparing this
memoir, and Loraine lent me the benefit of her proof reading skills at
the early stage and her lawyer's assessment of the coherence and read-
ability of the text. To all five I tender my regrets for neglecting them
and my thanks for their constant and invaluable support.

FOREWORD

This is an important treatise in which Ambassador Mahon Hayes has provided an account of the participation of the Irish delegation in the Third United Nations Conference on the Law of the Sea. In doing so he has made a significant contribution to the literature on the negotiating history of this important Conference that concluded with the adoption of the 1982 United Nations Convention on the Law of the Sea. The Convention is an important contribution to the rule of law and forms the basis of the modern legal framework for ocean governance. It has provided clarity, certainty and stability to the international law of the sea. Its widespread acceptance and application in state practice has earned it a place as one of the great achievements of the international community. It sets out principles and norms for the conduct of relations among states on maritime issues and in this way has made an immense contribution to the system for global peace and security of which the Charter of the United Nations is the foundation.

This treatise provides an important case study of how a small but effective delegation from a relatively small country planned, participated and pursued its national interests in what were difficult and protracted negotiations. The reader is presented with a rare insight into the internal processes of a country preparing for a major multilateral conference and the development and execution of national marine policy in one of the largest conferences with a complex and comprehensive agenda, the final outcome of which would change the political geography of nations and the world at large.

The study recounts the internal processes, which began with coordination meetings involving all government departments having competence in ocean-related matters. The law of the sea is multifaceted and deals with diverse issues, which are multidisciplinary in nature and therefore required input from experts in different fields. We are informed that the coordination involved the identification of issues of national interest for Ireland and the development of recommendations for policy decisions by government. The importance of selecting a competent delegation and ensuring at the national level that all key departments are adequately represented is highlighted.

The next phase is the actual participation in the Conference itself and the promotion of the national policy on a number of issues of critical interest to the country. The reader is provided with a narrative of the negotiating process covering more than twelve years, which includes three years of the preparatory phase. Ambassador Hayes was intimately involved in the preparation of national policies and in the negotiations at the Conference, eventually as leader of the Irish delegation. He has provided the reader with a fairly detailed session by session account from the perspective of the Irish delegation of the developments relating to some of the key issues at the Conference.

The negotiating process at the Conference was complex. As indicated in the text, the negotiations and discussions were held in diverse settings and the procedures followed differed according to the subject matter. There were formal and informal negotiations. Most of the difficult issues were resolved in informal meetings—either bilaterally or between coalitions of small or large groups having the same or similar interest on a particular issue. In addition, discussions on a number of key issues were held intersessionally at the initiative of individual delegations or groups of delegations most interested in the issue.

The Irish delegation played an active and constructive role in the negotiations on some of the core issues before the Conference that were of particular interest to Ireland and generally to the international community as a whole. These included issues such as the regime of islands, the definition of the continental shelf, the delimitation of boundaries between adjacent and opposite states, the regime for international navigation, the protection and preservation of the marine environment, and marine scientific research. An example of the delegation's constructive role was the proposal made by one of its members, Piers Gardiner, a geologist, on a technical formula for defining the outer limit of the continental shelf that formed the basis for an agreement on that difficult issue. Ambassador Hayes himself was the spokesman for one of the two groups that had taken different positions on the issue of the delimitation of boundaries between states with opposite and adjacent coasts. He also distinguished himself for his contributions to the resolution of other important issues of broader interest before the Conference. The Irish delegation was on the whole low-key, but quietly persuasive and effective in the resolution of a number of issues important to them. For the most part it was successful in achieving its national goal.

Ambassador Hayes has placed on record the Irish delegation's perspective on the negotiating history that led to the adoption of the 1982 United Nations Convention on the Law of the Sea. As he has stated this is not a comprehensive history of the Conference, but one that focuses on the developments relating to some of the key issues that were of interest to the Irish delegation and that were also central to the successful outcome of the negotiations. While this treatise will be of particular interest to Irish readers, it is nevertheless of interest to the larger international community. It will be welcomed by legal historians and those who study the progressive development of international law and the negotiating methods at multilateral conferences and by those interested in planning, preparation and execution of national policies at such conferences.

Satya N. Nandan CF, CBE
July 2009

Former United Nations Under-Secretary General for the Law of the Sea and Ocean Affairs, and the Special Representative of the Secretary-General for the Law of the Sea

Head of the Fiji Delegation to the Third United Nations Conference on the Law of the Sea, and Rapporteur of the Second Committee

PREFACE

This document is intended to be a narrative account of the negotiations at the Third United Nations Conference on the Law of the Sea (UNCLOS III) from the point of view of the participation of the Irish delegation. It does not purport to be a comprehensive overview of the Conference. Thus its focus is mainly on the issues in which Ireland had a significant interest and/or in which the delegation played an active role in intense negotiations, for example the questions of the outer limits of coastal state continental shelf jurisdiction, of delimitation of zones of marine jurisdiction between neighbouring states, of the marine zones appurtenant to islands, of fishery rights and conservation with special emphasis on anadromous species (salmon), of the rules applicable to marine scientific research (MSR) and transfer of technology (TOT) and of preservation of the marine environment. Some issues of national interest are more lightly touched on where the interest and its pursuit was shared with a wide number of other participants and/or where the negotiations were less intense, at least for the Irish delegation, for example the breadth and regime of the territorial seas and of the (new) exclusive economic zone (EEZ), as well as freedom of navigation. The account proceeds chronologically, following the successive sessions.

As a member state of the (then) European Economic Community (EEC), to which competences had been transferred by its members in some fields covered in the negotiations (notably at that time fisheries), Ireland acted in coordination with the other members and the EEC Commission in pursuance of common EEC interests in these fields. Ireland also had an interest in ensuring that the EEC's representation of the member states in the fields in which competence had been transferred to it, and the granting within the EEC of mutual and exclusive rights among member states, would be recognised and afforded priority in the future convention. In due course it became apparent that this objective could be adequately achieved only by securing the eligibility of the EEC to become a party to the convention. This became a significant issue at the Conference and one of great importance to the EEC. Accordingly it received considerable attention from the member states, which were all involved in furthering the objective, under the leadership of the successive EEC presidencies, including the Irish Presidency at two of the sessions. The Irish delegation, of course, participated in EEC coordination on these issues, which was conducted both at the sessions of UNCLOS III and between sessions.

The EEC's then practice (later intensified) of seeking cooperation among the member states in foreign policy fields not within the transferred competences, of course, also involved the delegation similarly throughout the Conference. Combined action under that practice then depended on unanimity of the member states, which was only infrequently achieved by them at the Conference, due to the diversity of their interests. However, there were also cases where delegations (including the Irish delegation) having no significant national interest in an issue, in a spirit of solidarity with their fellow EEC members that had such an interest, supported combined action in pursuit of that interest. As holder of the EEC Presidency for six months in both 1975 and 1979, the Irish delegation had the responsibility of organising this coordination and cooperation exercise at and around the Third Session and the second part of the Eighth Session. The delegation also represented the EEC and/or its member states at those sessions in the deliberations and negotiations, as appropriate, including negotiations on ensuring that the EEC was enabled to become a party to the convention.

There was a wide area of negotiation at UNCLOS III in which the Irish delegation was less active, including some issues that were very important in the overall context, for example the rights of passage through those straits that, if territorial sea limits were extended, would consist totally of territorial waters, whereas they had previously had high seas channels; and particularly the regime for the international seabed area (ISBA). However, the delegation was always concerned to promote consensus on reasonable solutions and maintained an awareness of all the difficult issues. In the later sessions it devoted considerable efforts to promoting solutions to some of these issues that were still outstanding. This attitude was inspired not least by the perception that adoption of, and subsequent wide adherence to, the intended convention was in Ireland's national interest.

The events preceding UNCLOS III are examined in Chapter I for the purpose only of setting the scene against which the negotiations were undertaken, and some developments of less importance in regard to the main issues addressed in the account are not mentioned.

The account ends with the final signature meeting in Montego Bay in Jamaica in December 1982, followed by an assessment of the results in the Conclusion. It does not deal with subsequent events such as the negotiations on the application of Part XI of the convention (on the regime for the ISBA) and straddle (fish) stocks.

Finally it should be indicated that this, as a narrative account, is concerned more with the thrust than the exact detail of developments and negotiations. Accordingly, references and citation of authorities are not as assiduous as would be appropriate in a purely legal treatise. Likewise, it is frequently the substance rather than the exact text of proposals that is addressed.

The UNCLOS III records are limited because much of the negotiation was conducted informally and without official record, although conclusions and formal decisions were, of course, reached in formal meetings. The official records are thus the authoritative source in this respect and were fully consulted. The University of Virginia Commentary contains much detailed information on the negotiations in general and was a most useful checking reference. However, the main source consulted was the Irish Government records. These are not always comprehensive in their treatment and are occasionally incomplete. In examining them the author was reminded that the purpose of civil service records is administration and not the facilitation of researchers or historians—or even a narrator. This source was complemented by reference to some personal papers retained by the author that occasionally served to fill *lacunae*. Contemporary published articles by members of the delegation were extremely useful, particularly in identifying the timing of developments in ideas as the Conference progressed. Publications by others were also consulted, although their varying emphases limited their usefulness for the specific purpose of this account. Personal memory was also a significant source, both that of the author and his delegation colleagues, and was occasionally the only source for some of the delegates' experiences. As this source is inevitably prone to fallibility, every feasible effort, including careful cross-checking with these colleagues and with contemporary documentation, was made to achieve accuracy. It would be rash to conclude that all errors have thereby been eliminated, but the author is satisfied that they have been reduced to an acceptable minimum. Insofar as errors have, nevertheless, survived, the responsibility is totally that of the author.

This account is, of course, neither exhaustive nor exclusive. The writer hopes that others will be encouraged to address the subject in whole or in part. In particular there is obviously scope in individual topics for more detailed treatment.

Mahon Hayes
September 2010

Chapter I

BACKGROUND

The post-medieval law of the sea could be said to date from the period following the great fifteenth- and sixteenth-century discovery voyages, with the writings of the distinguished Dutch scholar Hugo Grotius at the beginning of the seventeenth century as a milestone. As was the case with international law generally, the law of the sea emerged in the first instance as customary law through state practice (partly based on pre-Middle Ages rules, including codes adopted in the Roman Empire), supplemented by interstate agreements, the opinions of highly regarded jurists and common elements in national laws, etc. Thus, by evolution through generally accepted principles, rules of customary international law developed. At an early stage these rules largely divided the seas between narrow coastal belts (*mare clausum*, territorial seas), which were subject to national jurisdiction of the respective coastal states, and the rest of the oceans (*mare liberum*, high seas), which was free to all, subject to certain broad regulation. This development process was facilitated by the fact that the seas were an object of common use by states, thereby necessitating a regime as a practical requirement. The regime that emerged was naturally heavily influenced by the contemporary major maritime powers who, of course, tailored it to suit their own interests.

Efforts to achieve consolidation/codification of the rules at the end of the nineteenth century and, under the auspices of the League of Nations, between the two World Wars, including the 1930 Hague Conference, proved abortive. Nevertheless, draft codes produced in the course of these ventures by highly regarded non-governmental institutions were eventually helpful in moves towards codification. In the meantime there were new developments giving rise to new concerns and problems, for example conservation of fishery resources and coastal state desires for control of offshore fisheries, environmental protection (particularly from hazardous waste) and development of technology enabling exploitation of seabed mineral resources. New concepts were invented in response to these concerns.

After the Second World War the United Nations Organisation became the principal instrument of worldwide international cooperation. The UN General Assembly, in implementation of the United Nations Charter requirement to initiate studies and make recommendations for progressive development and codification of international law, set up the International Law Commission (ILC) in 1947, to undertake this task.

The ILC began its work in 1949 and, not surprisingly, one of the topics it addressed at an early stage was the law of the sea. In 1956 the ILC, in its annual report to the UN General Assembly, submitted a set of draft articles (with commentaries) on the territorial sea (without a provision on breadth), and the high seas (including the contiguous zone, the continental shelf, fishing and conservation of living resources and preservation of the environment). Coastal state continental shelf jurisdiction, mainly in respect of minerals, first formally promulgated in the 1945 (US) Truman Proclamations, was accepted in these draft articles.

In early 1957 the UN General Assembly convened a diplomatic conference, the United Nations Conference on the Law of the Sea (UNCLOS I), with a view to adoption of conventions on the law of the sea that would be generally acceptable and would, after wide ratification, comprise acknowledged rules of international law on the subject. The set of draft articles prepared by the ILC was the principal basis for the work of the Conference. UNCLOS I met in Geneva in early 1958 and adopted four separate conventions on, respectively, the Territorial Sea and the Contiguous Zone; the High Seas; Fishing and Conservation of the Living Resources of the High Seas; and the Continental Shelf. By 1966 all four conventions had entered into force, having received the requisite number of ratifications/accessions.

In 1958 the UN General Assembly convened another conference, UNCLOS II, to deal with the issues that proved intractable at UNCLOS I, notably the breadth of the territorial sea and of coastal state fishery limits. UNCLOS II met in 1960 but its efforts to resolve these issues also proved unsuccessful.

Ireland, as an island state, having security concerns, dependent heavily on international transport for trade vital to the well-being of its economy, having an economically important tourism industry reliant on *inter alia* clean waters and beaches, and also having significant offshore potential in both living (important for its expanding fishing industry) and non-living (to boost its limited land-based minerals) resources, had obvious national interests in law of the sea rules.

Moreover, it had a general interest in enhancement of international order and avoidance of potential conflict through broad acceptance of, and thus certainty in, such rules. Having been elected a member of the UN in 1955 it was also concerned to play its part in achieving these desirable developments. Ireland participated in both UNCLOS I and UNCLOS II. It signed all four 1958 conventions but, in the event, did not ratify any of them. A detailed examination of all the implications of each convention would have been an essential step towards a decision on ratification. At the time this could not have been undertaken by the relevant, but limited, staffing resources, which were fully taken up with more immediately urgent matters. A cursory consideration of the Convention on the Continental Shelf inclined towards its ratification to protect jurisdiction over the Irish state's potentially very extensive shelf area, bearing in mind that this convention was generally regarded as comprising progressive development of international law rather than codification of pre-existing law. However, some doubts arose as to the desirability of accepting the convention provisions on the outer limits of shelf jurisdiction and on delimitation of shelf areas between neighbouring states (although, interestingly, in preliminary correspondence in 1965 with the UK on division of the common Irish–British shelf, the Irish side indicated that the convention delimitation rule was acceptable). The doubts on both aspects were, however, significantly reinforced subsequently by the decision of the International Court of Justice (ICJ) in the North Sea cases in 1969 (see below).

Despite the entry into force of the 1958 conventions, law of the sea questions were still in a state of flux in the 1960s. The tendency of South American countries to claim coastal state jurisdiction over wide sea areas, dubbed successively and variously 'territorial sea', 'patrimonial sea', 'maritime zone', 'epicontinental sea', etc., with corresponding variations in the regimes proposed, had derived encouragement from the Truman Proclamations and were not inhibited by the results of UNCLOS I and II. Elsewhere, notably among the newly independent African states, support was emerging for wide coastal state exclusive fisheries or economic zones, a new concept. This position was inspired mainly by fears, not unjustified, of these underdeveloped countries that the fish stocks off their coasts would be severely depleted, or even exhausted, by long-distance fishing fleets (from developed countries), often accompanied by factory ships. Canada, sharing these concerns and also anxious about the threat of modern developments to its Arctic waters, claimed extended jurisdiction in some of its coastal areas, at least for conservation purposes. The Philippines and Indonesia renamed the seas between their myriad islands as archipelagic waters, claiming them to be part of their internal waters and, incidentally, greatly enlarging the areas of marine jurisdiction they claimed. The threat of pollution from shipping, especially the new fleets of enormous oil tankers (which emerged following the closing of the Suez Canal) and vessels carriers of hazardous waste, to fisheries and coastal amenities (soon to be realised in the *Torrey Canyon* disaster in 1967) was a source of anxiety, at least to coastal states other than maritime powers.

In 1961, following the failure of UNCLOS I and II to agree on the breadth of coastal state areas of jurisdiction over fisheries, Iceland implemented its previously signalled intention to declare an extension of its fishery limits to twelve miles, measured in part from straight baselines. Although similar and even greater extensions had been declared by several states across the world, it was the first such claim by a Western European state and triggered the famous 'cod war' between Iceland and the UK. The drawing of straight baselines between headlands and islands (from which the coastal state could measure its marine zones) had been upheld by the ICJ in 1951 in the Anglo-Norwegian fisheries case. This acceptance was reflected, with appropriate restrictions, in the 1958 Convention on the Territorial Sea and the Contiguous Zone. It was then implemented by several other states that had not previously done so (including Ireland, in 1959), thus effectively extending their areas of jurisdiction. Again following the failure of UNCLOS II to agree on the breadth of areas of coastal state fisheries jurisdiction, fourteen European states bordering on the Atlantic and the North Sea (including Ireland and one Eastern European country, Poland, but not Norway or Iceland) negotiated the London Fisheries Convention in 1964. This convention, which entered into force in 1966, reciprocally accepted establishment of coastal state fishery limits of twelve miles (and the straight baselines drawn by the participants), subject to rights in the outer six-mile band for those who had traditionally fished there.

In 1969 the ICJ delivered a very significant judgement in the North Sea cases concerning delimitation of the continental shelf between neighbouring states, in which the parties were West Germany (the Federal Republic of Germany (the FRG)) versus the Netherlands and Denmark. The judgement held that the provision in the 1958 convention on delimitation of the continental shelf between neighbouring states did not comprise a generally applicable rule of international law. It indicated the criteria that should therefore be applied, in accordance with generally applicable customary international law rules, in delimitation cases where not all of the parties were bound by the convention.

Delimitation should be by agreement between the parties and in accordance with equitable principles. In reaching its conclusion the ICJ also held that rights to the shelf did not depend on their being exercised, and set out the legal basis for coastal state shelf jurisdiction in terms of prolongation of the state's land territory. These findings also undermined the 1958 convention provision that based determination of outer limits of jurisdiction on alternative depth and exploitability criteria—already outdated and discredited by rapid advances in relevant underwater technology. The ICJ conclusions on the basis of coastal state continental shelf jurisdiction specifically cited Article 2 of the 1958 convention, which in turn drew heavily on the Truman Proclamations (see above). These conclusions, as well as the trend towards widening coastal state areas of jurisdiction, inclined towards Ireland's national interest.

On 1 November 1967 the Permanent Representative of Malta to the UN, Ambassador Arvin Pardo, addressed the General Assembly at considerable length on the resources and potential for development of the deep seabed. He advocated reservation of the seabed and ocean floor beyond the limits of national jurisdiction exclusively for peaceful purposes, and exploitation of its resources in the interest of mankind as a whole. He expressed concern about the dangers inherent in the potential extension of superpower rivalry to this sphere, and in a free-for-all approach to exploitation of its resources based on high seas rights and/or occupation. Among those who lauded his initiative was the Irish Minister for External Affairs, Mr Frank Aiken, who was greatly impressed (and, unusually, contributed to the subsequent debate). The General Assembly unanimously decided to set up an *ad hoc* committee of 35 member states to study the subject, including the possibilities of international cooperation in exploitation, conservation and use of the area. When the Committee reported in 1968 to the effect that further study was required, the General Assembly set up a more permanent and slightly larger (42-member) committee, the Committee on the Peaceful Uses of the Seabed and Ocean Floor (Seabed Committee), to consider the subject. In 1969 the US and the Soviet Union, both of whom were moving towards acceptance of a territorial sea of twelve miles breadth, which was already supported by a significant majority of states, floated the idea of convening a third conference with an agenda not much more extensive than that of UNCLOS II. However, in 1970 the General Assembly, having considered the annual report from the Seabed Committee, decided (with the support of the US *inter alios*) to convene a conference in 1973, with a wide agenda covering not only a regime for the seabed area but also effectively the whole field of the existing law of the sea. The Seabed Committee (enlarged to comprise 86 member states) was given a new mandate to prepare (a) a draft treaty on an international regime for the seabed and ocean floor beyond the limits of national jurisdiction and (b) a comprehensive list of subjects and issues relating to the law of the sea and draft articles on such subjects and issues.

In 1970 the General Assembly also adopted a Declaration of Principles (Res. 2749 XXV) in regard to the international seabed area (ISBA) (described as the area beyond the limits of national jurisdiction) to the effect, *inter alia*, that the area and its resources were the common heritage of mankind; that exploration and exploitation of its resources should be placed under an international regime and carried out for the benefit of mankind as a whole; and that in this context special consideration should be given to the interests of developing countries.

The Seabed Committee submitted its final report to the General Assembly in 1973. The General Assembly confirmed its 1970 decision to convene the Third United Nations Conference on the Law of the Sea (UNCLOS III) and described its mandate as adoption of a convention dealing with all matters relating to the law of the sea. The dates and venues for the First (procedural) and Second (substantive) Sessions were fixed. The General Assembly referred the reports of the Seabed Committee and all other relevant documentation of the Assembly and Committee to the Conference. UNCLOS III met for its First Session in December 1973.

Ireland was not a member of either committee but did attend as an observer at the meetings of the Seabed Committee in 1972 and 1973. Ireland enthusiastically supported the convening of UNCLOS III. Not only had UNCLOS I and II failed to achieve the desirable wide acceptance and consequent certainty of rules on at least some important issues, but developments in the meantime inclined towards a major reform of the law of the sea and an outcome on several issues of importance to Ireland that would be favourable to its interests. Ireland also felt that from a global point of view it was desirable to establish a regime for the ISBA.

Chapter II

THE DELEGATION

The question of the composition of the Irish delegation to UNCLOS III came under consideration in 1973. Bearing in mind the wide range of issues involved it was clear that several departments would have a direct interest. The most obvious interests were those of the (then) Departments of Agriculture and Fisheries in fishery matters; of Industry and Commerce in mineral resources and in marine scientific research (MSR) and transfer of technology (TOT); of Local Government in environmental matters; of Transport and Power in maritime transport; of Defence in security and surveillance matters; and of Finance in MSR and economic and financial considerations. As an international diplomatic and legal conference under the auspices of the United Nations, UNCLOS III necessarily involved the Department of Foreign Affairs both in regard to the substance and to providing the leadership of the delegation. As a legal conference it also engaged the interest of the Office of the Attorney General.

Already, in the later sessions of the Seabed Committee in 1972 and 1973, delegates from the Departments of Agriculture and Fisheries and of Industry and Commerce (the Geological Survey of Ireland (GSI)) and Finance (to which the National Science Council was attached) had joined with delegates from the Department of Foreign Affairs as members of the observer delegation. (The National Science Council was subsequently attached successively to the short-lived Department of Economic Planning and Development, the Department of the Taoiseach and the Department of Industry and Commerce. It was replaced in 1978 by a statutory body, the National Board of Science and Technology (NBST), which was attached to the Department of the Taoiseach.) The length of the UNCLOS III sessions—the Caracas Session lasted ten weeks—and the longer than anticipated duration of the Conference imposed a heavy servicing burden on departments that was sometimes partly alleviated by splitting sessions between delegates. The length of UNCLOS III also inevitably led to changes in delegation personnel over the years. In the early sessions when all issues were alive, delegation attendance at any given time comprised six to eight delegates with a support staff of three, consisting of an administrative assistant and two secretaries. In the later stages, as issues of vital national interest were judged to be effectively, if not formally, settled, the number of attending delegates was progressively reduced, as was the number of support staff.

Accreditation of the delegation for each session usually listed a large number of delegates, reflecting both splitting of attendance and, *ex abundante cautela*, inclusion of some delegates so that they would be available for specific tasks that might not in the event arise. In the support staff the role of administrative assistant was filled successively by Mary O'Regan (at the Second and Third Sessions) and Maureen Sweeney (at the Fourth to Tenth Sessions), both officers in the Department of Foreign Affairs Legal Division. They both quickly mastered the skills involved in dealing with the Conference demands (not least that of coping with and organising the copious flow of documentation) and of providing an excellent service to the delegation. Monica Murray and Frances Killilea (personal assistant to the Legal Adviser in Foreign Affairs) were the most regular secretaries to the delegation, each for most of the sessions, and fully lived up to their very high reputations. When only one of these two was available and another secretary was needed, a partner was normally provided variously from Department of Foreign Affairs headquarters, from the Missions in Geneva and New York and from the consulate in New York, all of whom were extremely assiduous and efficient.

The question of leadership was one of the first to be addressed. The precedents of UNCLOS I and II pointed to the Legal Adviser in Foreign Affairs (then the present writer). However, those were predominantly legal conferences at which codification of the law together with some progressive development was the objective. UNCLOS III, in contrast, was faced with establishing a regime in a totally new and politically sensitive field (the international seabed area regime) and with mooted radical changes, also politically charged, in many aspects of the existing law. Moreover the Legal Adviser's current commitments (including acting as agent of the Government in the Anglo–Irish human rights case under the Council of Europe Convention on Human Rights, dealing with legal aspects both of the relatively new membership of the EEC and with Anglo–Irish negotiations on Northern Ireland, and having a daily advisory function in the Department) suggested that it was unlikely that he would be in a position to devote the necessary time to leadership of the UNCLOS negotiations. The ideal solution was mooted by Patrick Power, then counsellor on the UN desk in the Department. He suggested as leader Ambassador C.C. (Con) Cremin, who was shortly to retire at the end of a very distinguished career, having just completed ten years as Permanent Representative (PR) to the UN. The suggestion was enthusiastically received in the Department and accepted by Ambassador Cremin. He anticipated these new duties, while still in office as PR, by leading the observer delegation to the final session of the Seabed Committee in Geneva in summer 1973. He led the UNCLOS III delegation into the Eighth Session, 1973–9. His experience, personal status and former office (as PR) rendered his leadership invaluable to the delegation, particularly as its membership otherwise had limited experience in such wide international negotiations. Indeed only two of the other delegates had previously participated in a major diplomatic conference. He ensured, from the beginning, delegation access to Conference personalities (mainly drawn from national diplomats accredited to the UN and from UN Secretariat officials) that would not have been easily achieved by a delegation whose membership was not otherwise very well known in those circles. His experience, wisdom and oversight were enormously supportive of delegates engaged in the detailed work.

Ambassador Cremin retired from the delegation in mid-1979 and was succeeded as head of delegation by Ambassador Seán Kennan, then Ambassador to Greece, and formerly PR to the EEC both before and after Ireland's accession—including the period of negotiation of accession. His experience of, and former office at, the EEC were major assets during the second part of the Eighth Session of UNCLOS in autumn 1979, when Ireland, for the second time during the Conference, held the EEC Presidency. The delegation was then responsible for the conduct of EEC cooperation and coordination and for acting as EEC spokesman in both formal and informal proceedings at that session.

In the event the (then) Legal Adviser in the Department (the author) attended part of the Second Session (1974) and effectively all of the succeeding sessions, including those subsequent to his appointment as Ambassador to Denmark, Norway and Iceland in 1977, and as PR to the UN Office in Geneva in 1981. Having been deputy head of delegation through the Second to Eighth Sessions, 1974–9, he led the delegation at the Ninth to Eleventh Sessions in 1980–2.

As well as supervising the delegation's work the head of delegation represented it at all meetings of the Plenary, of the General Committee and the Credentials Committee (Ireland being one of its seven members), as well as at meetings of the EEC heads of delegations, meetings of the Western European and Others Group (WEOG—one of the five UN regional groups) and in other meetings, consultations and representations as appropriate.

As a full listing of the accredited delegates for each session of the Conference would be misleading in the context of this document, an indication of the fields of expertise and responsibility of the most involved individual delegates is more appropriate.

Seamus Mallon (Séamus Ó Mealláin), a retired senior technical and engineering officer of the Fisheries section of the Department of Agriculture and Fisheries, had been a delegate also to both UNCLOS I and II. He attended the later Seabed Committee sessions and participated in UNCLOS III at the substantive sessions, (Second to Eighth Sessions, 1974–9) until the fisheries and related questions were effectively resolved. His wisdom and experience ensured that his influence in the delegation was not confined to his area of immediate expertise and responsibility. His wide linguistic ability (French, German, Spanish) was an added asset. On the fisheries side, the delegation also included during the early sessions Brendan O'Kelly (then) Chairman of Bord Iascaigh Mhara, as an adviser.

From the Geological Survey of Ireland (GSI), Robin Riddihough, Keith Robinson and Piers Gardiner all attended the Seabed Committee, with particular responsibility for geological aspects of the continental shelf issues, and continued to attend at UNCLOS III. Their duties at the home office usually resulted in their splitting attendance at the long sessions. Thus all three attended the Second Session. Keith Robinson and Piers Gardiner attended the Third to Fifth Sessions. Piers Gardiner was the main delegate in the middle sessions, during which time he devised the 'Gardiner formula', which formed part of the methodology finally adopted for identification of the outer limits of continental shelf jurisdiction. (This significantly facilitated acceptance of wide coastal state continental shelf jurisdiction, to Ireland's considerable advantage.) He was succeeded in the delegation by Ray Keary, at the first part of the Eighth Session in 1979, and at the second part of that session and at the Ninth Session by the GSI's deputy director, David Naylor, until the continental shelf negotiation effectively concluded at the Ninth Session. David Naylor's authoritative expertise was a priceless boon to the delegation in the vital late stage of the negotiations on the shelf, not only in safeguarding Ireland's interests but also in facilitating the delegation's leadership of the Margineers Group (see below), which it assumed during the Seventh Session in 1978. All of these delegates made valuable contributions to the work of the delegation on this vital issue.

The GSI officers also helped in the work on MSR, which fell mainly to officials from the departments to which the National Science Council and the NBST were successively attached. Exceptionally, Professor Colm Ó hEocha, head of the marine faculty in University College Galway and Chairman of the National Science Council, and Brendan Finucane, then a senior official from the Department of Finance, split attendance at the Second Session (1974) between them. Colm Ó hEocha was unavailable to continue as a delegate on being appointed President of University College Galway in 1975. He and Brendan Finucane were especially prominent in early informal exchanges, particularly at the Second and Third Sessions, contributing significantly to drafts on MSR that led in due course to a consensus on the points covered in them. Subsequently, Brendan Finucane also had to reduce his attendance due to increased duties at headquarters, until he also had to drop out of the delegation during the Seventh Session when assigned to the newly formed NBST in 1978. Unfortunately this occurred at a time when a campaign was launched by researching states, led by the US, which threatened Ireland's interests and required an active response. He was eventually succeeded by Agnes Breathnach, Department of the Taoiseach (to which the NBST was then attached), who attended the Ninth Session, where she was effective in recovering ground lost at the resumed Eighth Session. The topic was effectively settled at the Ninth Session. These delegates also were constantly helpful to the delegation in their willingness to assist in ways and areas not strictly within their direct responsibilities.

Most of the work in the sphere of the traditional law of the sea, including legislating for such new or relatively new concepts as the exclusive economic zone (EEZ), continental shelf jurisdiction, division of expanded national marine zones, regime of straits newly enclosed in territorial waters, etc., fell to Department of Foreign Affairs delegates, who cooperated on some of these issues with other delegates as already mentioned. Department of Foreign Affairs delegates deployed for this task were Raphael Siev and Charles Lysaght (Assistant Legal Advisers) at the Second Session, the author at the Second to Eleventh Sessions, Joseph Hayes (Assistant Legal Adviser) at the Ninth and Tenth Sessions and Geraldine Skinner (see below) at the Eighth to Eleventh Sessions.

The negotiations on the ISBA also fell to foreign affairs delegates. As Ireland was not a potential deep seabed miner its very slight direct interest in the seabed negotiations arose mainly from its status as a consumer of minerals and a producer of some. Nevertheless, the topic's central importance at the Conference, and the direct interests of some of Ireland's EEC partners, required that the delegation pay closer attention to it than its slight direct interest to Ireland would otherwise require. Ireland's policy, as indicated already at the Seabed Committee (to whose development a paper prepared by Charles Lysaght contributed significantly), was guided by the objective that the developing world, rather than the industrialised countries, would be the main beneficiaries of exploitation of the international area, in line with the UN General Assembly Declaration of Principles. This was a field in which there was a wide disparity of views among the (then) nine EEC member states, between the major industrialised countries with seabed mining capacity at one extreme, and Ireland and (to a lesser extent) Denmark at the other. This was highlighted at the Second Session when Ireland did not co-sponsor a proposal of the other eight on this topic, because it appeared to the delegation to be disproportionately weighted in favour of the industrialised countries. As the subject was not within EEC competence, a common position was not obligatory for members and could be reached only by unanimity through the cooperation consultation process. At that session the topic was covered by the author, Raphael Siev and Charles Lysaght, who split attendance at the session. (In addition to his assiduous work on the substance, Raphael Siev dealt very effectively with logistical problems arising for a delegation operating far away from any national support base.) A clear understanding of the topic by these three and the head of delegation were essential to enable them to vindicate Ireland's position, particularly vis-à-vis its EEC partners. Ireland's responsibility as EEC Presidency at the Third Session (1975) included conducting EEC cooperation in the ISBA field—obviously a difficult task and a delicate one in the light of the delegation's stance at the previous session. It was clear that, rather than continuing with shared responsibility in this field, it would be necessary to have a full-time delegate (preferably fluent in French) dedicated to it. Geraldine Skinner (Assistant Legal Adviser) was assigned to this duty and serviced the First Committee, which covered the ISBA topic, until late in the Conference. She was assisted by Justin Dillon (Assistant Legal Adviser) at the Seventh and Eighth Sessions, including the second part of the Eighth Session, when Ireland again held the EEC Presidency. Following Geraldine Skinner's appointment as Legal Adviser in the Department of Foreign Affairs in late 1978, her role at UNCLOS III and at intersessional meetings, both EEC and other, expanded to include all issues still unresolved. The primary servicing of the ISBA issue from then on was undertaken, under her supervision, successively, by Justin Dillon, by officers at the Permanent Missions to the UN in New York and Geneva, respectively Aidan Mulloy (Counsellor and deputy head of Mission) and Philip McDonagh (First Secretary) and by Micheál Ó Cinnéide (Vice-Consul at the Irish consulate in New York). All of these succeeded admirably in familiarising themselves rapidly with both the relatively arcane topic and the complexity of the negotiations, which they monitored very effectively.

As the two other departments that had a direct interest in preservation of the marine environment did not provide a delegate, coverage of this topic also fell to the Department of Foreign Affairs, specifically to its economic division. Among a succession of delegates were Counsellors James Kirwan and Paul Dempsey (who split attendance at the Second Session), First Secretaries Patrick Craddock (at the Third and Fourth Sessions), Margaret Cawley (at the Seventh and Eighth Sessions), all officers from the economic division; and Brian Nason (at the Fifth Session) and Isolda Moylan (at the Sixth Session), both First Secretaries from the New York Mission to the UN. At the Third Session Patrick Craddock devised a draft on one of the problems that contributed significantly to a consensus solution. However, the unavoidable frequent changes of delegates inhibited a build-up of Conference know-how and personal standing in this field. Thus in later sessions, the servicing delegate concentrated on straightforward protection of the Irish interest, a responsibility implemented very effectively by all. The topic was effectively completed at the Eighth Session.

The delegation's guidance on issues of TOT, including transfer of seabed mining technology, which was again a difficult topic within the EEC, came from the Department of Foreign Affairs economic division and the Department of Industry and Commerce. Assignment of a special delegate was not considered necessary and care of the topic in the delegation was normally combined with that of MSR. At the Fourth and Fifth Sessions (1976), John Moore of the Department of Defence undertook the servicing of issues relevant to security and fishery protection concerns, with particular interest in adoption of satisfactory hot pursuit provisions. The relevant texts were drafted at the Fourth Session, but a Department of Defence delegate continued to monitor the issue at the Sixth Session. At that stage the issue was effectively settled, thus rendering further attendance by a special delegate unnecessary. These delegates were most helpful in assisting on other topics when the delegation was stretched. A scheme of revenue sharing in respect of continental shelf production came under consideration from the Third Session in 1975, as part of the negotiation on extended coastal state continental shelf jurisdiction, and financing of ISBA bodies became a prominent issue at the Eighth Session in 1979. Delegates from the Departments of Finance and Industry and Commerce attended at these junctures and lent invaluable advice. These included Fionan O'Muircheartaigh and Patrick McGrath from the Department of Finance and Richard McKay from the Department of Industry and Commerce.

Matthew Russell, a Senior Legal Adviser in the Office of the Attorney General attended briefly at each of the Sixth to Ninth Sessions, 1979–80, to monitor developments, particularly in the field of delimitation of marine areas between neighbouring states. Bilateral negotiations had commenced in 1974 on delimitation of the continental shelf between Ireland and the UK.

Conference deliberations on settlement of disputes and on the preamble and final clauses were reserved for Plenary and were also the responsibility of the Department of Foreign Affairs legal officers. They were covered mainly by Geraldine Skinner, particularly from the Eighth Session (1979) on, when discussions on them intensified. Likewise the legal delegates covered the work of the Drafting Committee when this work came on stream at the later sessions, with the assistance of delegates responsible for the various topics and/or with advice from responsible officials in Dublin, as they came to be considered.

EEC meetings on coordination (in fields of EEC competence) and on cooperation (in other fields where members had interests and sought common positions in pursuance of the EEC's efforts at common foreign policy) were serviced by the head of delegation and by other delegates according to their fields of responsibility. They acted as chairpersons and spokespersons during Irish EEC presidencies in 1975 at the Fourth Session and in 1979 at the resumed Eighth Session. EEC meetings were held between as well as during sessions.

An important objective for EEC member states at UNCLOS III was to ensure that (a) the EEC's competence in some areas to be covered would be so acknowledged as to enable it to take responsibility in these areas under the future convention; and (b) mutual concession of exclusive rights between the member states as such in some of these areas (notably fisheries) would take priority over convention obligations to third parties. In 1975, at the Third Session, the delegates of the member states and the Commission, under the Irish Presidency, examined proposals geared only at facilitation of exercise of EEC competence mainly in the fisheries field—although considering whether the possibility of the EEC becoming a party to the convention should be explored. It was subsequently concluded, in the light of evolving competences, that it would be essential for the EEC to be enabled to become a party. At the level of deciding what measure was necessary this topic fell also to the Department of Foreign Affairs Legal Adviser, but implementation was pursued at the Conference through heads of delegation under the leadership of the current EEC Presidency.

The interest in the Conference at political level was particularly manifested in the attendance of Mr Declan Costello, then Attorney General, at the Second to Fourth Sessions in 1974–6, and of Mr Brian Lenihan, then Minister for Foreign Affairs, at the Ninth Session in 1980, as special representatives of the Government.

From the foregoing it is clear that the delegation was extremely well equipped, with the necessary expertise and knowledge to cope with its responsibilities. Although many of the delegates did not have significant previous experience of multilateral diplomatic negotiations, all took to the tasks of the Conference confidently from the outset, intervening at formal and informal meetings, preparing drafts, engaging in consultations and networking. Very soon a wide range of contacts was established extending across the regions and interest groups, as well as the Conference Secretariat. Obviously such contacts were used for the dual purposes of gathering information and promoting the delegation's objectives. The delegation entertainment fund, by no means lavish, was effectively deployed. Entertainment most frequently took the form of lunches or, less often, dinners, *tête-à-tête* or for relatively small groups, with concentration on specific issues. In addition the delegation, like most others, hosted a reception at each of the early sessions, to which a large number of delegates and officials were invited. The attendance at these receptions was always highly satisfactory, a feature reflecting the standing of the delegation (and also the popularity of the smoked (Irish) salmon that was always served). From the beginning, Irish delegates demonstrated a high level of expertise in drafting and negotiation and were prominent actors on several issues. As the sessions proceeded, Irish delegates were ever more frequently included in informal get-togethers of influential Conference personnel for discussions on general progress or on specific difficult issues. The delegation had a leading role in several interest groups, working groups and consensus seekers.

A senior New Zealand diplomat, reporting to his authorities on the Seabed Committee conclusions in 1973 and looking forward to UNCLOS III, advised that the most intractable issues at the Conference would ultimately be settled, near its end, in a small smoke-filled room. He assumed that New Zealand, due to its relative lack of size and global importance, would not be present in that room, and therefore urged that the New Zealand delegation should seek to secure satisfactory resolution of the problems affecting its serious interests before that stage was reached. His prognosis was correct except that, instead of one (metaphorical) small smoke-filled room, there were several, on different unresolved issues, including some affecting the serious interests of New Zealand and/or Ireland. Of course the major global powers were present in all. The Irish delegation, from a country similar in size and importance to New Zealand and others, was present in such (metaphorical) rooms as were concerned with issues affecting its serious interests, including one in which it represented New Zealand *inter alios*. Eschewing false modesty, the author has the temerity to claim that the delegation was much more influential at UNCLOS III than would be normal for a delegation from a country of Ireland's size and global importance. In short, it punched well above its weight, as is amply borne out by the account that follows.

Chapter III

PREPARATIONS AND PRIMARY INSTRUCTIONS

In 1972, at the proposal of the Department of Foreign Affairs, an Inter-Departmental Committee (IDC) on the UNCLOS III was convened to coordinate the work of the departments having responsibilities in the fields covered by the Conference agenda, and to formulate policy proposals for the negotiations. The participating departments were the Department of Agriculture and Fisheries, the Department of Industry and Commerce (and the associated Geological Survey of Ireland (GSI)), the Department of Finance (including the National Science Council and the Revenue Commissioners), the Department of Transport and Power, the Department of Defence, the Department of Local Government, as well as the Department of Foreign Affairs.

A pre-Conference review identified the following as the main issues: (a) establishment of an international regime for the exploration and exploitation of the international seabed area (ISBA), including operational international institutions; (b) the distance limits of exclusive or preferential fisheries rights for coastal states; (c) the distance limits of coastal state rights over the continental shelf; (d) the distance limits of the territorial sea and the rules in regard to passage through straits that would be newly enclosed through proposed expansion of those limits; (e) responsibilities and rights in regard to measures for preservation of the marine environment; (f) regulation of marine scientific research (MSR); and (g) obligations regarding transfer of technology (TOT). With the exception of (a) all of these issues were of direct importance to Ireland, as were implicit and related issues of delimitation of marine zones between neighbouring states, the role of islands in generating marine zones and in such delimitation, and preservation of high seas rights, in particular, freedom of navigation.

UNCLOS III was also the subject of major consideration in the EEC context. Representatives of the member states and of the

Commission met frequently, both at delegate and heads of delegation level, to examine implications in respect of fields in which competences had been transferred to the EEC and to reach common positions on these matters (coordination meetings). The nine member states also met separately to consider the possibility of adopting common positions on other matters in the context of implementing foreign policy cooperation (cooperation meetings).

In June 1974, as the Second Session of UNCLOS III (and the first to deal with substantive matters) was about to commence, the Minister for Foreign Affairs made a submission to the Government, dated 26 June, seeking instructions for the delegation. The IDC departments contributed directly to the preparation of the submission and, in addition, the Department of the Taoiseach and the departments of Justice, Health, Labour, Posts and Telegraphs, and the Office of the Attorney General were consulted on its terms. A minute from the Minister for Defence was submitted simultaneously, drawing attention to the implications for the defence forces of the obligations that would arise in the likely event that the areas of national marine jurisdiction were greatly expanded.

The submission, which was wide ranging, identified three broad interest groups at UNCLOS III—(i) the major maritime states anxious to maintain maximum freedom of the seas, particularly as regards navigation and fishing; (ii) a large number of coastal states (comprising the coastal states group—CSG) seeking control over all resources throughout a wide area off their coasts; and (iii) a number of land- and shelf-locked states (subsequently known as the group of land-locked and geographically disadvantaged states—LLGDS) urging minimum coastal state jurisdiction to the benefit of the ISBA, and to their own benefit, more directly, through exercise of high seas rights. These, which were not even then the only interest groups, evolved both as to membership and objectives as time progressed, and several other interest groups emerged. The Group of 77 (G-77), the group formed by the Third World (developing and underdeveloped) states in the UN General Assembly to pursue their common economic aims, was not mentioned, possibly reflecting Ireland's very limited direct interest in the ISBA regime in respect of which the G-77 were most active.

Ireland's broad interests were summarised in the submission as (1) safeguarding of its coastal fishery, particularly as regards shellfish and anadromous species (salmon); (2) securing as wide an area of coastal state resource jurisdiction as possible; (3) equitable distribution of the mineral resources of the ISBA and avoidance of damage to Irish industry, based on Irish onshore mineral deposits, through excessive supply of these minerals from the ISBA resources; (4) preservation of the marine environment; (5) maintenance of freedom of navigation; (6) guarding against arbitrary coastal state obstacles to MSR, while ensuring results of research in Irish coastal waters would be made available to the Irish authorities, as well as the results of research in the ISBA; and (7) exclusion of Rockall from entitlement to a continental shelf area or an exclusive economic zone (EEZ).

In the framework of this range of identified interests, recommendations were made in the Minister's submission as to the positions to be taken by the delegation on various issues. Not surprisingly, in the light of a lack of clear definition of the detail of many of the issues, the difficulty at that early stage of anticipating the course of negotiations and the uncertainty as to what action would have realistic prospects of success, many of the recommendations were relatively general. In addition, guidance by three broad considerations was suggested—(i) the safeguarding and promotion of national interests; (ii) sympathy with the reasonable requirements of Third World (developing and under-developed) countries in regard to specific issues; and (iii) attention to the views of EEC partners on matters outside those involving EEC competences (where coordination of positions would be the norm), and disposition to support them on such matters. Despite the third guideline, disagreement with some EEC partners was anticipated, for example in regard to the EEZ. Difficulties of reconciling solidarity with fellow EEC members with sympathy for Third World countries was recognised. It is clear that only the first of the three guidelines was intended to be absolute.

The recommendations were as follows:

(A) *territorial seas*—there was little enthusiasm for extension beyond three miles, partly because it would involve increased obligations of a policing nature, etc., but more so because a British twelve-mile limit would incorporate within its territorial waters some offshore islands currently outside, with a consequent possibility of enhancing the role of such islands in division of the continental shelf between Ireland and the UK. Opposition to a twelve-mile limit was considered unrealistic, but discretion for the delegation was recommended, to be exercised taking account of the implications for fisheries and continental shelf jurisdiction;

(B) *contiguous zone* (which under the 1958 convention extended to twelve miles and in which the coastal state could take measures to prevent infringement on its land territory or in its territorial sea of its customs, fiscal, immigration or sanitary regulations)—liberty for the delegation to support this zone extending a further twelve miles beyond the territorial sea, with a suggestion that this support might be used as a bargaining point;

(C) *straits* (to be newly enclosed by proposed extension of territorial seas)—support for a free/unimpeded transit regime (more permissive than innocent passage in allowing overflight and not requiring submarines to surface) or any reasonable alternative attracting wide general support (reflecting the Irish concern for preservation of freedom of navigation);

(D) *archipelagos* (i.e. concerning the move by states composed predominantly of islands to enclose waters between these islands by drawing straight baselines from the outermost points of the islands, thus effectively converting significant areas into internal waters as well as extending their territorial seas and other areas of coastal state jurisdiction)—acquiescence in enclosure by genuine archipelagic states subject to freedom of navigation being preserved;

(E) *islands*—support for the solution that would give Ireland the largest and most profitable area of marine jurisdiction. Under the 1958 Conventions on the Territorial Sea and the Continental Shelf the term 'island' was liberally defined and every island enjoyed a territorial sea and a continental shelf. If these provisions and a similar provision in the context of the proposed new EEZs were adopted by UNCLOS III, any small, isolated or even uninhabited island, such as Rockall, would be entitled to its own continental shelf and EEZ. Rockall would enjoy such zones of jurisdiction in an Atlantic area where Ireland would have aspirations for areas of shelf and EEZ jurisdiction. Moreover, British offshore islands, including such small islands as the Scilly Isles and the Smalls, could erode Irish claims in delimitation negotiations. Conversely, use of Irish offshore Atlantic islands for straight baselines would confer insignificant advantage in determining distance limits for the shelf or the EEZ, and there were no Irish islands off the east coast that could significantly affect division. The issue of islands was further complicated by uncertainties as to the future fisheries and continental shelf regimes, the nature of the intended subsequent adaptation of the EEC common fishery policy and whether there might be a distinction, in the future convention, between the entitlements of islands *simpliciter* and their role in division of zones between neighbouring states. In the circumstances the relatively general nature of the recommendation is not surprising.

The islands issue was described as one of the most crucial for Ireland. There was no separate recommendation on *delimitation* of areas of marine jurisdiction between neighbouring states. The 1958 Convention on the Continental Shelf effectively provided that delimitation should be in accordance with the median or equidistance line, unless otherwise agreed by the parties or where special circumstances justified variation. Presumably that provision was regarded as adequate subject to a satisfactorily limited role for offshore islands in determination of the median line. Apparently total dismissal of the 1958 provision, as in the International Court of Justice decision in the North Sea cases, was not regarded as essential for national interests, but the decision was looked on as being helpful in dealing with the role of offshore islands. Instructions would take a more trenchant line later;

(F) *EEZ*—support for an EEZ of up to 200 nautical miles width, involving coastal state jurisdiction over living (fish) and non-living (mineral) resources, control over MSR and in respect of pollution, and support for a wider zone (presumably for continental shelf jurisdiction) if likely to receive reasonable backing;

(G) living resources, i.e. *fisheries* (a separate recommendation although overlapping F)—support for a 200 nautical mile zone with coastal state jurisdiction for regulation of fisheries (not coastal state exclusive fishing rights) and for a proposal to confine of exploitation of *anadromous species* (salmon) to the state of origin. (The latter incorporated the only recommendation that a specific proposal should be made, or to support a proposal to the same effect.) The likely degree of coastal state control and the effect of the EEC common fishery policy and its evolution were speculated upon, and the overriding importance of conservation under coastal state supervision, particularly of anadromous species, was emphasised;

(H) non-living resources, i.e. minerals, and *continental shelf* jurisdiction (again a separate recommendation although overlapping E and F)—support for a 200-nautical-mile EEZ with coastal state jurisdiction over non-living resources (minerals) and opposition to granting of an EEZ to uninhabited islands. The base of the Irish continental slope being mostly within 200 nautical miles of the coast except north of the 53° line of latitude (where a potential rival claim based on Rockall could intrude) and the area of continental margin beyond the base being judged, at that time, not to have any great mineral potential, there was no great enthusiasm for seeking jurisdiction beyond the proposed 200 mile EEZ. It was suggested that a claim to such a further extension might be used as a bargaining counter. This position changed radically later;

(I) *marine environment* (relevant also to F, G and H)—support for coastal state rights to take measures to prevent pollution of its coasts and of waters under its jurisdiction, and to enforce regulations to that end without detriment to freedom of navigation; support for a 200 nautical mile wide coastal state pollution zone was specifically included; also support for obligations on states to prevent, within their own jurisdiction, activities giving rise to pollution, and for a positive contribution to international efforts to control pollution. The 1958 Convention on the High Seas (Articles 24 and 25) included an obligation on states to prevent pollution of the seas by oil discharges from ships or pipelines, by exploration or exploitation activities on the seabed, by dumping of radioactive waste or by activities with radioactive or other harmful material; but it did not provide for coastal state jurisdiction to regulate or enforce such obligation in regard to its marine areas. In the meantime other relevant environmental instruments had emerged, including the 1972 UN Stockholm Declaration on the Human Environment comprising non-legally binding principles. In addition, conventions (legally binding on their parties) relevant to the marine environment had been adopted under the auspices of the International Maritime Consultative Organisation (IMCO—the principal international body for promoting global international regulation of the rights and responsibilities of shipping) on vessel discharges and dumping. Moreover, three relevant regional conventions had also been concluded recently—the 1972 Oslo and London Conventions on dumping and discharges and the 1974 Paris Convention on land-sourced pollution. All of these of course applied in the context of existing law in relation to areas of jurisdiction, a law that was proposed to be radically changed by UNCLOS III. Uncertainty as to the likely approach at UNCLOS III in the light of these environment-related international instruments is mentioned, and obviously contributed to the general nature of the recommendation. As the negotiation on this topic proceeded the following main issues emerged: (i) whether to strengthen and widen the 1958 convention obligation for every state to prevent/control marine pollution originating under its jurisdiction—from its land territory, internal waters and territorial sea, from dumping (not just radioactive waste) under its authority or (other) pollution from its vessels at sea, from pipelines, from exploration or exploitation of the natural resources in its EEZ or on its continental shelf; (ii) a state's right to make laws and regulations to prevent/control pollution by others in its territorial sea, or EEZ, or on its continental shelf or in a pollution zone; (iii) whether such laws and regulations would have to be in conformity with internationally agreed standards, in respect of any or all of the sources of pollution and in any or all of the zones; and (iv) a state's right of enforcement against vessels (by stopping, boarding, inspecting, arresting, taking legal proceedings against them) whether by the flag state, the coastal state or the port state (i.e. a state into whose port the vessel had voluntarily entered). These complex interlocking issues and the obvious diversity of interest between coastal and maritime states made for difficult negotiations. Ireland's task was to balance its interest in preserving clean coastal waters and coasts with its concern to maintain freedom of navigation. This task was further complicated by claims (promoted by the EEC Commission and conceded to varying degrees by the EEC members) that the EEC had acquired ill-defined competences affecting some aspects of these issues, thus requiring a common EEC position on these aspects between members with occasionally opposing national interests. Not surprisingly the initial general instructions were subjected to review and more detailed development as the Conference proceeded;

(J) *MSR* (relevant also to F, G and H)—support for rules on MSR in areas of coastal state jurisdiction, which would ensure that coastal state interests would be protected without inhibiting research, and for rules on MSR in the ISBA, which would ensure rational performance and free availability of results. This approach, impliedly favouring maintenance of the *status quo* as set out in the 1958 Convention on the Continental Shelf (and applying it to the new EEZ, with something similar in the new ISBA), was based on Ireland's need of the results of research while having limited capacity to undertake such research. Article 5.8 of the 1958 Convention on the Continental Shelf required prior consent by the coastal state for conduct of MSR concerning its shelf, although such consent should not be unreasonably withheld in respect of requests for purely scientific research. Several questions of detail were not addressed in the instruction proposal (although mentioned in the submission), such as whether there should be distinctions in the rules for military research, for pure or fundamental research as compared with applied (including resource-related) research, and whether coastal state consent or merely notification should be required in regard to each of these. Presumably uncertainty about what would be realistic objectives dictated a relative lack of detail in the position at that stage. The detail would be developed later;

(K) *TOT*—support for appropriate measures in the light of the state's relatively low levels of expertise in the technology field. Reference was made to the fact that the question of TOT relevant to exploitation of ISBA had yet to be broached. This particularly general recommendation presumably also reflected the very high level of uncertainty as to the issues that would actually arise;

(L) *ISBA*—support for a constitution of an international authority (to administer the ISBA) that would ensure efficient conduct of its operations and give the poorer countries a significant say in its control; and rules that would ensure equitable distribution of the fruits of exploitation of the ISBA while taking account of the special needs of the poorer countries. An efficient authority with the right not only to licence, but also to engage directly in, exploitation was favoured. The basis of the position was a combination of, firstly, a feeling of obligation to support special benefit for the poorer countries (as envisaged in the UN General Assembly resolution) and, secondly, the fact that there was no potential Irish exploiter and that Ireland was unlikely in any case to be a significant beneficiary. At a time when exploitation of seabed resources seemed imminent the Minister for Foreign Affairs (Dr Garret FitzGerald) had a strong personal view that this exploitation should be an automatic source of revenue for underdeveloped countries. Nevertheless, the possibility of using the delegation position as a negotiating counter was again mentioned.

A number of other issues were flagged but without being the subject of specific recommendation, despite the obvious existence of a national interest, for example peaceful settlement of disputes, the claims of the LLGDS, the rules applicable in respect of artificial islands, high seas rights and radio transmissions from the high seas. Some of these were addressed in later revisions of instructions. The main issue to arise regarding high seas rights would be their preservation in the EEZ and on the continental shelf. The 1958 Convention on the Continental Shelf provided for general non-interference with specified rights by the coastal state on its shelf.

The need for flexibility was emphasised with the proposal that the delegation must have considerable discretion in its attitude to specific proposals, exercisable within the recommendations and only after consultation with the Minister for Foreign Affairs. It was also stipulated that no binding commitment would be entered into without prior approval of the Government.

The recommendations were approved by the Government in a decision dated 2 July 1974.

It is apparent that the submission's proposals were partly prompted by a concern to preserve traditional high seas freedoms, particularly freedom of navigation (despite the absence of a specific reference) and a not very aggressive stance on coastal state resource jurisdiction. Having regard to the three main interest groups identified in the submission, the overall position adopted was, not surprisingly, nearest to that of the CSG, but it fell far short of the more extreme positions taken by some states in that group.

The idea of using bargaining chips proved to be illusory, as UNCLOS III featured shifting alliances dictated by differing interests on individual issues. Negotiation was invariably between interest groups rather than individual states. Thus, bargaining was feasible only within a broad issue rather than across issues, as the parties on opposite sides on any two issues very rarely coincided.

The delegation reported on the proceedings after each session. The substance of each report was conveyed to the Government through a submission by the Minister for Foreign Affairs. The Minister also made a submission to the Government before each subsequent session, reviewing the delegation's instructions and proposing confirmation or adjustment of the detail of these instructions, as appropriate, in the light of developments.

Chapter IV

FIRST SESSION

UNCLOS III was convened at the United Nations headquarters in New York for its First Session for two weeks, from 3 to 15 December, 1973. It was formally opened by the UN Secretary-General, Mr Kurt Waldheim. Ambassador Shirley H. Amerasinghe of Sri Lanka, who had chaired the Seabed Committee, was elected President.

DELEGATION

The attending delegates were Ambassador Cremin, head of delegation, and Raphael Siev, both from the Department of Foreign Affairs.

PLENARY

The session concerned itself exclusively with organisational and procedural matters. Further informal meetings were required, leading to completion of this work at the commencement of the second (and first substantive) session in Caracas. It was decided that the Conference activities would be conducted through five main organs, the Plenary, three Main Committees of the whole and the General Committee. A Drafting Committee was also established that became operative only in the later sessions, when its essential purpose of ensuring the final text was correctly drafted in the five official UN languages came to be fulfilled.

The 48-member General Committee had the task of overseeing the work of the Conference, monitoring progress and making relevant proposals to Plenary. This Committee was presided over by the Conference President and its membership also comprised the Chairmen and Rapporteurs of the Main Committees, the Rapporteur General, and the Conference Vice-Presidents. The Chairman of the Drafting Committee could participate but without a right to vote. By agreement Ireland and Belgium shared a Vice-Presidency. The two delegations took turns in assuming the office at alternate sessions.

On decision-taking, the Conference broke with the tradition of previous UN diplomatic conferences where a proposal on which there was disagreement would normally have been put to a vote. At those conferences a simple majority was sufficient to carry a substantive issue in committee, which would then be referred to Plenary, where a two-thirds majority was required for adoption. At UNCLOS III, however, a 'gentlemen's agreement' applied, comprised in a President's declaration approved by the UN General Assembly and endorsed by the Conference. The agreement was to the effect that decisions on substance should preferably be taken by consensus, and that a vote should be resorted to only after all efforts at reaching consensus had been exhausted. While this move obviously made decision-taking more difficult, it was inspired by the view that the issues should be considered as a whole (as was expressed in the 'gentlemen's agreement'). Moreover, the actual rules provided for deferral of votes, and tightened the conditions for adoption in Plenary by requiring that the necessary two-thirds majority must also comprise at least half of the Conference participants. These arrangements reflected, on the one hand, states' concerns to avoid being outvoted on issues involving vital national interests and, on the other hand, a general desire to reach a widely acceptable convention. In addition, the number of Third World (developing) countries had increased significantly over the years until, by 1973, they were so numerous as to be in a position under the previous rules, if they were united, to vote through what they wanted. This raised the unwelcome possibility of adoption of a convention that would be rejected by the major powers at least, and thus be rendered practically unviable. The decision-taking arrangements were intended to meet all these concerns. In the event, votes on substantive issues were held only at the Eleventh (last) Session—on formal proposals of amendments to the Draft Convention and on its adoption. There were also votes on non-substantive questions, including a decision in regard to the Presidency at the Seventh Session, decisions on the seats of the International Seabed Authority and of the International Tribunal for the Law of the Sea between rival candidates at the Tenth Session and on the holding of some of the sessions.

On the question of allocation of the many topics it was decided that the peaceful uses of ocean space and zones of security would be reserved to Plenary, as was also subsequently decided with regard to peaceful settlement of disputes (although also subject to consideration by any of the Main Committees if relevant to its mandate) and the final clauses. Of the Main Committees, which were required to report to Plenary, the First Committee was assigned the international regime of the seabed and ocean floor beyond national jurisdiction—the international seabed area (ISBA). The Second Committee agenda was most of the hitherto traditional law of the sea, including rules determining jurisdiction and regimes in regard to the territorial sea, the high seas, living resources (fish) and non-living resources (minerals other than those in the ISBA). The Third Committee had three main topics, preservation of the marine environment, marine scientific research (MSR) and transfer of technology (TOT).

Although the rules of procedure were discussed fully at the session, their finalisation and the allocation of topics among Plenary and the Main Committees were not definitively adopted until the beginning of the Second Session.

Those elected Chairmen of the Main Committees were (First Committee) Ambassador Paul B. Engo of Cameroon; (Second Committee) Ambassador Andres Aguilar of Venezuela; and (Third Committee) Ambassador Alexander Yankov of Bulgaria. Ambassadors Engo and Yankov had chaired the corresponding subcommittees in the Seabed Committee. By agreement of the Latin American and Caribbean (LAC) Group, Ambassador Reynaldo Galindo Pohl of El Salvador was Chairman of the Second Committee at the Third Session (having chaired the corresponding subcommittee at the Seabed Committee). Ambassador Aguilar resumed as Second Committee Chairman at the Fourth Session and for the following sessions. Each Main Committee had two Vice-Chairmen and a Rapporteur, who together with the Chairman formed the Committee Bureau. Ambassador J. Alan Beasley of Canada was elected Chairman of the Drafting Committee. Thus the Conference followed the usual UN practice of dividing the main offices between the five regional groups. Mr Kenneth J. Rattray of Jamaica was elected Rapporteur-General. The usual Credentials Committee was also established and Mr Heinrich Gleisner of Austria was elected as its Chairman. Its membership of nine included Ireland. The UN Secretary-General was formally Secretary-General of UNCLOS III and was represented at the sessions by an Under-Secretary-General as his special representative, Mr Constantin Stavropoulos at the First and Second Sessions and Mr Bernardo Zuleta at subsequent sessions. (Mr Stavropoulos had retired from his post as UN Legal Counsel after the Second Session and acted as head of the Greek delegation at the following sessions.)

Chapter V

SECOND SESSION

The second (and first substantive) session of UNCLOS III was held in Caracas for ten weeks, from 20 June to 29 August 1974. At the opening meeting it was addressed by the United Nations Secretary-General, the President of Venezuela and the Conference President.

DELEGATION

The delegation, led by Ambassador Cremin, included Seamus Mallon from the Department of Agriculture and Fisheries, Keith Robinson and Piers Gardiner from the Geological Survey of Ireland (GSI)(assigned by the Department of Industry and Commerce), Colm Ó hEocha from the National Science Council (assigned by the Department of Finance) and Brendan Finucane from the Department of Finance, as well as the author, James Kirwan, Paul Dempsey, Raphael Siev and Charles Lysaght from the Department of Foreign Affairs.

GENERAL

The Conference contrasted with the Seabed Committee in that all the attending states had equal status. Thus, Ireland was a full participant and not a mere observer.

A feature of the session was the crystallisation of the group phenomenon. The traditional UN political/regional alignment was maintained through the five regional groups and the Group of 77 (G-77, which in fact comprised more than one hundred of the developing countries from Africa, Asia and Latin America). The regional groups were the African Group, the Asian Group, the Eastern European Group (EE), Latin American and Caribbean Group (LAC) and the Western European and Others Group (WEOG). These met regularly. Only the G-77 had a wide range of shared Conference interests, most notably its members' position on the international seabed area (ISBA) regime. However, the already existing trend towards groups based on shared

31

interests on various issues and crossing the regional groups accelerated. Thus, for instance, the coastal states group (CSG) evolved to include members from all of the regions and, although there were significant differences of emphasis among its many members, it met regularly and sought to cooperate on common objectives. In the opposite corner, so to speak, was the group of land-locked and geographically disadvantaged states (LLGDS—evolving from the Land-Locked Group at UNCLOS I and II), which crossed the regional groups. Issues generated other interest groups both at this and later sessions. Of special interest to Ireland was the emergence at this session of embryonic opposing groups on the issue of islands and the coming together of a few wide margin states, the latter being the forerunner of the Margineers Group (see below in the chapter on the Third Session). A small group of major maritime states also held meetings. As the Conference proceeded the Arab states became cohesive as the Arab Group and were active on several issues, not least on the outer limits of the continental shelf. The EEC member states were not a group related to UN membership but they followed their usual conference practice of meeting regularly. These meetings included both coordination on issues coming within EEC competence (mainly fisheries) and discussion of other issues where the possibility of common positions of the nine member states was explored (in the context of political cooperation), particularly in regard to the high seas and the ISBA. A novel development was the Evensen Group, an unofficial group convened by Mr Jens Evensen, Norwegian Minister without Portfolio and head of the Norwegian delegation. It began as a small number of heads and legal experts of mostly Western delegations, thus not widely representative, invited by Minister Evensen to an informal exchange of views on Second Committee topics, in fact mainly the exclusive economic zone (EEZ). The early members included France, the FRG, the Netherlands and the UK from the EEC member states. It evoked a certain resentment at both the fact that its participants were predominantly from developed countries and its practice of meeting at the same times as the Conference Committees. Inevitably, this practice detrimentally affected attendance at the Committee meetings.

PLENARY

The early days of the session were taken up with finalisation and adoption of the rules of procedure and allocation of subjects and issues among the Plenary and the Main Committees. This was followed by two weeks of general debate, in which states broadly indicated their positions and the nature of the provisions they expected to emerge. Priority was given in this procedure to countries that had not been members of the Seabed Committee. In the event this was among only a few protracted periods of formal meetings in UNCLOS III. Most of the substantive work was done in negotiating or working groups or informal meetings of Plenary and the Committees, although advances in the negotiations usually required endorsement in formal meetings of Plenary.

The Attorney General, Mr Declan Costello, attending as Special Representative of the Government, spoke for Ireland in the general debate on 11 July. His statement identified the objective of the Conference as adoption of a convention comprising rules of law that were binding, just and reasonable. He made suggestions for guiding principles for the Conference and comments on issues of Irish concern. He urged that states' self-interest should be enlightened and that advantage should not be used to override the common good of the world community. He felt that the 1958 conventions should be built on, although with appropriate improvement.

The statement, of course, reflected many of the recommendations adopted by the Government, mainly those involving important Irish interests, such as the proposed EEZ, fisheries with particular reference to anadromous species (salmon), continental shelf, islands and rocks, MSR and preservation of the marine environment, as well as some of lesser national importance, such as the breadth of the territorial sea and the regime for the ISBA. There were some elaborations on the recommendations. On the EEZ, the statement spoke of a pluralist regime to accommodate the differences in responsibilities, rights and obligations accruing in respect of the individual fields of jurisdiction (to which control of navigation was added as a coastal state function). The state of origin of a stock of anadromous species (salmon) alone should manage, control and exploit that stock. This would not only protect the livelihood of coastal communities heavily dependent on salmon fishing, but also, and even more importantly, avoid a situation in which the state of origin would no longer regard as worthwhile the maintenance of the economically onerous measures necessary for the conservation of the stock. The statement advocated continental shelf jurisdiction based on the fact that the shelf was a submerged part of the coastal state land-mass, and that the definition should be one that distinguished geologically and geomorphologically between the continental and oceanic crusts (which implied enabling extension of jurisdiction to the edge of the margin). A combination of distance and geomorphological criteria could suffice to define the outer limits. On islands and rocks, there was a call for definitions and laws that respected equity and fair-dealing in regard to the effects on the limits of coastal state areas of jurisdiction, both seaward and between neighbouring states.

On preservation of the marine environment, the statement supported coastal state rights of enforcement of international regulations in the EEZ, and added a reference to existing pollution-related instruments. Likewise on MSR, while making the converse points about avoiding undue restriction on research and the overriding interest of the coastal state in its EEZ (without mentioning the continental shelf), the statement included both a cautionary reference to military research and support for transfer of technology (TOT) in the MSR field to developing countries.

The desirability of a twelve-mile territorial sea was accepted, provided baselines were drawn in accordance with fair criteria and the right of innocent passage was not restricted.

On the ISBA, the statement described Ireland as not being among the states intimately interested either as a potential seabed miner or as a principal beneficiary. Establishment of an international authority was urged, with an assembly as its supreme organ, and a council. The authority should not be precluded from undertaking exploitation, and the principal beneficiaries of the regime should be developing countries, on the basis of clear criteria for benefit sharing. There should be a compulsory settlement of disputes procedure. A novel idea was suggested—that if differences on this issue appeared insurmountable, a limited regime should be considered, with a view to future evolution and with a safeguard against creation of new rights that might impede such evolution.

When the general debate ended the Committees commenced work. Most of the work was undertaken in informal meetings of the Committees or negotiating or working groups. The objective of adopting this procedure was avoidance of formal records of detailed exchanges with a view to facilitating flexibility in negotiation. Many additional proposals were tabled and added to the existing documentation.

The main focus of the Irish delegation's interest was on issues in the Second and Third Committees. However, it also became involved in First Committee issues, not least because many of its EEC partners had a direct interest in these issues—and positions on them that varied widely from the Irish position.

Ambassador Aguilar chaired the informal meetings as well as the few formal meetings of the Second Committee. The agenda items were considered *seriatim*.

Delimitation and regime of islands

Two statements were made by the Irish delegation, on continental shelf delimitation between neighbouring states, on 30 July, and on fisheries, on 31 July. The former concentrated on the role of islands in delimitation and entered into more detail than the Attorney General's address. The statement did not reject the equidistance method (median line) of the 1958 Convention on the Continental Shelf, but drew attention to the possibility of a distinction between the capacity of an island to generate continental shelf jurisdiction and whether it should have an influence on division of areas of jurisdiction between neighbouring states. (Article 1 of the 1958 Convention on the Continental Shelf expressly included islands among territories entitled to a continental shelf. Article 6 on delimitation had no express reference to islands. Although the wording of the delimitation provisions differed between adjacent and opposite states, the method of division based respectively on the median line or equidistance from the respective baselines would prevail in both situations in the absence either of agreement otherwise or of special circumstances). The statement proposed that low tide elevations (i.e. ground totally under water at high tide), islands outside territorial seas and uninhabited islands, wherever situated, should have no relevance in determining a delimitation line; that in regard to other offshore islands, their size relative to the size of the owner state as a whole and their proximity to the mainland should be criteria for determining whether their use as base points would be in accordance with equitable principles; and that the low-water-mark rather than straight baselines should be the measuring point for continental shelf jurisdiction because, as the International Court of Justice had explained in the North Sea cases, such jurisdiction arose from the fact that the continental shelf is an extension of the land mass of the coastal state. The statement referred favourably to proposals by Malta (in a draft convention submitted to the Seabed Committee) and Romania (A/Conf.62/C.2/L.18) in this context, and also to part of a Netherlands proposal (C.2/L.14), which provided for delimitation by agreement in accordance with equitable principles. Notable in the Irish statement was the general reliance on the ICJ judgement. (In the subsequent long-drawn-out negotiations on this issue Romania was on the same side as

Ireland but Malta was on the opposite side, and the Netherlands was in between.)

On 6 August the delegation submitted to the Second Committee a draft article on delimitation of the continental shelf (C.2/L.43) on the lines of the statement. It provided primarily for delimitation by agreement in accordance with equitable principles—drawing on the ICJ decision. It accepted the median line as the main method of division but subject to its being consistent with equitable principles. It also provided for measurement of the median line from the low-water-mark rather than from straight baselines; and it specifically required that an offshore island could be taken into account only if it was inhabited and either within the breadth of the territorial sea (measured from the low-water-mark) or containing at least one tenth of both the land area and of the population of the owner state. Pending agreement, exploration or exploitation would be prohibited in any bona fide disputed area.

Neither the Irish statement nor the proposal related to the emerging EEZ, whose jurisdictional basis, unlike that of the continental shelf as identified by the ICJ, would rest on a simple distance criterion. Extension of the ICJ delimitation decision to the EEZ would lack authority. In so far as the EEZ covered fisheries, its delimitation was less important to Ireland in the light of elements of the EEC common fisheries policy, which provided for access for all member states to one another's fisheries and which were unlikely to be significantly changed in the pending revision. The separate definitive negotiations on shelf and EEZ jurisdiction in due course resulted in an overlapping of the two bases and areas of jurisdiction. Likewise, as the delimitation negotiations proceeded they covered the EEZ as well as the shelf. The possibility of having different delimitation provisions for the EEZ and the shelf was raised later but not pursued, probably because it would have added further complication to an issue that proved to be one of the most intractable at the Conference. Similarly, the apparent distinction in the 1958 convention as regards delimitation between opposite or adjacent states was not maintained. (This distinction also figures in the ICJ judgement).

The issue of delimitation was by its nature one of controversy between neighbouring states with adjoining areas of marine jurisdiction, mainly involving continental shelf jurisdiction. It inevitably featured confrontation between such states, perhaps most notably between Greece and Turkey in regard to the Aegean Sea with its multitude of Greek islands, many of them much closer to the Turkish than to the Greek mainland. Indeed the most controversial element in delimitation issues was often that of the effect, if any, on the dividing line, of islands situate between the states. Thus Greece included, in each of a series of proposals on the continental shelf (C.2/L.25), the EEZ (C.2/L.32) and other marine zones (C.2/L.22), a provision on delimitation that established the median line as the dividing line unless the states concerned agreed otherwise and gave all offshore islands full influence. This was based on the 1958 convention provision, but was more extreme in its addition of the provision on islands and omission of the modifying element of special circumstances. In a proposal on regime of islands (C.2/L.50) (reiterating in more detail a provision in C.2/L.22) Greece proposed that all islands would have the same entitlement to marine zones as continental states. Proposals by Japan (C.2/L.31) on delimitation and Uruguay (C.2/L.75) on regime islands followed the same line, and the Irish delegation report identified Italy as another supporter of that position.

Conversely Turkey, in a series of proposals on the territorial seas (C.2/L.9), on the continental shelf (C.2/L.23) and on delimitation of the EEZ (C.2/L.34), incorporated provisions calling for delimitation by agreement in accordance with equitable principles (as in the ICJ decision—see above), taking account of all relevant factors and of special circumstances (including the configuration of the coasts and the presence of islands, islets and rocks), and using method(s) appropriate to reaching equitable delimitation based on agreement. In a proposal on regime of islands (C.2/L.55), Turkey would deny any marine zone to low-tide elevations or rocks or to islands without economic life and situate outside the territorial seas of their states, and would deny EEZ or continental shelf jurisdiction to an island in the EEZ or on the continental shelf of another state unless it contained at least one tenth of the land area and population of its owner state. Proposals on the same lines were made on delimitation by Romania (C.2/L.18), by Kenya and Tunisia (C.2/L.28), by the latter two and sixteen other African states (C.2/L.82 on the EEZ, Article 8) and by France (C.2/L.74); and also on regime of islands by Romania (C.2/L.53), and fourteen African states (C.2/L.62), with both the substance of the two topics (delimitation and islands), and the co-sponsors, overlapping. The Netherlands proposal already mentioned (C.2/L.14) was also on the same lines, except that it gave significant status to the median line by making it an interim measure pending agreement. It also provided for compulsory settlement of disputes. Clearly these proposals were to varying degrees close to Irish interests.

The rival delimitation proposals reflected respectively a rejection and an embracing of the ICJ decision. Thus the stage was set for long and difficult, and sometimes bitter, negotiations.

In regard to generation of zones of marine jurisdiction by islands it was anticipated that many of the G-77 would take a negative attitude, fearing the use of colonial islands as a basis for claims by Western states in Third World regions, including claims to the newly emerging EEZ. Proposals by New Zealand, Fiji, Tonga and Western Samoa (C.2/L.30), Turkey (C.2/L.55) and Argentina (C.2/L.58) reflected concerns to protect rights for the indigenous peoples, and drew the wrath of the US *inter alios*. This subsequently became a separate issue under the rubric of 'territories under foreign domination' and was not ultimately an element of the negotiation of the regime of islands. However, archipelagic and island states among the G-77 were naturally resistant to any restriction of marine jurisdiction accruing to islands. The Irish statement sought to separate this issue from that of the role of islands in delimitation but, even if they were separated, the question of generation was not totally irrelevant to delimitation. Thus Turkey and others pursued both issues. The Irish delegation report on the session correctly anticipated the likelihood of Ireland being drawn into a similar position.

Exclusive economic zone and fisheries

The delegation statement relating to the EEZ and fisheries enlarged on the remarks in the Attorney General's address. It emphasised that the main purpose of the provisions should be to ensure, through careful management and exploitation, the maximum yield, year after year without depletion, of fishery stocks, and urged coastal state exercise of control in a wide fisheries zone as the most effective means of achieving that purpose. While the coastal state should have prior right of exploitation, other states also had legitimate interests. Coastal state control should include determination of the total allowable catch (TAC) in consultation with conservation organisations, and its allocation and enforcement. There should be appropriate settlement of disputes procedures. Again it advocated sole control over and exploitation of anadromous species by the state of origin as the only means of maintaining maximum yield.

Subsequently eight of the EEC members (the UK being the exception) tabled in the Second Committee, on 5 August, a set of draft articles (A/Conf.62/C.2/L.40) on fisheries (expressly as a basis for discussion rather than as a definitive position). This draft had been prepared in EEC coordination meetings over the previous eighteen months. The draft would give the coastal state less than total control over fishing in a zone (of undefined width), subject also to a compulsory consultative role for international fishery organisations. The coastal state would have the right to regulate fishing in the zone and calculate the TAC as well as enjoying preferential fishing rights, all within guidelines to be set out by a regional/sectoral organisation, and subject to an arbitration settlement of disputes system. Rights in the zone for other states, including those who had traditionally fished there and land-locked states, were provided for although subject to conditions. Flag state enforcement of zone regulations would take priority over enforcement by the coastal state. A provision intended to ensure that fishing rights under the EEC common fisheries policy would be unaffected by the new convention was unacceptable to the UK. It regarded the provision as implying support for the access arrangements of that policy, which the UK was seeking to change in the context of the on-going internal EEC negotiations on its revision. Although Ireland shared the UK's desire for such a change, the delegation accepted that this provision was necessary in any case to enable EEC member states to accord rights to one another in preference to rights for non-member states in the categories set out in the draft. It could not realistically or reasonably be expected that there would not be any special rights for member states, not necessarily rights of access, in a revised EEC common fisheries policy. Moreover, review of the policy was an internal EEC matter rather than one that should become an issue between the delegations of the EEC member states at the Conference, and the provision proposed was not inconsistent with review of the policy as distinct from an abandonment of it.

The draft clearly represented a compromise between the coastal EEC members (for example Ireland, the UK, France) and the LLGDS member states (for example Benelux, the FRG). It reflected closely the Irish position as set out in the delegation's statement in the Committee, which of course was influenced by the likely impact of the EEC fishery policy on any extended fishery waters acquired by Ireland and by the EEC consultations leading to the draft and its tabling. It fell far short of the positions (and not only the most extreme ones) of many of the members of the CSG at the Conference, which, however, had never been supported by Ireland. The issue became more controversial among the EEC members as the Conference proceeded and a regime more favourable to coastal states gathered support. It was already clear that there was general support at the Conference for an EEZ of 200 miles width, and that the future negotiation would concentrate on the regime applicable to it.

Anadromous species

On 5 August the Irish delegation also submitted a draft article (C.2/L.41) on confining exploitation of stocks of anadromous species to the state of origin within waters under its jurisdiction, and permitting exploitation by any other state only within waters under the latter's jurisdiction and in agreement with the state of origin. Among states with similar positions were Canada (most notably), the US, the UK, the Soviet Union and Iceland. Canada tabled a paper (C.2/L.81) illustrating that conservation and maximum yield of salmon could be achieved only by the state of origin through often difficult and economically expensive measures. Thus it must enjoy both the main control of its stock and the cooperation of other exploiting states. Denmark and Japan, exploiters rather than states of origin, also submitted proposals (C.2/L.37 and C.2/L.46), respectively) calling for agreement on exploitation between interested states, and/or international regulation. The Japanese proposal, unlike the Danish proposal, acknowledged a preferential position for the state of origin. As indicated in the Irish delegation report on the session, it appeared that the bulk of the G-77 members were resistant to any position restrictive of a coastal state's rights in its own EEZ, including restriction on a right to exploit anadromous species originating elsewhere. The US particularly was unenthusiastic for a confrontation with the G-77 on this issue. Yet, in its proposal on the EEZ etc. (C.2/L.47), the US included a provision prohibiting exploitation of anadromous species outside the territorial sea unless authorised by the state of origin. Ireland and Canada, albeit more reluctantly, subscribed to this view, more conservative than their own view but less conservative than the privately expressed US view. Hence confinement of exploitation solely to the state of origin was not suggested in the Canadian paper or the Irish proposal.

Continental shelf

The question of definition of the outer limits of continental shelf jurisdiction was one of the most controversial, and at the same time, most open, issues at UNCLOS III. The 1958 convention relevant provision, setting out a combination of depth and exploitability criteria, had been undermined by advances in exploitation technology, and fatally wounded by the ICJ (North Sea cases) decision. This decision was to the effect that, under international law, continental shelf jurisdiction derived from the fact that the shelf was a natural prolongation of the coastal state land-mass. However, the North Sea cases were not concerned with outer limits and the judgement did not therefore give any direction on precise identification of outer limits. Specifically, it did not clearly indicate whether jurisdiction extended to all the areas having continental rather than oceanic crust, i.e. the whole margin comprising the geological shelf, slope and rise. While coastal states with wide margins wished to claim these areas in full, the LLGDS group (part of whose *raison d'être* was opposition to extension of coastal state jurisdiction) and others who sought the widest possible area for the ISBA, were opposed to such claims.

Several proposals to fill this void were made, including a combination of 500-metre isobath and 100-miles distance (by the Soviet Union), and a definition purely in terms of natural prolongation. For different reasons neither of these was regarded as viable in itself. The two most practical (and mutually opposed) proposals were (i) amalgamation of continental shelf jurisdiction into the proposed EEZ with a 200-mile limit, and (ii) continental shelf jurisdiction throughout the EEZ and extending to any margin beyond the EEZ in any individual case. The US floated the idea that combining a degree of revenue sharing with this approach might make it more acceptable. The Irish position, as per instructions, was predicated on the assumption that prolongation ended at the base of the slope, which in Ireland's case coincided generally with the 200-mile distance. However, proposal (ii) would give Ireland a greatly enhanced area of jurisdiction on the slope and rise, provided it was not cut off by an area of jurisdiction accruing to Rockall. Accordingly, the delegation, mindful of the guideline in its instructions to safeguard and promote national interests and the definition of a wide area of coastal state resource jurisdiction as a national interest, did not commit itself to either of the two proposals at the session. Nevertheless, the Attorney General's address, with its references to a distinction between oceanic and continental crusts, to combined distance and geomorphological criteria and to jurisdiction possibly reaching the edge of the margin, hinted strongly at the line of proposal (ii). Even if the proposal had not specifically emerged at the time of the statement the delegation would have been aware that it was pending. Certainly the delegation discussed the matter thoroughly internally during the session, taking into account *inter alia* the Rockall and ISBA aspects, and opposing views were expressed. It was felt that further discussion at headquarters would be necessary to determine whether the delegation position and/or instructions needed adaptation or revision.

Territorial sea, straits, high seas and archipelagos

There was wide consensus that the breadth of the territorial sea could be extended to twelve miles. However, for the major maritime states, with their shipping and navy concerns, their acceptance was subject to parallel acceptance that there would be unimpeded passage through ('on, over and under' as understood by the US) straits enclosed in territorial seas by such an extension. Thus, led by the US and the Soviet Union, these states sought free transit through straits with limited coastal state control and traditional immunity for naval vessels. (This, unlike the traditional right of innocent passage through territorial seas, would include uncontrolled overflight and permission for submarines to remain submerged). The Irish delegation was not very active in this area of negotiations. The contiguous zone received little attention. Some thought it superfluous in the light of extended territorial seas but it received greater consideration at later sessions.

There was little discussion of the high seas topic, probably reflecting a wide acceptance both of a twelve-mile territorial sea limit and of the high seas regime as set out in the 1958 convention, subject to adaptation to other developments (notably the EEZ) and perhaps a need for further elaboration. This trend was apparent also in a working paper submitted on 12 August by the EEC member states (including Ireland) acting in political cooperation in a field not with EEC competences—the EEC-9. This also proposed draft articles providing for some exceptions from high seas freedoms, with a view both to reducing abuses connected with flags of convenience and to enabling stricter measures against illegal trafficking in narcotics and unauthorised broadcasting. On archipelagos there was little if any movement with the main problem still outstanding, i.e. ensuring a moderate approach to enclosure and reconciling the consequences of enclosure with maintenance of freedom of navigation. The maritime states advocated that modified versions of free transit and innocent passage should apply to different parts of newly enclosed waters, depending on the circumstances. The Irish delegation did not take a public stand on the issue at the session.

Uganda tabled the Kampala Declaration, adopted at a meeting of developing LLGDS in March 1974, as a Conference document. It made claims for LLGDS rights of access to the sea and related rights, rights in regard to coastal states' zones of jurisdiction and rights in regard to the ISBA with a corollary that that area should be extensive. Of these issues the only ones considered at the session were questions of access to the seas for land-locked states and rights of exploitation for the LLGDS in the marine zones of their neighbours. The former question was controversial only on the aspect of whether the future convention should have explicit provisions or the matter could be left to be worked out in detail in individual agreements. As none of the LLGDS was a neighbour of Ireland the delegation did not participate in the exchanges. Other LLGDS pursuits would prove more intrusive in Irish interests at later sessions, particularly in regard to the outer limits of the continental shelf.

Nearing the end of the session the Second Committee Bureau prepared a set of informal working papers, based on the documentation (including new proposals) before the Committee and intended to reflect the main trends, often multiple, on controversial issues. It was specifically indicated that this did not prevent tabling of and deliberation on further proposals. These papers were comprised in a single document (A/Conf.62/C.2/WP.1). A partial discussion of the document in informal meetings was undertaken in the remaining part of the session. The Irish delegation was pleased at the progress so made and satisfied its preferences were reflected in the document.

THIRD COMMITTEE

Marine scientific research and transfer of technology

The Committee resorted to informal meetings at an early stage. Meetings on MSR and TOT were chaired by Mr Cornel Metternich (FRG). Under existing law the coastal state's territorial seas jurisdiction included full control over MSR and, under the 1958 Convention on the Continental Shelf, its consent was required for conduct of MSR by others on its shelf (such consent not to be unreasonably withheld in respect of purely scientific research). The pending ISBA regime and the proposed establishment of the EEZ and extension of continental shelf jurisdiction raised new questions. The CSG and G-77 proposed that the coastal state should have exclusive right to conduct and regulate MSR in all marine areas under its jurisdiction, and that MSR in the ISBA should be conducted by, or under the direct effective control of, the international authority—thus avoiding disguised commercial exploration or military activities. In opposition (promoted particularly by the US) it was proposed that outside the territorial seas conduct of MSR should be free unless concerned with exploration or exploitation of resources in a coastal state zone, in which case consent of the coastal state should be required. The EEC-9, most of which were advanced industrially, including some with deep seabed mining capacity, were initially split three ways on the issue. Some of them joined with other states in proposing that MSR should be free outside the territorial seas but subject to obligations if in the EEZ, including notification of the coastal state and making the data available to it. Others of the nine joined with the Soviet Union and others in differentiating between applied (including resource-related) and pure research and making the latter absolutely free outside territorial seas.

The Irish delegate made a statement on 19 July indicating the Irish position and elaborating on the Attorney General's address. The statement said the distinction between applied and pure research was difficult to define, and any attempted definition was liable to be rendered obsolete with development of technology. Thus MSR in the EEZ should be subject to the consent of the coastal state, which, however, should not be arbitrarily refused or withheld for an unreasonable length of time. The coastal state also should have the right to regulate MSR and the researchers should be obliged to observe its regulations. In the ISBA conduct of MSR should be free but subject to notification to the authority to facilitate it in seeking coordination and efficiency of programmes. The authority should also seek coordination with states having jurisdiction in areas adjacent to the ISBA. Results of ISBA research should be disseminated as widely and quickly as possible. The statement also supported those developing countries that had advocated establishment of suitable mechanisms for TOT.

The statement reflected the overall concern to facilitate MSR. Other like-minded states (including Mexico, Australia, Canada, New Zealand and Spain), varying only slightly from the Irish position, spoke in terms of consent not being normally withheld if the coastal state's conditions were met. The Irish delegation report suggested a slight inconsistency between the statement and a view that MSR in the ISBA should be under the jurisdiction of the authority. However, the instructions were unclear on this point. The report also indicated that the delegation refrained from submitting a written proposal on MSR in the expectation that one could be more effectively submitted later as a compromise.

Environment

Mr Jose Vallarta (Mexico) chaired informal meetings on preservation of the environment as he had done in the Seabed Committee. There was general agreement, carried over from the Seabed Committee, on obligations of states to preserve the marine environment, as favoured in the delegation's instructions. However, some developing countries suggested that the level of preventive measures required to be taken by individual states should be varied in accordance with their stage of development. The delegation did not add to the Attorney General's statement in the general debate that supported coastal state rights of enforcement in the EEZ. Such a right in regard to seabed exploration and exploitation activities was generally acceptable. However, the main issue was coastal state jurisdiction in regard to dumping and (other) vessel-source pollution, and attitudes depended on the extent and nature of that control, including whether national, as distinct from international, standards could be imposed and enforced. The major industrialised and maritime states were strongly opposed to that possibility. In the cooperation consultations of the EEC-9 the Irish delegation reserved its freedom to support a proposal giving the coastal state the residual right to impose in the EEZ, in limited circumstances, standards higher than those prescribed in international conventions (going beyond the trend of the Attorney General's statement but in conformity with the very general instructions). This attitude drew heavy criticism from all the others of the EEC-9, none of which was willing to accept enforcement of national standards by the coastal state in the EEZ in regard to dumping or other vessel-source pollution. This difference was hardly surprising, bearing in mind that all were more industrially advanced than Ireland and several were major shipping powers, while few had as much potential for an EEZ area.

At the end of the session the Third Committee Bureau, following the example in the Second Committee, prepared main trends documents in regard to MSR and TOT (A/Conf.62/C.3/L.15) and (partially) the environment (C.3/L.17). The Irish delegation again was pleased with the progress so made and satisfied that the documents covered its concerns.

FIRST COMMITTEE

This Committee held a one-week general debate before moving to informal negotiating and working group meetings. The latter were chaired by Mr C.W. Pinto (Sri Lanka), continuing a role he had undertaken in the Seabed Committee.

International seabed area

There was no significant discussion of the limits of the ISBA that was already accepted (in the UN General Assembly Declaration) as the area beyond the limits of national jurisdiction. Indeed there seemed to be tacit acceptance that the ISBA would effectively begin at the edge of the continental margin, i.e. it should comprise the ocean abyss where the known resources were manganese nodules rich in such minerals as nickel, copper, zinc and cobalt as well as manganese.

The discussions concentrated on the operational international institutions, their functions and powers, and particularly the ensuing question of what entity (or entities) should carry out the work of exploitation There were two competing views for the overall regime, that of the G-77 and that of a group of industrially advanced countries, which included most of those with seabed mining capacity. The G-77 envisaged an international authority with exclusive control over exploration and exploitation and conduct of MSR in the ISBA and over marketing of the products and distribution of profits. While the G-77 also saw an organ of the authority (the enterprise) as the entity to be primarily given the task of exploration and exploitation, it seemed to realise that there would be a need to employ other entities (states, corporations including multinationals), at least initially, to carry out that work. In such circumstances the authority would need adequate powers to enable it to hold its own in negotiations with these entities. Within the authority a universally representative assembly should be vested with the fundamental powers rather than the second organ, the council. The latter, which was seen as the instrument for carrying out the day-to-day work of the authority, would have limited membership (with the possibility that the industrialised countries would have greater influence in it than in the assembly). The group of industrialised countries, led by the US, on the other hand, favoured a more limited authority, having as its main function the issuing, through the council, of exploration and exploitation licences only to states or companies sponsored by states, on terms to be laid down in the convention. It should not have power to regulate MSR in the ISBA or to control marketing of the minerals produced. The assembly should be confined to establishing general policy.

The Irish position, adhering closely to the General Assembly Declaration of Principles and based on the view that the resources of the ISBA should be used to narrow the economic gap between the richer and poorer nations (with a flexible approach to the method of achieving that objective), was set out in a delegation statement on 17 July. The statement elaborated slightly on the earlier address by the Attorney General. It anticipated that the desirable outcome would be more likely if control rested with an organ in which poorer countries had a predominant voice. Thus a universally representative assembly should have the overall powers, although a smaller council, but not one dominated by industrialised countries, would be necessary for efficient operation. Distribution of profits should lean in favour of disadvantaged countries on the basis of criteria to be laid down in the convention. The authority should be free to operate through licensing, joint ventures, service contracts or other commercial arrangements with states or corporations, or by direct exploitation, according to whatever methods it considered most likely to achieve the greatest profit. Security of investment and a compulsory settlement of disputes procedure would be essential to engender confidence in potential state or corporation explorers and exploiters. The authority should also control marketing and in doing so should be particularly concerned not to damage primary producers of minerals, many of whom were extremely economically disadvantaged. (Interestingly the Irish and US delegations drew diametrically opposed deductions from a presentation by a UN Conference on Trade and Development (UNCTAD) official regarding the likely effect on land-based producers).

As is apparent, the Irish statement was much nearer to the G-77 position than that of the industrialised countries, and evoked severe criticism from the others of the EEC-9. The main concern these eight countries expressed was that access to the minerals of the ISBA, which they regarded as essential for their future prosperity, would be denied by an authority dominated by G-77 countries (shades of the then recent first oil crisis). They rejected Irish arguments that the authority need not be dominated by either partisan group, that many of the G-77 were mineral consumers and that it would be in the interest of all of them to make the minerals available if they would profit most from the sale. These eight countries felt that the interests of land-based producers (of minerals with which the ISBA-sourced minerals would be in competition) in the G-77 would override those of consumers. Their overriding objective was guaranteed market access to the ISBA minerals without artificial restraint or price-fixing, regardless of the possibility of depression of prices and of consequential damage to land-based producers.

Consultations within the EEC-9 led to preparation of a set of draft articles on the regime to which all agreed, except Ireland. The delegation felt the articles leaned too far in favour industrialised countries to be compatible with its instructions. The draft articles (A/Conf.62/C.1/L.8) were submitted on 16 August with eight co-sponsors. Prior to its tabling the delegation was subjected to very heavy pressure by the others of the nine, directly experienced by the author in his capacity at the time both as First Committee delegate and as acting head of delegation (in the temporary absence, of Ambassador Cremin, who was in hospital at that time). The French (current holders of the EEC Presidency) and Dutch were particularly pressing, as were the Danes for different reasons—the other Scandinavians had adopted a position similar to Ireland's and the Danes had pleaded EEC-9 solidarity as the reason for not joining them. The UK delegation, severely disappointed at the Irish unwillingness to join it in rejecting the earlier fisheries draft proposed by all the member states except the UK, combined their criticism of the Irish position on this issue with a certain wry satisfaction that, on this issue, the Irish delegation was experiencing similar isolation among the members, even if on a topic outside EEC competences.

The session discussions concentrated on the system of exploitation of the resources more than on strictly institutional issues. Thus such questions were addressed as whether exploitation should be carried out by the authority itself or by other entities, conditions of exploitation and economic implications for land-based producers. While the Seabed Committee had forwarded to UNCLOS III alternative texts on many issues, they did not include any drafts on rules and regulations for seabed mining, which the G-77 regarded as a matter for the proposed authority. Proposals by the US (C.1/L.6), by eight of the EEC members (C.1/L.8 as mentioned above) and by Japan (C.1/L.9) set out the position shared by the seabed mining countries. For quite some time it looked as if there might be a breakdown on the question of who could exploit, with veiled threats of the possibility of unilateral exploitation, despite the thrust of the General Assembly Declaration of Principles. The situation calmed with the submission at a relatively late stage of a G-77 paper (C.1/L.7) on basic conditions regarding exploitation that accepted that the authority could, while retaining direct and effective control, enter into arrangements with other entities for exploration and exploitation, and that the convention could contain regulations concerning the authority's power of so contracting. This development more precisely defined, and even narrowed, an area for negotiation.

PLENARY

Peaceful settlement of disputes

An informal group of about 30 interested delegations (in which Ireland and all others of the EEC-9 except Denmark participated) discussed the question of peaceful settlement of disputes under the joint chairmanship of Ambassador Galindo Pohl (El Salvador) and Ambassador Ralph Harry (Australia). There was general agreement that a procedure for settlement of disputes arising out of the future convention was highly desirable. A working paper (A/Conf.62/L.7) co-sponsored by the Benelux countries, Australia, and El Salvador *inter alios*, but not claiming the support of all the participants in the group, was tabled in Plenary. It was introduced by Ambassador Galindo Pohl on the last day of the session and thus not discussed. The paper was quite extensive and included many alternatives, thus resembling the main trends documents that emerged from the Second and Third Committees.

On 27 August the Plenary decided to recommend to the UN General Assembly that the Third Session of UNCLOS III be held in Geneva from 17 March to 2 May 1975, with the possibility of extending for a further week, and that its final session be held in Caracas. Thus an invitation from the Austrian Government to hold the Third Session in Vienna was declined as suitable dates were not available at that venue. The Plenary's decision to recommend that the final session be held in Caracas refrained from indicating any dates, although the General Committee had suggested the period of July–August 1975.

CONCLUSION

The session had two main features. Firstly, delegations (particularly those that had not been members of the Seabed Committee) had the opportunity to set out in full their positions on the Conference, generally and on the various issues, and to submit proposals. These procedures served to highlight further the enormous disparity in positions already apparent from the huge amount of documentation before the Conference, particularly proposals carried forward from the Seabed Committee. Secondly, the Second and Third Committees sought to clarify and even modify the disparity by preparing the main trends documents. The Irish delegation, presumably like others, saw this as a welcome step towards facilitating negotiations. Moreover, it could be said to have begun laying the foundation for achievement of a convention. Nevertheless, the ensuing negotiations proved to be more difficult and protracted than then anticipated. The continuing optimism that UNCLOS III could be completed rapidly was apparent in the discussions in the General Committee and Plenary on dates and venue for the Third Session. Several delegates anticipated a signature session in Caracas in autumn 1975 or early in 1976—an attitude that was partly reflected in the ensuing decision. In addition some post-session remarks, by officials as well as commentators, suggested that anticipation of the Third Session had slowed progress, by discouraging delegations from taking difficult decisions on concessions at the Second Session. The Irish delegation took the less sanguine view that at least two more sessions would be required to complete the work—a view that was itself proved to be wildly optimistic.

The logistical arrangements for the Second Session, put in place at short notice by the Venezuelan authorities (following Chile's reluctant withdrawal, at the final session of the Seabed Committee, of its invitation) were very satisfactory. The session was held in the city-centre custombuilt Parque Central, which provided all the needed facilities, including many and varied accommodations for meetings and consultations as well as a delegation room for each delegation. (However, the Irish delegation had to bring English language typewriters from New York). It also provided an individual apartment for each head of delegation in the Parque Central. The other delegates secured accommodation in hotels around the city. The Irish delegates stayed at the Hotel Avila, a relatively old-fashioned hotel in the hills between the centre city and the sea, where they had some EEC Commission delegates for company. While comfortable, it had some disadvantages. It was some distance from the Parque Central. Its restaurant was seriously unsatisfactory and there were no other restaurants nearby. Thus there was a constant transport problem. For one of the delegates, Seamus Mallon, assistance was unexpectedly at hand. The Venezuelan authorities, without explanation, provided him with a daily car and driver/bodyguard. Whether this had anything to do with his personal history as a member of a family intimately involved in the national struggle 1916–23, or his not unconnected emigration to Venezuela as a young engineer in the 1920s, was never revealed. The two gentlemen who provided the service were most pleasant and helpful to all the delegates, and not at all averse to having additional passengers.

There were other, less pleasant, experiences. Ambassador Cremin was taken ill and spent some time in hospital. However, he recovered in time to resume his duties as head of delegation for the final fortnight. Mary O'Regan, the delegation's very efficient administrative assistant, was knocked down on the street and robbed, and the author had his wallet stolen by a pickpocket. Other acquaintances were even more unfortunate in being robbed at knifepoint. The stark contrast between the city centre hotels, in which many delegates were accommodated, and the incredibly congested flimsy dwellings of the overcrowded *barrios* nearby afforded a convincing, if regrettable, rationale for such events.

Chapter VI

THIRD SESSION

The Third Session was held at the United Nations Office (Palais des Nations) in Geneva from 17 March to 9 May 1975 for eight weeks, including an optional extra week.

PREPARATIONS

The Inter-Departmental Committee (IDC) met several times to consider the developments at the Second Session and to review policy in that light. Likewise the EEC delegations met for the same purpose, concentrating on fisheries, the international seabed area (ISBA), environment and marine scientific research (MSR).

The Minister for Industry and Commerce, Mr Justin Keating, called a meeting with the members of the delegation engaged in the continental shelf negotiation. At the Second Session, delegations of some states with broad margins, led by Argentina, Australia and Canada, had advocated coastal state continental shelf jurisdiction over the whole geological continental margin, i.e. the shelf, slope and rise, relying on a certain interpretation of *dicta* in the judgement in the North Sea cases. Of the other states having broad margins (estimated at 35–40, including Ireland) some (including the UK) privately supported the approach so advocated. The Irish delegation had not taken a position pending further consideration at headquarters. The British delegation had also spoken privately in Caracas of the possibility of an early British continental shelf designation order (i.e. an order indicating areas of shelf claimed by the UK in respect of which the British Government was ready to consider granting exploration/exploitation licences) covering areas extending across the Rockall Trough and on to the Faeroes Plateau. Such an order was in fact made on 8 September (very shortly after the end of the Second Session). In Ireland the Minister for Industry and Commerce, personally, and his

Department, were strongly of the view that Ireland should seek jurisdiction over the whole margin, and were encouraged in that view by
the UK action. At the opening meeting with the British (10
December 1974) on bilateral delimitation of the continental shelf
between the two countries, the recent British designation was criticised by the Irish side, but only insofar as it covered an area disputed
between the sides, i.e. it crossed a dividing line proposed by the Irish
side in a letter dated 12 July 1974. A similar Irish designation order
followed, made by the Government on 20 December that, in designating areas as Irish continental shelf, both covered an area already
designated by the UK and extended across the Rockall Trough on to
the Faeroes Plateau. Crossing the Rockall Trough involved claiming
jurisdiction in an area of rise sedimentation in the Trough, thus
implicitly claiming coastal state jurisdiction extending over the
margin. This designation was of course a response, not only to the
encroachment in the recent British designation, but also, effectively,
to the question whether Ireland should support at UNCLOS III the
position of those broad margin states claiming jurisdiction over the
whole margin. In the latter context both designations could be
regarded by some participating states as unilateral action, particularly
states opposing the broad margin states' position, and rejecting the
interpretation of *dicta* in the judgement in the North Sea cases (see
above) on which that position was based.

In EEC consultations it was anticipated that the emerging exclusive economic zone (EEZ) would provide for exclusive rather than
preferential coastal state fishing rights, and that the fisheries proposal
submitted by eight of the members would not prove viable. There
were indications of willingness, at least by some members, to prepare
a proposal that would have better prospects of general acceptance
and would favour the needs of poorer coastal areas in such member
states as Ireland, Italy and the UK. It was also hoped that the UK
would join with the other eight members in co-sponsoring a revised
proposal.

The EEC-9 review of the ISBA item again reflected the fears of the
industrialised countries regarding sterilisation of production and/or
procrastination or discrimination in sale of minerals. Nevertheless,
some members, particularly the Netherlands and Denmark, felt the
proposal of the eight needed modification, and were willing to explore
the possibility of an EEC-9 draft more amenable to the Group of 77
(G-77). However others, particularly France, the Federal Republic of
Germany (the FRG) and the UK, were opposed.

INSTRUCTIONS

Following these developments and deliberations, the Department of Foreign Affairs prepared a submission on instructions for the Third Session, which, when agreed with the IDC departments and other interested departments, including the Department of the Taoiseach and the Attorney General's Office, was submitted by the Minister for Foreign Affairs to the Government on 18 March 1975.

The submission proposed confirmation of the existing instructions in regard to the territorial sea, the contiguous zone, high seas, straits, archipelagic waters, islands, the EEZ, fisheries, MSR, transfer of technology (TOT), and the ISBA. It elaborated on some of these topics—the EEZ, fisheries and anadromous species (salmon), the ISBA regime and, to a lesser extent, MSR and TOT.

With regard to anadromous species it was felt that the prospects for the Irish proposal submitted at the Second Session were promising. The planning of a campaign was under way, together with the main other interested parties, Canada, Iceland, the Soviet Union, the UK and the US, with a view to persuading uncommitted countries of the need for a provision along those lines. The existing instructions were adequate.

On MSR and TOT it was recounted that at the Second Session the delegation had been one of a group of delegations advocating a middle course between the extremes represented by some of the G-77 on the one hand and the US on the other. Confirmation of existing instructions on this issue would be appropriate.

The submission suggested adjustments to the instructions re continental shelf jurisdiction and preservation of the environment, and proposed, for the first time, instructions on peaceful settlement of disputes (PSD) provisions.

Continental shelf

On the continental shelf the submission, in the context of the steps taken since the Second Session, rehearsed the arguments for (the advantage of jurisdiction over areas on the Faeroes Plateau and on the western rise, which were now regarded as having mineral potential) and against (expected difficulties in identifying the limits of the margin in the west, and the risks and expense involved in exploitation in such deep waters) supporting coastal state claims for jurisdiction over the margin. A further consideration was that such claims applied world wide would reduce the ISBA. Irish support would not chime very well with its stated position on the ISBA regime and might forfeit the sympathy of some G-77 members on other important issues, for example in regard to anadromous species or delimitation of marine zones between neighbouring states. The submission also speculated that among the EEC-9, only the UK and France, for obvious reasons of self-interest and with no similar concern about reducing the ISBA, were likely to favour this attitude, unless the benefits of the shelf resources were to accrue to the EEC as a whole—not an attractive proposition for Ireland (or the UK or presumably France). Obviously, bearing in mind the action already taken, support for coastal state jurisdiction over the whole margin was advocated. An adaptation of instructions would be needed to enable the delegation to pursue this line. Accordingly, a new instruction was proposed to the effect that the delegation should support (i) an EEZ of 200 miles, including jurisdiction over non-living resources (minerals) together with similar jurisdiction beyond the EEZ over the continental margin (including the slope and rise), provided this enabled Irish jurisdiction on the Faeroes Plateau and (ii) no EEZ or continental shelf for isolated and uninhabited islands.

Environment

On the environment the submission adverted to general acceptance at the Second Session of coastal state jurisdiction in the EEZ in regard to pollution from seabed activities, for example exploration or exploitation of resources. There had also been a tendency to accept coastal state jurisdiction in the EEZ in regard to dumping and (other) vessel-source pollution, depending on the extent and nature of such jurisdiction.

However, attention was drawn to the serious differences that had arisen about another issue—whether the coastal state should be permitted to apply standards to ships, including those sailing under foreign flags, that were more strict than those internationally agreed (particularly in the International Maritime Consultative Organisation (IMCO) Convention following the *Torrey Canyon* disaster). Most of the EEC-9, anxious to maintain traditional high seas freedoms in the EEZ, opposed application of stricter national standards and favoured leaving enforcement in any case to the flag state. Some maritime states, however, (including the Netherlands of the EEC-9 and the US) could accept enforcement by the port state (where the vessel docked voluntarily). On the other hand, states that were more coastal than maritime (including Australia and Canada), concerned at the role of flags of convenience, supported coastal state right of enforcement concurrent with that of the flag state and the port state. The submission mentioned the threat of contamination of the beaches on the south and west coasts of Ireland from vessel-source pollution, and speculated that IMCO sponsored standards might not always provide adequate protection. Nevertheless, it suggested, in the interest of maintaining freedom of navigation, that the coastal state should be permitted to apply only internationally agreed standards in the EEZ and should have limited rights of enforcement, including prosecution only if the flag state failed to prosecute within a specified period. This policy, varying from the original instructions and thus from the line taken by the delegation *en marge* at the Second Session, would also bring Ireland more into line with the positions of the others of the EEC-9. There was a negative attitude to suggestions made at the Second Session for creation of special areas with more stringent anti-pollution standards; for covering state liability for pollution in the convention; and for accepting lower standards for pollution prevention by developing countries. Inclusion of a right of action in national courts, for non-nationals who had suffered damage from pollution originating from areas within the state's jurisdiction, was advocated. Revised instructions were proposed, differing from those given in 1974 in (i) opposing coastal state application, in respect of vessel-source pollution in the EEZ, of national regulations more stringent than those internationally agreed; (ii) supporting a requirement of advance notice to the coastal state of intended dumping in its EEZ, and support for specifying of measures that could be taken by the coastal state in regard to vessels so engaged, including inspection, boarding, arrest for breach of international dumping regulations and residual right of prosecution; and (iii) supporting a requirement that states ensure that polluters could be sued in national courts by non-nationals suffering damage from pollution originating from an area within the state's jurisdiction.

Peaceful settlement of disputes

The submission mentioned the delegation's participation at the Second Session in the group conducting informal discussions on PSD, and the working paper that emanated and was tabled in Plenary, but not discussed there. Compulsory procedures for settlement of disputes, incorporating variations to suit different areas of the convention, were favoured, invoking Article 29.2 of the Constitution (with its affirmation of Ireland's adherence to the principle of peaceful settlement of international disputes) and the Attorney General's address to the Second Session. An instruction to support adoption of compulsory procedures for settlement of disputes, including appropriate preliminary procedures, was recommended. This very general recommendation left room for evolution of detailed policy in the light of developments at the Conference.

Flexibility was again proposed to allow the delegation to react to unexpected developments at the session, but within the limits of policy, after consultation with the Minister for Foreign Affairs and without entering into any binding commitment.

The Ministers for Defence and Finance attached observations to the submission in regard to the surveillance resources implications of expanded zones of jurisdiction. These revealed differences between their attitudes, the latter being, not surprisingly, the more conservative on the need for additional resources. The Minister for Justice attached an observation mentioning possible difficulties in regard to vessel liability and raised the possibility of including an appeal mechanism in the PSD procedures.

The Government, in a decision taken on 4 April, approved the proposed adjustments to the delegation's instructions.

DELEGATION

Following the Second Session Ambassador Cremin and the author discussed the organisation of the delegation, in the context of the Irish EEC Presidency during the Third Session involving additional tasks of EEC organisation, spokesmanship and representation. It was agreed that the Committees should all be serviced consistently by delegates dedicated to specific topics. As a consequence Geraldine Skinner, Assistant Legal Adviser in the Department of Foreign Affairs, joined the delegation as full time First Committee delegate, and the author undertook mostly Second Committee duties. Seamus Mallon continued to look after Irish interests in the fisheries sphere, where he was joined by Brendan O'Kelly. Keith Robinson and Piers Gardiner, splitting the session, took turns as the source of the vital technical expertise on the continental shelf. Keith Robinson and Piers Gardiner also lent assistance to Brendan Finucane, who was the main delegate on MSR and TOT questions, as Colm Ó hEocha was no longer available to the delegation. Patrick Craddock, counsellor in the Department of Foreign Affairs economic division, took over servicing of environment in the Third Committee. Thus, in addition to Colm Ó hEocha, James Kirwan, Paul Dempsey, Raphael Siev and Charles Lysaght, all of the Department of Foreign Affairs left the delegation.

GENERAL

Interest groups continued to meet *en marge*, including a group of seventeen industrialised and maritime states, which became known as the Maritime Group, or Group of 17 (G-17). Six of these were from the EEC-9—Belgium, Denmark, the FRG, Italy, the Netherlands and the UK. Other interest groups also emerged. The Evensen Group became more prominent than at the Second Session despite continuing its practice of meeting at the same time as the Committees. Its Chairman (like the working groups—see below) sent texts, at first on the territorial seas and the EEZ, to the Second Committee Chairman, but expressly without general support within the group. He later sent a text on continental shelf jurisdiction. In due course, despite its lack of formal status, the Evensen Group became significantly influential, partly due to its becoming more representative as participation expanded to approximately 40 delegations covering all geographical regions. Its deliberations undoubtedly contributed to progress on formulation of compromise texts.

EEC coordination and cooperation meetings addressed respectively fisheries and the ISBA regime. The fisheries draft submitted by eight members (excluding the UK) at the Second Session included a clause intended to enable EEC members to accord exclusive fishery rights to one another in their zones (as required in the EEC common fisheries policy) that would have priority over rights that might accrue to other states under the future convention. Examination of this problem led to consideration of a wider question—how to accommodate EEC competences generally in the context of the future convention. Capacity to implement convention obligations in certain fields would, through existing and future transfers of competences, rest with the EEC rather than with the member states individually. The question of whether it would be desirable, or even necessary, to have a general clause in the convention covering this situation was raised in the context of future widening of EEC competences. The legal experts of the EEC member delegations, under the Irish Presidency, discussed this question at length. Only the UK expert disputed the need for such a clause—reflecting opposition to the fisheries draft and possibly influenced by the imminence of a UK referendum on EEC membership. The legal experts devoted their attention to the difficult task of drafting a clause that would be legally adequate and could be credibly presented to the Conference as being necessary for the EEC members, as not giving EEC members an unfair advantage and as not amounting to a derogation from the convention provisions. Progress was made among the eight positive members mainly on the basis of an approach promoted by Ireland and the FRG. Finality was not reached during the session and no proposal was made. The eight felt that they could devise a text without undue difficulty, and it was hoped that the UK would reconsider its position in due course. During the discussions an even more fundamental question was raised: whether it would be necessary for the EEC itself to become a party to the future convention in respect of its relevant areas of competence, to enable implementation of obligations in those areas. Although the discussions on this were necessarily preliminary, only the UK delegate voiced clear opposition. The difficulties of achieving acceptance of any such provision by the general body of Conference participants were not underestimated.

Eight states with broad continental margins formed a group subsequently known as the Margineers. The eight comprised Argentina, Australia, Canada, New Zealand, Norway, the UK, the US and Ireland (under its revised instructions on continental shelf jurisdiction).

PLENARY

At the beginning of the Third Session it was agreed that the time for general debate was past and that negotiations should begin immediately. Nevertheless, progress was again very slow, partly because of the absence of single texts on which to base negotiations. After a reading in the Second and Third Committees of the appropriate parts of the main trends documents, informal working groups on specific topics were set up, under the auspices of those Committees, with a view to establishing agreements or at least reducing the number of texts on each topic. A single working group was set up by the First Committee. Ireland participated in the First Committee working group; in groups on the EEZ, the continental shelf, regime of islands, and delimitation between neighbouring states under the Second Committee; and in groups on the environment and MSR under the Third Committee. Where texts were formulated they were forwarded to the Committee Chairmen. Ireland also continued to participate in the working group on settlement of disputes.

At a meeting of Plenary on 18 April (in the fifth week of the session) to assess progress, the Conference President, recalling the value of having a single text as a working document, proposed the preparation by each Committee Chairman of single texts reflecting his assessment of the consideration of the topics in his Committee. These, he explained, would not be negotiated texts but a procedural device to facilitate future discussions. The Plenary adopted this proposal, and the Chairmen duly prepared such texts that comprised the informal single negotiating text (the ISNT). However, they were circulated only after the session had ended and were therefore not discussed at it. The Co-Chairmen of the informal working group on PSD also transmitted a text on that subject to the Conference President. Although not discussed in Plenary or included in the ISNT, this text served a similar purpose.

The ISNT appeared in document A/Conf.62/WP.8 Parts I, II and III, the parts corresponding to the respective mandates of the three

Committees. The texts were presumably based on documents before each Committee following the Second Session (including the main trends documents), the texts forwarded to each Chairman by the working groups and interest groups, and each Chairman's assessment of the discussions and negotiations and his judgement of the solution on each issue that seemed the most promising platform for further, hopefully decisive, negotiations. The process was a calculated risk that nevertheless provided a very significant outcome to the session. The Irish delegation (presumably like other delegations) saw the ISNT as a forerunner of a convention, and gauged how its interests were faring on the basis of the drafts relating to those interests.

The Attorney General, Mr Declan Costello, again attending as Special Representative of the Government, addressed the Plenary, speaking in the assessment debate following the President's statement and request to the Chairmen. His statement concentrated on the need for an early conclusion to UNCLOS III to avoid a breakdown, unilateral action or loss of common ground already achieved. He listed some issues requiring speedy resolution to protect the interests of those, such as fishermen, whose livelihoods were at stake; to avoid international difficulties; and to maintain a supply of urgently needed resources. (The issues mentioned were ones of interest to Ireland—the EEZ, continental shelf jurisdiction and delimitation of marine zones, including the role of rocks and islands.) He supported the President's request for single texts, which he felt could be prepared on an ongoing basis in the light of progress (thus anticipating the mode of advance subsequently adopted). He urged the need for agreement on PSD procedures and advised against unilateral action.

SECOND COMMITTEE

Ambassador Galindo Pohl was Chairman of the Committee for the session. When a reading of the main trends document had been completed in informal meetings of the Committee without achieving any significant progress, subgroups were set up on various topics with a view to reducing the alternative texts on each topic.

Exclusive economic zone and fisheries

One subgroup dealt with the EEZ, including fisheries. The EEC consultations on the topic again demonstrated a will on the part of some to modify the fisheries paper submitted at the Second Session. This tendency, however, was strongly countered by the fundamental non-acceptance of the concept of the EEZ by Belgium, the FRG and

Italy, and continued reluctance of the UK for different reasons. In the meantime a paper on the topic in preparation by Jens Evensen in his group, although with limited support among that group's members, leaned in favour of coastal state fisheries interests. This was used by the UK, in the EEC consultations, as a basis for criticism of some of the suggestions made for preparation of a revised text to be proposed by the EEC. While the Committee's subgroup did not succeed in producing a text, Evensen sent the Committee Chairman a text at a late stage, but with indications that it did not enjoy full support in his group. Even later the eight of the EEC members, again excluding the UK, agreed on a mildly revised proposal, which the Irish Presidency sent to the Committee Chairman, also with an indication that not all of the pro-posers accepted all of the text's provisions. This text again did not specify the width of the zone. It heavily emphasised the conservation duties of the coastal state, and also sought to constrain it in calculating both the total allowable catch (TAC) and its own harvesting capacity, by com-pulsorily requiring an input from international fisheries organisations in that process. As to rights for third parties to fish in the zone, habitual fishers would rank first. The Evensen text, unlike that of the eight, was a comprehensive set of EEZ articles that would set the limit of the EEZ at 200 miles. In regard to fisheries, while accepting both a limited role for international organisations and the possibility of other state partici-pation in exploitation, it would give the coastal state effective control. For instance, the coastal state would have the main role in setting the TAC, and would be obliged to permit other state exploitation only where its own harvesting capacity could not take up the whole TAC. His text also included a provision on anadromous species based on a Canadian proposal into which the Irish delegation also had an input.

When the Chairman's ISNT emerged (Part II, Articles 45 to 60) it was seen to have taken much more from the Evensen text and the pos-itions of coastal states group members than from the text conveyed by the EEC eight. The ISNT provided for an EEZ not wider than 200 miles. It enabled the coastal state to determine both the TAC and its own harvesting capacity without any input from international fisheries organisations. It confirmed the maintenance in the EEZ of high seas freedoms (for example in regard to navigation, overflight and commu-nication) not incompatible with EEZ rights, without treating the EEZ as part of the high seas. It was strong on conservation (but not as strong as the EEC text), with a cooperative role for international fisheries organisations in this matter. Third state rights were confined to the surplus (i.e. excess of TAC over the coastal state harvesting capacity) and land-locked and geographically disadvantaged states (LLGDS) or habitual fishers' rights were not particularly strong. (Part III of the ISNT also established a coastal state role in the EEZ in regard to MSR and protection of the environment, these matters being within the mandate of the Third Committee.) The ISNT included substantially the Evensen provision on anadromous species that identified the state of origin as having primacy of interest and of responsibility. This latter provision, although less limiting on other states than the Irish proposal, was probably the best likely to be successful, and it still faced opposition, notably from Japan and Denmark.

Regime of islands and delimitation

Concentrated work began on the topics of regime of islands and delimitation of maritime areas between neighbouring states. They became more closely linked at this session than previously, although separate subgroups to discuss them were set up by the Second Committee. During the reading of the main trends document a statement was made by the Irish delegate on 4 April on the regime of islands, mainly asserting that not all islands should have the capacity to generate areas of marine jurisdiction, and also confirming the delegation statement at the Second Session concerning the role of islands in delimitation.

The Irish delegate subsequently participated in consultations with members from other delegations having a similar approach, including Algeria, Madagascar, Romania, Thailand, Tunisia and Turkey and, later, Morocco and Senegal. The aim was to devise texts on the two topics that these delegations could put forward as a consolidation of, and replacement for, those they had already submitted individually. Despite the small number involved, these consultations were long and often difficult, but texts on the topics were finally agreed.

The text on delimitation followed the indication in the International Court of Justice (ICJ) decision that delimitation should be by agreement in accordance with equitable principles, but added to that the requirement of an equitable result. It did not specify any method of division but envisaged that negotiation would determine the method or combination of methods appropriate to achieve the stated objective. It required that account be taken of all relevant circumstances and specifically included the presence of islands and configuration of coasts (a feature in the ICJ decision—see above) as coming under the rubric 'special circumstances'. It listed size, population and proximity to the coast as factors to determine the role, if any, of an island in delimitation.

The text on islands provided that no marine zones should accrue to rocks or low-tide elevations, or (other than narrow security zones) to islands or islets without economic life and unable to sustain a permanent population. To accommodate a difference between Tunisia and Romania the text had an illogical exception for a group of such islands close to the mainland state, a provision accepted by Ireland only when a delimitation provision was also added reflecting the provision on islands in the group's delimitation text. Islands that were the principal islands or group of islands of an island state and also archipelagic states were excluded from application of the text.

Both texts were transmitted as informal proposals to the Committee Chairman under cover of two letters from the Irish delegation, that on regime of islands on 25 April and that on delimitation on 30 April. Both were introduced in the subgroups by the Irish delegate on behalf of the proposing delegations on 29 April and 2 May respectively. In the subgroups both proposals were naturally opposed by those states with offshore islands, and those favouring the median line as the exclusive delimitation method with full effect for islands in calculating it (including Greece, Italy, Norway, the UK, etc.). The regime of islands proposal was also opposed by the Pacific Ocean small island states and their ally, New Zealand. Inspired by the extreme economic dependence of the Pacific small island states on resources of the seas, they had tabled a proposal at the Second Session (A/Conf.62/C.2/L.30) to the effect that islands had the same rights to marine jurisdiction as other land territory. They felt the exclusions in the text transmitted by Ireland were not adequate to cover their concerns. The Irish delegate, particularly, conveyed a willingness to seek a solution to this problem. These countries were critical of only some of the detail in the delimitation text, and suggested that satisfactory delimitation provisions would dispense with the need for an article on regime of islands. The subgroups were still deliberating when the session came to an end.

The provision on regime of islands that appeared in the Chairman's ISNT (Article 132) excluded low-tide elevations from the definition of islands, and provided that rocks that could not sustain human habitation or economic life of their own should not have an EEZ or continental shelf. Other islands would have both. This provision obviously derived in part from the text transmitted to the Chairman by Ireland, although not going nearly so far. It would benefit Ireland at least by depriving Rockall of EEZ or shelf jurisdiction, but was not adequate for some of Ireland's allies. On delimitation the ISNT (identical Articles 61 and 70 addressing the EEZ and continental shelf respectively) drew heavily on the Netherlands proposal (C.2/L.14) submitted at the Second Session. These articles provided for solution by agreement in accordance with equitable principles but (unlike L.14) mentioned the median line as a method to be used where appropriate, but not to prevail in absence of agreement. They required that account be taken of all relevant circumstances (as in the ICJ judgement) as compared to the narrower reference to special circumstances (as in the 1958 convention). They set the median line as an interim measure pending agreement or settlement, with compulsory settlement procedures in default of agreement. Bearing in mind that the fundamental Irish ambition was that the use of the median line method should be modified without necessarily being omitted, the text was appreciated by the delegation in that respect but was a disappointment to some of Ireland's allies in the interest group. All of the allies, including Ireland, were unhappy with the interim measure provision. Those of the allies who had not ratified the 1958 convention could justifiably argue that they should not be required to accept any part of its provisions that were inconsistent with the generally applicable principles as identified in the ICJ decision, thus making a compromise between the two positions extremely difficult. Many of these allies, not including Ireland, were opposed to a compulsory settlement of disputes procedure. It was decided that the group would not have a position on this point, thus avoiding later efforts to make it a bargaining counter.

Continental shelf

Continental shelf jurisdiction was also referred to a subgroup after discussion of the main trends document in the informal meetings of the Committee. The main contention was between those who wished to subsume continental shelf jurisdiction into that of the EEZ, thus confining it to that 200-mile zone, and those who advocated that it should cover the margin. Ireland had of course moved to the latter position for the session and joined in forming the Margineers Group, under Australian Chairmanship. The Margineers regarded it as tactically very important in the negotiations to find a satisfactory, and generally acceptable, solution to the often technically difficult problem of identification of the outer edge of the margin, which would prevent exaggerated claims. There were varying views among the group members as to how to deal with this problem. The group arranged for preparation, mainly by the geological experts from its delegations (including the Irish expert), of a text on the topic that would include coverage of this problem. The text was passed to Minister Evensen, for inclusion in discussions of the issue in his group, in which the question of revenue sharing was also raised. The Margineers text, firstly, provided for coastal state continental shelf jurisdiction extending over the EEZ and, beyond the EEZ, throughout the natural prolongation of its land territory to the outer edge of its continental margin (drawing on the ICJ judgement). It further provided that each coastal state would be required to identify the geological limit of its continental margin according to a definition and criterion set out in the text, with supervision of that process by an international commission established for that purpose and largely composed of geological experts. (The criterion, based on a distance measurement beyond the foot of the continental slope, was devised by a geologist member of the US delegation, and was subsequently dubbed the Hedberg formula, from the name of its author.)

Following discussion in his group, Evensen forwarded a text to the Committee Chairman. It was more comprehensive than the Margineers text in that it also addressed the resources involved, the rights and the duties of the coastal state and other states. It also included a provision on revenue sharing, i.e. payment to the (ISBA) international authority of an unspecified percentage of the production from the part of the shelf beyond the EEZ, an idea floated by the US at the Second Session. In regard to extent of jurisdiction, limits and definition it conformed closely to the Margineers' text. However, reference of coastal state identification of the limits of its margin to the proposed international commission would not be strictly compulsory, but could be done by the coastal state, another state with a particular interest or the international authority.

The Chairman's ISNT (Articles 62 to 69) incorporated most of the Evensen text, but omitted clauses relating to the identification of the edge of the continental margin. This was a relatively satisfactory outcome from the Irish point of view in so far as Article 62 reproduced verbatim the first paragraph of the Margineers text, which provided for coastal state jurisdiction beyond the EEZ to the edge of the margin. It also, however, included the Evensen text provision on revenue sharing (Article 69). This, while not particularly welcome (being contrary to Irish interests), would be a concession to the ISBA interests, and was already realistically recognised as likely to be a necessary ingredient of a widely accepted package on broad shelf jurisdiction. Moreover further progress was required on resolution of the vital question of an acceptable method of identification of the edge of the margin. The text also repeated the 1958 continental shelf convention provision that shelf rights did not affect the status of the superjacent waters or airspace, although omitting to refer to them as high seas.

Territorial seas, contiguous zone and high seas
Acceptance of a twelve-mile maximum limit was consolidated, and concentration was on elaboration of the details of innocent passage as compared with the 1958 convention provisions. Details of the coastal state regulating power emerged from the discussions, including a right

to apply national standards on pollution (overlapping the mandate of the Third Committee) provided innocent passage was not thereby hampered. There were some changes to the rules on baselines (as comprised in the 1958 convention) of no relevance to Ireland. The Chairman's ISNT (Articles 6 to 32) reflected these developments. Maintenance of the contiguous zone beyond the territorial seas was also included (Article 33). On the high seas the Chairman's ISNT (Articles 73 to 107) defined it as the sea area outside the EEZ. Otherwise it reiterated the 1958 convention with some limited modifications to high seas freedoms, including provisions on measures to deal with illegal traffic in narcotics and unauthorised broadcasting, as proposed by the EEC-9 (at the Second Session). These provisions (Articles 94 and 95) effectively reproduced the EEC-9 draft, although omitting the coastal state right of arrest of a ship not bearing its flag.

Straits and archipelagos

On straits the ISNT (Articles 34 to 44) drew from the main trends document in providing for unimpeded transit passage through newly enclosed straits waters, a solution that seemed to have wide acceptance despite initial opposition from some straits states. On archipelagos the ISNT (Articles 117 to 131) defined the concept moderately and also described the newly enclosed waters as archipelagic waters that were subject to a combination of innocent passage and transit passage.

Article 136, to the effect that convention resource rights of a territory whose people did not have full independence should vest in its inhabitants and be exercised for their benefit, reflected the Second Session proposal of Argentina, New Zealand, etc., in the context of islands.

THIRD COMMITTEE

The Committee met informally for a half of each day, dealing alternatively with preservation of the environment, MSR and TOT, leaving the other half days for meetings, for example for working groups.

Environment

A drafting group of about 20 delegates (including the Irish delegate) prepared texts for consideration at the informal meetings. Progress was made on texts on monitoring, environmental assessment, land-based sources of pollution, and ocean dumping. These were included in the Chairman's ISNT (Part III, Part I, Articles 13 to 16, 19, 22 and 25). The text on environmental assessment (Article 13) was substantially an Irish draft, representing a less stringent and more widely acceptable approach than a US draft based on US internal legislation. Among the issues on which wide agreement was not forthcoming were those relating to less onerous preventive obligations on developing states, and the extent of a coastal state's jurisdiction, including a right of enforcement of international regulations in its EEZ or on its continental shelf. Nevertheless, the main feature was the failure to have a meaningful discussion on vessel-source pollution. Hopes of a decisive Evensen Group input and of a G-77 common position on this issue were not realised. A group of 17 (G-17 Maritime Group) proposal at least addressed the question of enforcement of pollution regulations against ships. However, it would leave enforcement almost completely to the flag state, with a limited role for the port state and even more limited role for the coastal state. This approach did not involve a special coastal state role in any pollution zone outside its territorial sea. An earlier G-17 draft considered in EEC cooperation meetings had recognised such coastal state jurisdiction, and its omission in a subsequent version ensured opposition from Ireland and France. After the G-17 text had been tabled, France submitted in EEC cooperation deliberations a text providing for a pollution zone in which the coastal state would have power to inspect and prosecute. Ireland indicated general support for this text but other member states opposed it. France, encouraged by an indication in the Evensen Group that the US delegation could accept a pollution zone in which the coastal state would have powers of enforcing international regulations, transmitted its text to the Committee Chairman. The G-17 co-sponsors nevertheless maintained their position and also transmitted their text to the Chairman.

On vessel-source pollution the Chairman's ISNT allowed application of national standards by the coastal state in the territorial seas (Article 20, Paragraph 3), but only in special areas of the EEZ (not relevant to Ireland). Otherwise internationally agreed standards could not be exceeded. Enforcement rested predominantly with the flag state, which would be required to impose international standards (Article 20 Paragraph 2 and Article 26). A port state had limited enforcement powers (Article 27). A coastal state's powers were even more limited (Articles 28, 30 and 31). In regard to dumping, however, express coastal state approval was required for dumping within a zone of undefined width (Article 19 Paragraph 3), and the coastal state could enforce international anti-dumping regulations on vessels dumping within its EEZ or continental shelf (Article 25).

Marine scientific research

The exchanges regarding MSR featured a stand-off between the G-77, favouring coastal states, and a US-led position, favouring researchers. The Soviet Union promoted requirements of notification to the coastal state for pure research and its consent for applied research. The distinction between pure and applied research was again widely rejected. Meanwhile the Irish and Mexican delegates, seeking as at the Second Session to establish a middle ground, consulted widely, following which the Irish delegate prepared a discussion paper. This set out *inter alia* (i) a general obligation to facilitate MSR conducted exclusively for peaceful purposes; (ii) unspecified preferential treatment for developing LLGDS; (iii) a distinction between fundamental and resource-related research in regard to MSR in the EEZ or on the continental shelf. For the former notification to the coastal state and dissemination of the results would be required; for the latter express consent of the coastal state would be required and the results given to it alone. Any disagreement as to which category applied to the research would be subject to a settlement of disputes procedure; and (iv) a requirement to notify the (ISBA) authority of MSR in the ISBA and to disseminate the results. This approach was taken up by Colombia, El Salvador and Nigeria, who together with Mexico tabled it as a proposal, omitting the settlement of disputes provision. The Irish delegation was reluctantly persuaded not to co-sponsor, on the basis that the proposal would have a better chance of acceptance by the G-77 if it did not have a developed state among the co-sponsors. The Chairman's ISNT (Part III, Articles 1 to 24) largely included this proposal and added a settlement of disputes provision. The latter had, however, in place of the detail of procedures in the Irish draft, a reference to the general settlement procedures anticipated as part of the future convention.

Transfer of technology

Discussion of TOT was resisted by several industrialised countries, including Denmark, the FRG, the UK and the US, who maintained that the Conference was an inappropriate forum for the topic, which was under consideration elsewhere in the UN system. In fact there was little discussion, although two papers were tabled by developing countries that would require heavy commitments from developed countries. In response to a suggestion from the Irish delegation, a postponement pending tabling of papers by developed countries was accepted. Meanwhile lengthy EEC-9 deliberations under the Irish Presidency produced a text that the Irish Presidency transmitted to the Committee Chairman on 5 May. It provided for promotion of TOT through cooperation and with due regard to the interests of others, including the holders of technology. The Chairman's ISNT substantially reproduced this text in the opening articles on TOT, incorporating parts of it verbatim.

First committee

The discussions centred on two elements of a regime for the ISBA— (a) who may exploit and (b) the constitution of the authority. The contrast between the positions of the G-77 and of the industrialised states on these issues continued, although slightly reduced by the G-77 paper tabled late in the Second Session. This had accepted the possibility of exploitation by entities other than the authority, had set out basic conditions on exploitation and provided for some limits on the discretionary powers of the authority in entering into exploitation contracts. This evoked a positive response from some of the industrialised countries, including the US, whereas others still opposed any direct exploitation by the authority. The Soviet Union tabled a proposal (A/Conf.62/C.1/L.12) on 21 March that accepted direct exploitation by the authority. The exchanges were not very productive. In the EEC-9 consultations Denmark and the Netherlands showed signs of flexibility, but France, the UK and, particularly, the FRG maintained a hard-line stance against any direct authority exploitation. Most of the nine favoured an authority council of 36 members, with voting procedures that would preserve the influence of the industrialised countries in the face of a likely numerical superiority of the developing countries. There was no meeting of minds among the EEC-9 as a basis for a common position on the fundamental issues, and it was thus decided that no EEC-9 proposal would be put forward. There was a certain relief in the Irish delegation that there was not yet another stand-off with the other eight, especially during the Irish EEC Presidency. France and the FRG transmitted proposals to the Committee Chairman, both of which provided for council membership based on interest groups. On 28 April the LLGDS group tabled two proposals (C.1/L.13 and 14) covering distribution of the ISBA revenue, and advocating that membership of the authority institutions should be on the basis of interest groups, including the LLGDS group.

The Chairman's comprehensive ISNT (Part I, Articles 1 to 75 and an annex on conditions of exploitation) not surprisingly took as its starting point a reflection of the 1970 General Assembly Declaration of Principles. In developing the regime it largely reproduced the G-77 position. On the council (Article 27) it provided for a membership of

36. A complicated mixed election process was mostly on the basis of the traditional UN geographical/regional representation, with provision also for interest-based representation. The overall effect of this process would not be likely to meet the objectives of Ireland's partners in the EEC-9, particularly as the council would establish its own rules of procedure, presumably including decision-making procedures. The ISNT had self-contained settlement of disputes procedures, including a special tribunal, and no possibility of reservations from these procedures. Surprisingly it also included formal final clauses, as if anticipating that this part would comprise a separate convention. These clauses included an article (Article 73) on provisional application to be brought into effect by notification on signature.

PLENARY

Peaceful settlement of disputes

The informal group on PSD resumed its discussions with a view to reducing the alternative texts comprised in A/Conf.62/L.7 tabled at the Second Session. There appeared to be wide agreement that there should be a separate chapter in the future convention on the topic, as suggested by Ambassador Galindo Pohl of El Salvador (Second Committee Chairman at this Session) when introducing L.7 in Plenary at the end of the Second Session. The EEC-9, following the usual internal consultations, agreed to favour compulsory procedures with the minimum of exceptions or possibilities for reservations. They sought a progressive process of negotiation, conciliation and ultimately binding procedure, whether arbitration or judicial, with a choice of fora. The informal group responded positively to this approach. It transmitted a paper (which did not have universal support in the group) to the Conference President. It provided for conciliation, arbitration and a special law of the sea tribunal (as envisaged also in Part I of the ISNT for ISBA regime disputes). It was not included in the ISNT. There were, however, several provisions in various sections of the ISNT anticipating a settlement of disputes chapter. The President undertook to prepare his own paper on the topic.

Following the assassination of King Faisal of Saudi Arabia on 25 March a commemoration meeting of Plenary was held on 27 March. The meeting lasted most of the day. The Conference President made the opening statement followed by tributes and condolences on behalf of the UN Secretary-General; the five UN regional groups; other groups, including the Arab Group, the League of Arab States, the

G-77, the Association of South East Asian Nations, the EEC-9 and the Nordics; the US; and all the Arab states individually as well as several other states. On behalf of the EEC-9 the Irish Presidency, in the person of Ambassador Cremin, delivered a short statement that was a minor classic of diplomacy. The Saudi Arabian delegation duly replied to the tributes.

On 9 May the Plenary decided that a fourth session should be held in New York from 15 March to 7 May 1976, and to leave over until then a decision regarding a further session in 1976, for which provisional UN General Assembly authorisation was also requested. The holding of interim informal consultations was encouraged and the UN Secretary-General was requested to allocate funds for the servicing of such consultations. (The anticipation of a further session, not a signature session, was witness to a reduced optimism regarding a speedy conclusion of the Conference.)

Conclusion

The Irish delegation, like most others, welcomed the emergence of the ISNT as a significant aid to negotiation, and thus a considerable step towards fulfilment of UNCLOS III's objective of adoption of a generally acceptable convention. The Irish welcome was all the more enthusiastic because the solutions proposed in the ISNT were largely satisfactory from an Irish point of view on most issues. The exceptions included (i) the provisions on delimitation of marine areas between neighbouring states, which were, however, only a little short of Irish aspirations; (ii) the absence of any provision on definition of outer limits of continental shelf jurisdiction perceived as needed to facilitate general acceptance of the extended jurisdiction provided for in the ISNT; and (iii) the provision for revenue sharing in respect of the product of the part of the shelf beyond the EEZ, although it would probably also be needed to facilitate general acceptance. If these issues were few it was not anticipated that improvements would be easily achieved. Other delegations, of course, were less satisfied with the ISNT and, bearing in mind that many issues still featured wide disagreement among the participants, general agreement on a convention was far from guaranteed. The Irish delegation's future objectives would be threefold—to preserve the ISNT provisions that served Ireland's interests, to seek appropriate changes in those that did not fully do so and to promote general agreement across the whole field. Some balancing in the pursuit of these objectives was also likely to be required.

The Irish delegation was not free from personal travail during the session. Ambassador T.J. (Joe) Horan, the Permanent Representative to the Geneva UN Office, died suddenly at the end of the first week of the session. The delegates, who had been among his guests at his St Patrick's reception at the beginning of that week, were all shocked. The impact particularly affected Ambassador Cremin, Seamus Mallon and the author, who had been among his personal friends. His removal, which was also attended by the Minister for Foreign Affairs, Dr Garret FitzGerald, was an affecting occasion.

Near the end of the session one of the delegation's very assiduous and conscientious secretaries, Ms Mary Davitt, was taken ill suddenly, seriously enough to be hospitalised, if briefly. Fortunately she recovered enough in time to travel home with the rest of the delegation. While her illness was a matter of concern to all the delegates, it was especially so to her secretarial colleagues, who were very solicitous and helpful, and to the author, to whom she was a close work colleague in her regular duties as his personal assistant. Happily she was quickly restored to full health.

Chapter VII

FOURTH SESSION

The Fourth Session was held at the United Nations headquarters in New York for eight weeks, from 15 March to 7 May 1976.

Preparations

The Inter-Departmental Committee (IDC) considered the results of the Third Session and, in particular, examined the informal single negotiating text (ISNT), on the basis that it was intended to be the platform for future negotiations at the Conference. Mr John Kelly, Minister of State at the Department of Foreign Affairs (having responsibility for the work of the legal division *inter alia*), arranged a meeting of several ministers from interested departments, attended also by members of the delegation, for a broad discussion of policy on the basis of a letter, addressed to the ministers by him, setting out the issues of importance to Ireland.

European Economic Community coordination and cooperation meetings continued, dealing with many of the Conference topics and, even more importantly, the new 'Community clause'. Its intent was to enable the EEC to become a party to the future convention, now regarded as necessary by all the members, including the UK.

The Evensen Group convened intersessional meetings open to all delegations in August–September and December 1975 and in February 1976. The Irish delegation attended the group for the first time at these meetings, in the persons of Ambassador Cremin and the delegates concerned with the topics on its agenda. These included the ISNT provisions on the continental shelf and the environment. A text subsequently prepared by Evensen, to make good the omission of a provision on identification of the outer limits in the ISNT articles on the continental shelf, was acceptable to Ireland, but not generally agreed in the Margineers Group. This and a text he prepared on the environment figured at the session.

On 11 August 1975 Mr Henry Kissinger, the US Secretary of State, in an address on UNCLOS III to the American Bar Association, described rapid and fundamental changes of circumstances relevant to the law of the sea, including advances in technology, which required expeditious response from the international community. He outlined the US position on most issues at UNCLOS III, including a fairly detailed treatment of those concerning the international seabed area (ISBA). He believed that such issues as the breadth of the territorial sea, establishment of a 200-nautical-mile exclusive economic zone (EEZ) and right of transit through new straits were effectively settled. He urged an early conclusion to the Conference to avoid its being bypassed by developments and by unilateral actions under pressure of events.

Intersessionally, the Conference President prepared draft articles (A/Conf.62/WP.9) on peaceful settlement of disputes (PSD), based partly on the paper transmitted to him at the end of the Third Session by the informal working group on the topic.

INSTRUCTIONS

With the agreement of the IDC departments and the Departments of Transport and Power, of Justice, of Health, of Labour, and of Posts and Telegraphs and the Office of the Attorney General, a submission to the Government was prepared by the Department of Foreign Affairs and was transmitted by the Minister for Foreign Affairs on 12 March 1976.

The submission proposed confirmation of existing instructions in regard to the territorial seas and contiguous zone, high seas, archipelagos, establishment of an EEZ, anadromous species (salmon), the ISBA and PSD.

International seabed area

At the meeting of Irish ministers and delegation members (see above) there was no inclination to change the Irish position in the direction of that of the more conservative among the EEC partners. The submission proposed basically unchanged instructions, although with more elaboration, particularly on safeguarding the interests of land-based producers of relevant minerals.

Exclusive economic zone

On (the regime of) the EEZ and fisheries, islands and delimitation, marine scientific research (MSR) and transfer of technology (TOT), slight adaptation of the existing instructions was sought in the light of Conference developments, particularly the greater clarity of the issues that resulted from the emergence of the ISNT. More significant adaptation of the instructions in regard to the continental shelf and preservation of the environment was sought in the light of conference progress on these topics. The topic of straits was not mentioned.

Fisheries, regime of islands, delimitation, marine scientific research and transfer of technology

More emphasis on the role of international fisheries organisations was proposed and no change to the instructions on anadromous species. On regime of islands and on delimitation, mention was made of support at the Conference as a factor that should be taken into account in determining the details of proposals that should be promoted. On MSR it was proposed to add advocacy of specific settlement of disputes procedures. On TOT, support for the provisions of the ISNT, which provided for encouragement of TOT rather than legal obligation, was suggested, together with opposition to the articles in Part I of the ISNT, giving the International seabed authority a controlling role.

Continental shelf

It was proposed that the delegation should be enabled to accept revenue sharing in respect of resources beyond 200 miles if this were necessary to achieve acceptance of extended jurisdiction, but only in the form of a share of profits. On the environment support was proposed for (i) a coastal state zone of jurisdiction including the continental shelf as well as the EEZ; (ii) prohibition of dumping in this zone except with the consent of the coastal state; and (iii) coastal state powers of arrest in this zone in case of flagrant and serious violations of international regulations.

Peaceful settlement of disputes

The submission referred to the President's text prepared after the Third Session. It commented that there might not be general acceptance of a provision in the text giving a proposed new law of the sea tribunal priority over other procedures.

'Community clause'

It was proposed that the delegation should join in promoting the 'Community clause', devised by the EEC member states both to enable the EEC to become a party to the future convention and to give internal EEC arrangements (for example the common fisheries policy) priority over convention obligations to third parties.

The Government by decision dated 23 March approved these recommendations.

DELEGATION

John Moore, a Principal Officer in the Department of Defence, joined the delegation to undertake monitoring of developments with implications for the Naval Service. Otherwise the delegation was the same as for the Third Session.

GENERAL

Ambassador Galindo Pohl resigned as Chairman of the Second Committee and was definitively replaced by Ambassador Aguilar, who had been Chairman at the Second Session. Group meetings were resumed, particularly of the Evensen Group and interest groups such as the group of land-locked and geographically disadvantaged states (LLGDS), the Group of 77 (G-77) and the coastal states group (CSG), but under a Conference constraint that they could not meet at times for which Committee meetings were scheduled. The Evensen Group discussed successively the environment, MSR, LLGDS rights and the continental shelf, and transmitted texts on these topics to the Chairmen of the Third and Second Committees, in their respective areas of responsibility. EEC members also continued their coordination and cooperation meetings, particularly regarding the 'Community clause'.

In an address to the US Foreign Policy Association on 8 April, Mr Henry Kissinger, the US Secretary of State, described UNCLOS III as the most important international negotiation ever to be held. Following his theme from the previous autumn, and in conciliatory language, he outlined proposals for settlement of the issues expeditiously. He urged a further session in 1976 to complete the substantive work, dramatically indicated that the US President had suggested that he lead for the US in the negotiations, and urged other states to participate also at decisive political level. He said that in absence of agreement at the Conference the US would proceed unilaterally. In an interview with the *New York Times* around the same time the Conference President expressed a similar view with regard to the proposal for a final substantive session in 1976. The Attorney General, Mr Declan Costello, visiting the conference as Special Representative of the Government, also at that time, had private conversations with several Conference personalities about its progress and prospects.

The Irish delegation, reporting to Dublin on these developments, was sceptical of the feasibility of finalisation in the time scale advocated by the US Secretary of State and the Conference President.

FOURTH SESSION

PLENARY

The President's proposals for organisation of work included (1) all Committee meetings should be informal; (2) the ISNT should be the basis for discussion; (3) at a given stage of the session, probably at the end of the fourth week, the ISNT should be revised and given formal status; and (4) the draft articles on PSD, prepared by the President intersessionally, should be discussed in informal meetings of Plenary from a date to be fixed. These proposals were accepted. The President also requested the Chairman of the Drafting Committee to prepare, with the assistance of the secretariat, drafts of a preamble and final clauses. The document prepared in response to this request appeared in late July, shortly before commencement of the Fifth Session.

The LLGDS opened their campaign at the session with a letter to the President seeking for LLGDS (i) free access to the oceans; (ii) rights in the EEZ of coastal states; and (iii) representation as a group in the organs of the international authority. This evoked a sharp and unusual written response from Peru, a prominent member of both the G-77 and the CSG, apparently designed to indicate that virtually all states suffered disadvantages, even if not necessarily geographical.

As the session proceeded it became apparent at a very early stage that the target for revision and formalisation of the ISNT as at (3) above could not be met, and eventually that only revision could be achieved at the session. The ISNT was revised by the Chairmen in the light of the discussions, and the revised version (A/Conf.62/W.P.8/rev.1 Parts I, II and III) was entitled the revised single negotiating text (RSNT). It was distributed on 7 May, the last day of the session.

The Irish delegation was convinced from the beginning that the substantive work could not be advanced at the session to the stage envisaged in the plan to formalise the revised text.

SECOND COMMITTEE

The articles falling within the mandate of the Second Committee were those in Part II of the ISNT—Articles 1 to 137. The President's organisation proposals were supplemented by further proposals by the Chairman and accepted by delegates: (a) to work article by article; (b) that discussions should be confined to comments on the ISNT without proposing amendments (a proposal that was largely ignored); (c) that the Chairman would hold consultations *en marge*, and would produce a revised version of the ISNT; and (d) that a rule of silence would apply, to the effect that a delegation that did not comment on a provision of the ISNT would be assumed not to object to that provision being carried forward in the revision (although it would not be assumed to approve the provision as acceptable). If the last rule tended to increase the interventions in the discussions it also facilitated the Chairman's revision task.

Territorial sea

The G-77 indicated that acceptance of (so narrow) a limit as twelve miles was conditional on adoption of a 200-mile EEZ with a satisfactory regime. There was also considerable controversy regarding the details of innocent passage rules, particularly whether notification to, or even consent of, the coastal state for passage of warships and nuclear powered vessels should be required. The Irish delegation intervened to object on two scores. Firstly, to a Spanish suggestion in regard to Article 2 that tended towards enabling archipelagos belonging to mainland states to be treated the same as archipelagic states for purposes of determining the territorial sea, because of its detrimental relevance to Irish objectives in regard to regime of islands and delimitation of marine zones. (This issue arose more broadly later in the discussion on Article 131 on such archipelagos). The second objection was to a US suggestion that coastal states should be obliged to produce charts showing the low-water lines and straight baselines from which marine zones were to be measured (Articles 4 and 6), as being disproportionate and excessive. On Article 18 (innocent passage) Ireland sought to clarify in Paragraph 1 that the paragraph list of matters on which the coastal state could make regulations was not exhaustive, but advocated retention of Paragraph 2, which excluded design of ships from such regulation. Its only other comment was on Article 13 (delimitation of territorial seas, see below). The RSNT did not make any significant change to the ISNT in these matters.

The EEC members sought to cooperate in preparing written suggestions of changes to Articles 1 to 44 for submission to the Chairman after the debate on each article. Ireland's only suggestion in this process was in regard to Article 13 on delimitation of territorial seas between neighbouring states but, not surprisingly, it did not achieve the necessary unanimous support among the partners.

Exclusive economic zone and fisheries

Progress was slow and the articles on the EEZ and (specifically) fisheries were reached on 1 and 8 April respectively. Meanwhile the EEC delegations sought to reach agreed positions on the ISNT on both of these topics. The main obstacles to agreed positions were, respectively, the continued Belgian rejection of the EEZ and UK reluctance to agree on fisheries proposals. In the event, the FRG proposed amendments in the Committee confined to seeking explicit preservation of high-seas rights in the EEZ (Article 47). These were supported by all the EEC members, and by other maritime powers, for example the US, Japan and the Soviet Union. Proposals on the EEZ regime were made by the Netherlands, ostensibly individually rather than as representing the EEC (as part of its current Presidency responsibilities), as Belgium was not prepared to support some of them. The UK delegation, after contact with London, was able to accept, at the last minute, a covering note for submission of EEC fisheries amendments, and to support the Netherlands amendments. (The commission delegation in its subsequent report to the Council of Ministers commented on the fact that the latter had not been overtly proposed as EEC proposals.) The amendments affecting fisheries were aimed at (a) eliminating arbitrariness in coastal state decisions, for example regarding the total allowable catch (TAC) and its harvesting capacity, by giving a significant role regarding these decisions to international fisheries organisations; (b) strengthening the claims of traditional third-country fishers in the EEZ (echoing the London Fisheries Convention); and (c) eliminating an indicative list of matters on which the coastal state could regulate third-country fishing in the EEZ, which was seen by some EEC members as facilitating arbitrary restriction. The amendments were thus an attempt to promote salient parts of the eight member proposals made at the Second and Third Sessions that had not been incorporated in the ISNT, and reflected only slightly the inclination of several members to moderate their original position. The amendments were introduced by the Netherlands article by article (Articles 45, 47, 50, 51 and 54) and supported briefly by each of the other EEC members, with the exception of Belgium in regard to Article 45 (due to its non-acceptance of the EEZ). Support, or similar proposals, came from other countries, including the US, Japan, Greece, the Soviet Union and other Eastern European Group (EE) countries. A significant feature of developments in EEC deliberations from the Irish point of view was the acceptance by Denmark of the provision on anadromous species, with some slight changes proposed by the Netherlands. In the meantime a stalemate had developed around Articles 57 and 58 (rights of LLGDS) between the LLGDS and the most trenchant members of the CSG (issues that did not impinge on direct Irish interests). CSG members also suggested changes (counter to those of the EEC) reducing third-country rights in the EEZ. The EEC members also proposed amendments on conservation on the high seas, with a view to strengthening the role of international fisheries organisations in this context also.

The RSNT changes as compared with the ISNT were negligible in this area. Only a few minor points made by the EEC were adopted. No changes were made to the provisions on LLGDS rights, which gave land-locked states fishing rights in the EEZ of adjoining states on an equitable basis and subject to the coastal state's own rights (which probably confined LLGDS rights to the surplus of the TAC beyond the coastal state's harvesting capacity). On anadromous species the only change was to extend explicitly the conservation obligations of the state of origin to its territorial seas and internal waters as well as its EEZ.

The Chairman's covering note accompanying the RSNT addressed the controversy as to whether the EEZ should be defined as high seas, and the fact that he had made no change in this respect. He described the EEZ as *sui generis* and anticipated that the controversy should be resolved in the form of residual rights (as was the thrust of Article 46). He also explained his view that any change in provisions on LLGDS rights at that stage would jeopardise future negotiations.

Continental shelf

The Margineers' consultations tended to a conclusion that a package that would have genuine prospects of general acceptance at the Conference would have to include three elements—(1) an addition to the definition (which included the whole margin) of a workable and comprehensible method by which the coastal state would identify the actual outer limits of its jurisdiction; (2) a boundary commission to oversee coastal state application of that method; and (3) revenue sharing (which alone of the three elements was already covered in the ISNT). Element (1) presented difficult technical problems. There were differences among the Margineers regarding (2), whether the boundary commission decisions to accept or reject should be conclusive, and also regarding (3), whether revenue sharing should be based on production or on profits (the latter favoured by the UK) or even opposed (by Australia and Argentina simply, and by Ireland because the ISNT based revenue sharing on production, whereas Ireland, like the UK, favoured a profits basis). The Margineers (including new members India and Uruguay) worked on the text that had emerged from the Evensen Group intersessional meeting, with a view to formulating amendments in the form of additions to Article 62. When amendments were agreed, subject to some reservations by India, they were presented in the Committee by the Irish delegation and became known as the Irish amendment. These were provisions (a) specifically indicating that the slope and the rise were included in the margin; (b) requiring the coastal state to establish the actual outer limits of jurisdiction on the margin by reference to two alternative geophysically based formulae (the previously proposed Hedberg formula, and the newly proposed Gardiner formula devised by Irish delegate Piers Gardiner); (c) requiring the coastal state to submit the limits, so identified, to a continental shelf boundary commission, whose acceptance of the submission would be final and binding; and (d) requiring the coastal state to deposit with the UN Secretary-General charts indicating the limits and the data relevant to their identification. The amendments left the details of the boundary commission for later elaboration and did not address the question of the consequences of rejection of a submission by it. (With the Chairman's permission a draft annex on the proposed commission was tabled by Canada at the end of the Committee's deliberations. It was agreed within the Margineers but again did not address the issue of rejection of a submission.) Together with a clarifying suggestion by Chile, the Margineers' amendments received considerable support. There was also some, but less, support for suggestions by the Soviet Union and Japan, and by Austria and Belgium (both LLGDS members) that would depart from the ISNT Article 62 to limit jurisdiction to 200 nautical miles (as the EEZ) or where a depth of 500 metres was reached. Malta suggested incorporating shelf jurisdiction into the EEZ. Some supported Article 62 without change.

As there was no agreed Margineer position on revenue sharing the group did not make a proposal on the subject, although individual members spoke in favour of the principle. Thus the US supported the ISNT Article 69 on the subject, and submitted a proposal for payment of a percentage of the volume or value of production from the area beyond 200 miles. It would apply only from the sixth year of production, and the percentage would increase from 1 per cent, in that year, by 1 per cent yearly to a ceiling rate of 5 per cent. There was no provision for exemption for developing countries, and the proceeds would not be paid to the (ISBA) international authority but rather to development organisations recognised by the UN. Most of the Margineers (not including Ireland) found this acceptable. Austria, supported by Belgium and the Netherlands, suggested revenue sharing should apply to production from areas beyond a distance of 50 nautical miles or a depth of 500 metres, and widely varying percentages were mooted. There was little opposition to the principle as distinct from differences about the details.

Other continental shelf articles attracted little attention, but the LLGDS (with Austria prominent) suggested changing Article 63 to give all states in a region equal, or near equal, rights on the shelf of the region.

The RSNT preserved Article 62 as in the ISNT and did not incorporate any provision on identification of the outer limits. The Chairman explained that he was satisfied that the definition was widely supported, and that he was sympathetic to the idea of precise identification of the outer limits. However, he obviously felt unable to assess unaided the technicalities or the consequences of the formulae in the Irish amendment, and suggested an expert study of this question at the following session. On revenue sharing the RSNT incorporated the US-proposed system, with its grace period for the first five years of production. Gradation of payments and a ceiling were provided for but no percentage figures were given. The ISNT provisions for payment to and distribution by the (ISBA) international authority, and for the possibility of exemptions for developing countries, were retained.

Delimitation

On delimitation the Irish delegate spoke, largely for tactical and solidarity reasons, to support a Turkish proposal that the provision on delimitation of the territorial sea (Article 13) should be amended to add equity as a basis for departing from median line division (and sought unsuccessfully to have this suggestion included in the EEC written submissions, see above). Others did likewise and those of like mind with Ireland on delimitation were pleasantly surprised and heartened at the number of interventions that supported the proposal. Consultations between the Irish and Turkish delegations produced amendments to delimitation Articles 61 (EEZ) and 72 (continental shelf) of the ISNT, which the Irish delegate introduced in the Committee. Other like-minded delegations, including those associated with the similar proposal made at the Third Session, supported them. These were revised versions of the draft proposed at the Third Session. They were aimed at total elimination of the role of the median line as set out in the 1958 convention provision, which had been significantly reduced in the ISNT. They would emphasise equitable principles as the prime determining factor, as in the International Court of Justice (ICJ) decision (in the North Sea cases), and stress the need to have regard to special circumstances, including specifically the presence of islands. They also excluded the role of the median line as an interim measure. Conversely, proposals by Greece, Spain and Cyprus, supported by others, sought to strengthen the role of the median line. Greece sought to make it mandatory between opposite, as distinct from adjacent, states—probably drawing on an *obiter dictum* in the ICJ judgement. A majority of the speakers supported the Irish proposal, particularly exclusion of the median line as a solution in the absence of agreement.

Regime of islands

Consultations between Irish and New Zealand delegates on Article 132 on regime of islands drew a New Zealand offer to support the Irish position on delimitation in return for acceptance of that article. However, Ireland's delimitation allies were not prepared to accept the condition for the offer. Thus, while the Irish delegate, in solidarity with those allies, supported a proposal to amend the article on islands so as to reduce further their capacity to generate zones of marine jurisdiction, the support was low key. Within the allies the Irish delegate proposed, as an alternative, a cross-reference in the islands article to the delimitation articles, which would indicate that in a delimitation situation the latter provisions would prevail.

The RSNT retained the ISNT provision on regime of islands. On delimitation it replaced Paragraph 3, featuring the median line as an interim measure (or even a default solution), with a provision calling for interim measures taking account of the provisions of Paragraph 1 (which set out the basis for agreement). The latter was a move in the direction of Irish interests. Paragraph 1, with its mention of the median line as a possible division, was retained.

Straits and archipelagos

The ISNT texts on straits and archipelagos were carried over with some changes (mainly drafting changes).

Article 136 of the ISNT regarding territories whose people did not have full independence was retained in the RSNT, but without a number and after all the other articles. Its title was changed to 'Transitional Provision' (from 'Territories under Foreign Occupation or Colonial Domination') and it was slightly redrafted to clarify its effect.

THIRD COMMITTEE

The ISNT articles coming within the mandate of the Third Committee were those in Part III. Confusingly these were further divided into Part I (environment), Part II (MSR) and Part III (TOT), in each of which the articles were numbered from Article 1. It was agreed that the three topics would be dealt with in informal meetings under special Chairmen, and that consideration should proceed article by article.

Environment

The informal meeting on the environment articles began on 17 March with Jose Vallarta (Mexico) again as Chairman. The issues in Articles 1 to 15 (general, cooperation, technical assistance, monitoring, assessment) were the least controversial, so consideration began with the chapters on standards (Articles 16 to 21) and on enforcement (Articles 22 to 40). Agreement was reached quickly on Paragraphs 1 to 3 of Article 16 (control of pollution from land sources) and Article 22 (general provision on enforcement). Articles 17 and 18 (pollution from exploration or exploitation) were deferred because of overlaps with the work of the Second and First Committees. It was accepted that the flag state would have an obligation to regulate dumping and (other) vessel source pollution by its vessels and the right and duty to enforce those regulations (Articles 19 and 20). Developing countries were resistant to the requirement (Article 19 Paragraph 4 and Article 20 Paragraph 2) that such regulation should not be less effective than internationally agreed regulations, effectively those in the 1972 London Convention on Dumping. Maintenance of this position by the G-77 evoked strong resistance by developed countries and a stalemate ensued.

The main other controversies related to the question of coastal state regulation and enforcement. Coastal state sovereignty in the territorial sea was generally accepted, but not the claim of some coastal states to a right to apply national standards stricter than international standards (on which Article 20 was ambiguous), including rules on design and other similar aspects of vessels (which were expressly excluded in Part II of the ISNT dealing with innocent passage—Article 18 Paragraph 2). Maritime states rejected coastal state rights of regulation and/or enforcement outside the territorial sea. This applied, if not identically, in respect of both dumping and (other) vessel-source pollution. Thus a Mexican proposal on Article 19, supported by Australia and Canada, that the zones in which a requirement of coastal state approval for, and control of, dumping would apply (Paragraph 3) should include the EEZ and the continental shelf as well as the territorial sea, met strong opposition from the US and other maritime states. This Mexican proposal, of course, coincided with the Irish position. The provision in Article 25 (Paragraph c) for coastal state right to enforce dumping regulations on vessels dumping within its EEZ and on its continental shelf met similar opposition. In EEC-9 consultations Ireland's support for coastal states' right to regulate within the EEZ and continental shelf and to stop ships in these zones was opposed, but not totally, by all the other members. There, and in the Committee discussions, the idea of a narrower pollution zone, for example 50 miles, was floated. Wide disagreement also emerged on the priority given by the ISNT to flag states (over port and coastal states) in prosecution rights for both dumping and vessel-source pollution.

The Chairman of the informal meetings proposed, for discussion in a smaller drafting group (of which the Irish delegate was a member), an outline of issues on dumping and vessel-source pollution. This outline drew also on drafts that had emerged from intersessional meetings of the Evensen Group. The Chairman revised the outline in the light of the drafting group discussions and transmitted the revised version to the Third Committee Chairman for his guidance. It set out roles of regulation and enforcement for the flag state, the port state and the coastal state respectively, varying according to marine zones. Flag states would have regulation rights and duties in respect of their vessels everywhere, and corresponding enforcement rights and obligations. Coastal states would have right of regulation and enforcement, including prosecution, in their territorial sea; rights of enquiry and limited rights of boarding, inspection and prosecution in the EEZ. Port states would have rights of enforcement, including prosecution, on vessels docked in their ports.

The RSNT (i) included a new provision (Article 6) aimed at preventing the introduction of new or alien species to a particular part of the environment where it might cause harmful change; (ii) asserted the right of the coastal state to permit, control and regulate dumping within its EEZ and continental shelf (Article 20) and to enforce its regulations (Article 26); (iii) defined 'dumping' by reference to the 1972 London Dumping Convention (footnote to Article 20.1); (iv) authorised the coastal state to regulate, in accordance with agreed international standards (other) vessel-source pollution within its EEZ; and (v) gave stronger rights of enforcement to port and coastal states, including in certain circumstances right of prosecution (Articles 28 and 30), while retaining in most cases the priority of flag state prosecution. The RSNT, therefore, largely met Irish concerns.

Marine scientific research

The informal meetings on MSR were chaired by Mr Cornel Metternich of the FRG. There was much discussion on (general) Articles 1 to 7, although these had developed from broad agreements apparent already at the Second Session. Nevertheless a more precise definition of MSR was not achieved. On the international cooperation provisions (Articles 8 to 12) the G-77 sought changes to strengthen the obligation to transfer information to developing countries, which they saw as inadequately acknowledged in Article 10. On the provisions on conduct of MSR (Articles 13 to 26) the G-77, supported by Canada, rejected the distinction between fundamental and resource-related research, and thus sought the consent regime for all MSR in the EEZ. The G-77, more radically, regarded the EEZ as an area in which the coastal state would exclusively control and regulate MSR, as it did in the territorial sea. The developed countries, including most of the EEC-9, sought to preserve the ISNT without confrontation, and the US and the Soviet Union maintained a particularly low profile. EEC members' activity took the form of suggestions by individual delegations supported by the others. There was, according to an Irish delegation report, an objection by seven of the EEC-9, excepting Ireland and the UK, to inclusion of the continental shelf as well as the EEZ (in Articles 14 and 15) in the coastal state zone of jurisdiction, on the basis that this prejudiced the work of the Second Committee on the nature of coastal state jurisdiction on the shelf. The subsequent EEC Commission report on the session indicated that coastal state MSR jurisdiction as set out in the 1958 Convention on the Continental Shelf was accepted by all members. The LLGDS sought specific recognition of MSR rights for them. Nothing was achieved in regard to a settlement of disputes provision (Article 37), partly because of the separate treatment in Plenary of PSD as a general topic. Likewise, some delegations regarded MSR in the ISBA (Article 25) as a matter for the First Committee. Little attention was paid to the other articles. Progress was slight. An informal group (eighteen delegations including only the Netherlands and the FRG of the EEC-9) convened by Ambassador Keith Brennan (Australia) worked on an Evensen text but without results. The EEC-9, following their usual practice, sent by letter to the Committee Chairman those amendments on which they had reached agreement.

The Chairman's RSNT included some changes (basically drafting changes) to the ISNT general provisions and those on cooperation. Article 26 of the ISNT on MSR on the high seas was revised to refer only to the water-column, omitting MSR on the seabed. On conduct of MSR in the EEZ and on the continental shelf a consent regime was provided for all research. However, there were only four reasons for which consent could be withheld—(i) if the research related to exploration or exploitation; (ii) if it involved drilling or explosives; (iii) if it interfered with economic activities of the coastal state; or (iv) if it involved construction of artificial islands, etc. Having regard to these four as the only grounds for refusal and the researcher' right to proceed in the absence of a reply to its application within months, the difference from the notification regime of the ISNT for non-resource-related research was significant only in giving the coastal state a more intrusive role; and the distinction between fundamental and resource-related research was preserved in the first ground. The Second Committee ISNT Part II Article 49, which had a similar but not identical consent regime for MSR in the EEZ, was changed in the RSNT to refer to Part III provision in regard to conditions, thus avoiding any inconsistency between the provisions.

Transfer of technology

The informal meetings on the TOT were also chaired by Mr Metternich. Discussions were somewhat overshadowed by a simultaneous meeting in Nairobi of the UN Conference on Trade and Development. This dealt with TOT generally, and Western countries in particular were concerned that those deliberations should not be undermined by what was going on in UNCLOS. A general discussion at the beginning was followed by an examination of the ISNT article by article. A major point of contention was the powers given by the ISNT (Articles 8 and 9) to the (ISBA) international authority to transfer ISBA technology to developing countries. The G-77 strongly supported these articles against opposition from developed countries, including the EEC-9, which sought deletion of all references to the authority in Part III and negotiation of the matter only in the First Committee. The G-77 put forward drafts to strengthen further the central role of the authority, and also to impose more imperative obligations on developed countries. The LLGDS were dissatisfied at resistance to their claims for extra concessions or special treatment. The EEC-9, like other developed countries, regarded the ISNT as favourable to developed countries (apart from the role of the international authority) and were concerned to prevent its being changed to become less favourable to them. They conveyed agreed comments to the Chairman. These received some support at the informal meetings.

The changes in the RSNT as compared with the ISNT were mainly of a drafting nature. However, there was a slight shift of emphasis by way of references to transfer of technology to other than developing countries, although the latter continued to be regarded as the primary recipients. This was a slight improvement for Ireland. There was no substantive change to the LLGDS references. The articles on ISBA TOT were modified to take account of the rights of owners of technology.

FIRST COMMITTEE

International seabed area

The articles dealing with the ISBA regime, and thus falling within the mandate of the First Committee, were those in Part I of the ISNT, Articles 1 to 68 and Annex 1 (on conditions of exploration and exploitation). Most of the deliberations were conducted in an informal working group (of the whole) and in smaller groups of experts on particular issues. Ireland did not participate in the latter. The texts were progressively revised leading finally to the Chairman's RSNT. This moved towards the interests of the industrialised countries as compared with the ISNT, which had reflected mainly G-77 positions. The changes inevitably evoked G-77 resistance. The advances made by the industrialised countries may have been facilitated by Henry Kissinger's speech outside the Conference on 8 April (see above), in which he addressed the First Committee issues at length. His statement was quite conciliatory to G-77 concerns on some of the fundamental issues, including direct exploitation by the authority, distribution of the revenues by it, reservation of sites for it and for developing countries and the economic threat to developing producers of land-based minerals. Although he took a hard line on other issues his statement probably encouraged both the G-77 and the industrialised countries to engage in a search for viable compromises, which led to the RSNT.

The subject first discussed was conditions of exploration and exploitation (as in Annex 1), including pre-exploitation activities, system of granting contracts, requirements for operations and reservation of areas (for exploitation by the authority and for developing countries). There was disagreement as to whether areas in the ISBA should be open to pre-exploitation activities unless closed by the authority, as favoured by industrial states, or only if permitted by the authority, as favoured by the G-77. On the question of the authorisation of such activities, the G-77 tended towards acceptance that they could be conducted on the basis of an undertaking by the operator to the authority rather than under contract. On granting of exploitation contracts the G-77 insisted world economic factors should be among those to be taken into account by the authority, whereas the industrialised countries argued that the vagueness of this and other factors gave the authority excessive discretion. They sought clear objective conditions, whose non-observance would justify appeal of the authority decision to the PSD procedures. They were also concerned at the requirement of an operator's bond and the authority's facility to invest in operations, fearing that the former would inhibit operators and that the latter might be a factor in refusal of a contract. Thus they urged that the operator should have the decision as to the extent of authority investment. They did, however, incline towards acceptance of reservation of areas. France, concerned that the most advanced states might scoop all the best sites, promoted within the EEC-9 the idea of an anti-dominant clause (to which Ireland was sympathetic). Although the idea of preventing monopoly had been approved earlier, the French proposal met with opposition from others of the nine, particularly the UK, the FRG and Belgium, and discussion was deferred. The Kissinger statements were also against the idea. Other aims of the industrialised countries in regard to contracts were security of tenure and guarantee of no change in the terms for a specified time.

The RSNT provided for operations to be carried out directly or through contracts with states, state-sponsored enterprises (effectively international consortiums, some already in existence) or companies. A contract could be granted on an application in respect of effectively two mining sites (a Kissinger proposal), one of which would be reserved by the authority when it gave a contract for the other (which became known as the parallel system). The conditions would be as in an annex. There would be security of tenure and no unreasonable change in the terms.

Little progress was made on the powers and functions of the authority. Several aspects of this topic were controversial, with the industrialised countries fearful, as ever, that access to the ISBA and availability of its production would be restricted. Their fears were reflected in positions on granting of access; on the respective roles of the assembly and the council of the authority; on the composition of and voting rules in the latter; on measures to protect land-based producers of minerals, particularly of developing countries, heavily dependent economically on the minerals; and on any authority role in preservation of the environment. Thus they sought that access should not be at the discretion of the authority, and strongly opposed a G-77 proposal that the assembly could review council decisions. The G-77 supported the ISNT on the authority's powers and functions and insisted that its 'direct and effective' control of the ISBA (as in the ISNT) was necessary to ensure compliance with contracts, but did not extend to interference in details of operations. They favoured a council elected on a basis of equitable geographical representation. They saw the assembly as having powers to make policy, to take executive action, to interpret policy and to review decisions, while the council would be responsible for day-to-day management. The US advocated an assembly with recommendatory functions only, while the council would decide policy after universal consultation and subject to objection by a third of its membership. France proposed a category voting system in the assembly, with a majority in each category necessary for a decision, which the US regarded as a possible basis for assembly policy-making powers. The G-77 saw this as creating an unacceptable veto, and within the EEC-9 there was minority opposition to it, from Denmark as well as Ireland. The industrialised countries' position on composition of the council was that it should be based on interest groups, for example operators, land-based producers, consumers, LLGDS, etc.

The RSNT provided that the assembly would have the function of establishing general policy. The council would also make policy decisions, it would grant contracts and make rules and regulations. The RSNT made no change to the ISNT provisions on composition of, and voting in, the council.

In regard to land-based producers most of the industrialised countries were prepared to accept that the authority could become party to international commodity agreements, but only in respect of its own direct production, whereas the G-77 felt it should cover all production from the ISBA. The industrialised countries were also amenable to authority production control for an initial limited period, but were negative on compensatory financing for land-based producers. As to the source of such compensation, if nevertheless adopted, they suggested it should come from the authority revenues.

The RSNT provided for production control for twenty to twenty-five years; for authority participation in commodity agreements in respect of all production from the ISBA; and for compensation for affected land-based producers.

The establishment of a separate body, called the enterprise, as the operating arm of the authority was widely acceptable, and specifically accepted by Henry Kissinger for the US, in his speech of 8 April (see above). However, among the EEC-9, Belgium, in the context of its position on authority operations, opposed it. In signalling acceptance, industrialised countries suggested the enterprise should be independent of the authority and financed by revenue from the ISBA, although there was recognition that initial financing from other sources would be necessary. The Committee Chairman undertook to prepare an enterprise draft statute, although its content had not been discussed in the Committee.

The RSNT provided for the enterprise as the operating arm of the authority, acting in accordance with the policy of the assembly and under the direction of the council. It would be a separate body having as members all assembly members and a governing body of the same composition as the council. It would have title to its production and powers to process it and to dispose of it at market prices, with the possibility of offering more favourable prices to developing countries.

The Chairman also undertook to prepare a draft statute of the proposed new law of the sea tribunal. The US insisted that there should be a permanent tribunal or an arbitration system, but France opposed the former. The Chairman's draft statute appeared at the end of the session and discussion was deferred to the next session.

The final clauses included in the ISBA articles in the ISNT were not carried over into the RSNT except the clause on provisional application (Article 63).

Within the EEC-9 there was a softening of positions by France, the FRG and the UK, for example in accepting both direct exploitation by the authority and establishment of the enterprise as the operative arm for that purpose; processing by the enterprise of its production and authority participation in commodity agreements in respect of that production. However, Belgium opposed all of these. Ireland refused to join efforts to confine the authority's powers to exploration and exploitation, maintaining that it must have general control of the ISBA, and that its powers as defined in the ISNT did not give it functions of processing and marketing other than in respect of its own direct production. The Netherlands eventually spoke for the EEC-9 (including Ireland and Belgium) in seeking clear definition of the authority's discretion in granting access, and also in indicating acceptance of authority participation in international commodity agreements. It also made a statement accepting a non-exclusive function for the authority in regard to MSR in the ISBA.

PLENARY

Peaceful settlement of disputes

The consideration of the President's articles on PSD (A/Conf.62/WP.9) in Plenary began on 5 April. The Attorney General, again attending as Special Representative of the Government, spoke in the general debate on 9 April to the effect, *inter alia*, that procedures for settlement of disputes must be compulsory and binding with minimal exceptions. (The exceptions permitted by Article 18 were regarded among the EEC-9, and in Western circles generally, as excessive). The procedures must also be comprehensive, simple, capable both of speedy decision and of granting interim relief, and inexpensive. He advocated a range of choices of procedure (as in Article 9). He was doubtful about a special law of the sea tribunal. His statement was commended privately by both the UN Secretary-General's Special Representative and the President.

The discussions revealed wide acceptance of the need for compulsory and binding procedures. However, China disagreed; the Soviet Union (traditionally resistant to compulsory and binding procedures on the grounds that they infringed state sovereignty) did not object to PSD procedures but insisted that state consent should be required; Poland and some other EE states nevertheless accepted a compulsory element; Romania and Turkey suggested an optional protocol. Some Latin American states in the CSG objected to application of the procedures to the EEZ, on the grounds that it was an area of exclusive coastal state jurisdiction. There was also general support for establishment of a special law of the sea tribunal, although some wished to deny it the central role proposed in the articles and to confine its jurisdiction to ISBA matters. Others were concerned that it might detract from the role of the ICJ. There was some disagreement with the provision that, in the absence of a common choice of procedure between disputing parties, the law of the sea tribunal should be the residual forum. As alternatives it was proposed that arbitration or the forum chosen by the defendant should be the residual forum.

The President undertook to revise the articles and to present them to a working group of Plenary for detailed examination similar to that of the ISNT in the Committees. However, the revision (A.Conf.62/WP.9 rev.1) appeared only at the end of the session, and detailed discussion was deferred to the Fifth Session. Although entitled as Part IV of the text, it was not included as part of the RSNT. The most significant change in the revision was that Article 9 provided for the defendant's choice as the residual forum.

Preamble and final clauses

The preamble and final clauses were not discussed pending the production of the paper requested by the President. Thus there was not an opportunity for the EEC members to advocate the 'Community clause' intended to enable the EEC to become a party to the future convention. The declared intention of the EEC Netherlands Presidency of engaging in informal soundings seeking support for the proposed clause was effectively limited to a lunch with the Conference President, some senior secretariat officials and a few prominent heads of delegations. Subsequent remarks suggested that these interlocutors did not fully understand the problem posed. No text was circulated, even informally, in the face of UK opposition. Accordingly, no significant progress was made on the issue.

At an early stage the Conference President had suggested a further session in Geneva in the autumn, as allowed for in the UN General Assembly decision. The G-77 was reluctant, citing the short time for consideration of the results of the Fourth Session, the demands of servicing other conferences and the inconvenience of Geneva as a venue. The G-77 reluctance was still evident late in the session, perhaps reinforced by a feeling of lost ground in the RSNT on the ISBA. However, when the President later proposed a session in New York from 2 August to 17 September, the G-77, after a short delay, acquiesced, and it was so decided. The President also suggested a change in working methods, including identification of and concentration on the most difficult issues, and a search for solutions to these issues through negotiations between interest groups. He also raised the possibility of resorting to voting, even if only of an indicative nature.

Conclusion

The emergence of the RSNT was clearly a further progressive step in the negotiations, and as such was a welcome development in the view of the Irish delegation, all the more so as Irish interests were adequately reflected in it.

Chapter VIII

FIFTH SESSION

The Fifth Session was held at the United Nations headquarters in New York for seven weeks, from 2 August to 17 September 1976.

PREPARATIONS

In view of the short interval since the Fourth Session, intersessional consultations were less intensive than before previous sessions. Nevertheless, EEC coordination and cooperation meetings were held. UK opposition to formal proposal of the text of the 'Community clause' was withdrawn, and the EEC Council of Ministers adopted a decision that such a clause should be sought.

The Inter-Departmental Committee (IDC) met and the delegation instructions were reviewed in the light of developments. In the Department of Foreign Affairs a fairly detailed outline of policy on the international seabed area (ISBA) regime was approved at ministerial level.

INSTRUCTIONS

As usual, following consultations among the concerned departments, both those in and those not in the IDC, the Minister for Foreign Affairs made a submission to the Government on 9 August on instructions for the delegation. The Minister for Finance separately conveyed observations regarding aspects of the submission on the ISBA regime, the continental shelf and the exclusive economic zone (EEZ). The submission by the Minister for Foreign Affairs proposed that existing instructions on the territorial sea and contiguous zone, the high seas, straits, archipelagos, and marine scientific research (MSR) be confirmed.

International seabed area

On the ISBA regime it also indicated that no change was called for, but there was some elaboration on detailed positions to be adopted by the delegation on the basis of the existing instructions. Thus there was reference to opposition to weighted voting in the authority assembly and to support for (i) representation in the council on an interest group basis; (ii) non-discriminatory access to the ISBA subject to reservation of sites for the authority and developing countries; (iii) the French proposal for an anti-monopoly clause; (iv) initial financing of the administrative expenses of the authority by the contracting parties (to the future convention); (v) establishment of the enterprise as the operational exploitation arm of the authority; (vi) if necessary, financing of the first operations of the enterprise; (vii) measures to minimise damage to land-based producers; and (viii) inclusion of a compulsory and binding settlement of disputes procedure. Most of these and some other points were reflected in lettered specific recommendations on instructions for support of proposals, including (d) financing of the initial administrative expenses of the authority; (e) financing of the first operations of the enterprise (without indicating a source); (f) financial arrangements (for contractors) likely to encourage exploitation; (g) measures to safeguard land-based producers and (h) equitable sharing of authority profits among developing countries. The observations of the Minister for Finance suggested that the delegation's general approach should move closer to that of the EEC partners with a view to manoeuvrability on financing issues. On production limitation and related matters the stance should conform more closely to Ireland's position on raw materials, etc., in other fora, and financing of compensatory arrangements by developed countries should not be accepted. Opposition to weighted voting in the assembly was queried on the grounds that such a system could ensure protection of the economic and financial interests of developed countries, including Ireland. Any obligation on Ireland to contribute financially to any operations of the enterprise was objectionable and indeed the need for any direct operation was questionable. Amendments to specific instructions (d) to (h) in conformity with the views expressed were proposed. Those on (d) to (g) relating to costs to Ireland were incorporated in the Government decision, some as proposed and others with some softening. Amendments regarding distribution of profits (h) and on weighted voting were not incorporated.

Exclusive economic zone and fisheries

On the EEZ no substantive change was suggested. There was additional emphasis on support for coastal state control of fisheries in the zone, together with support for the EEC proposal that would strengthen the role of international fisheries organisations, and for the EEC-9 proposal for preservation of high-seas rights in the zone. It was suggested that the revised single negotiating text (RSNT) provision on anadromous species (salmon) was unlikely to be susceptible to improvement, but no softening of the instructions was proposed. The observations of the Minister for Finance repeated his indication before the Third Session that his acceptance of support for extended coastal state jurisdiction did not constitute a commitment to any corresponding increase in patrol and control resources.

Continental shelf

On the continental shelf it was proposed that in addition to existing instructions the delegation should be enabled to accept the boundary commission, as proposed by Canada and agreed by the Margineers at the Fourth Session, with the function (only) of validating coastal state identification of outer limits, and also to accept revenue sharing in the form of a percentage of production (instead of the preferred percentage of profit). In his observations the Minister for Finance advocated that efforts should be made to secure exceptions from revenue sharing where it would inhibit production or be inequitable to the country of jurisdiction (although the Foreign Affairs submission expressed the view that there would be virtually no support at the Conference for any exception). A proposal to amend instructions in the light of the observations of the Minister for Finance was incorporated in the Government's decision, albeit in terms of appropriate revenue-sharing arrangements rather than of exceptions.

Delimitation and regime of islands

On delimitation and regime of islands more detailed instructions were suggested directly related to the RSNT. It was proposed that the RSNT be supported subject to (i) exclusion of all reference to the median line in Articles 62 and 71 (regarding division of EEZ and continental shelf respectively); (ii) inclusion of a reference to equitable principles in Article 14 (regarding division of territorial seas); and (iii) a cross-reference in Article 128 on regime of islands confirming the priority of the delimitation provisions in delimitation situations.

Environment and transfer of technology

On the environment, addition of an instruction to support the new provision (Article 6) on alien species was proposed. On transfer of technology (TOT), support for the RSNT (with its reliance on promotion rather than binding commitments) was proposed, except for the provision on the (ISBA) authority's role (Article 86).

Peaceful settlement of disputes

There was more detail than previously on peaceful settlement of disputes (PSD) in the context of the intended detailed examination of the President's text. An account was given of reactions in the EEC-9 to the text. Mention was made of their concerns that the permissible exceptions from binding procedures were excessive, particularly the exception in regard to disputes arising in respect of exercise of sovereign rights and jurisdiction. In addition the French and UK delegations felt, as did the Irish delegation, that arbitration should be the residual forum (i.e. where the choices of disputants did not include a common forum). Others of the EEC-9, including the Federal Republic of Germany (the FRG) and the Netherlands, while accepting this view and favouring arbitration in the ISBA context also, considered a compulsory and binding system so important that they would, if necessary, accept the text as it was. The instruction suggested that the delegation should continue to advocate compulsory settlement of disputes procedures and, if consistent with that objective, to favour arbitration as the residual procedure.

Preamble and final clauses

The question of instructions regarding the preamble and final clauses of the future convention was raised for the first time. At the Fourth Session a direction had been given by the Plenary to the Chairman of the Drafting Committee to prepare, with the assistance of the Conference Secretariat, drafts on these topics for consideration by the Plenary. Provisions for provisional application of the convention and for permissible reservations to it were foreseen in the submission as likely to be the most problematic. Provisional application was probably desirable to inhibit unilateral action that, if inconsistent with the convention, could undermine its status. Yet, unless carefully constructed, it could lead to selective application with similar dangers for the convention's status. Again to preserve the convention as a package, reservations ideally should not be permitted at all, or at worst should be extremely limited. An instruction was sought to (a) support enablement of provisional application with adequate safeguards and (b) oppose permission of excessive reservation. An instruction to support and/or propose the 'Community clause' as decided in the EEC was also suggested.

Conference procedures

Finally authority was sought to support Conference procedures seen as likely to lead to an expeditious and successful conclusion, while taking account of the views of our EEC partners. This was in the context of the Conference President's suggestions, at the end of the Fourth Session. This was to the effect that that progress might best be made through identification of the most difficult issues and their negotiation between interest groups for a period of three weeks, after which indicative voting might be used to point the way to solutions not yet reached. The delegation again felt the President's assessment of the time needed was over-optimistic. It also felt that indicative voting might be a two-edged sword—useful in some situations to inject realism and face down intransigence, but potentially counter-productive if used prematurely. Obviously the Conference needed a Solomon's wisdom to distinguish these situations. Not surprisingly in the circumstances, a flexible instruction was proposed.

Land-locked states

The submission also referred to the land-locked and geographically disadvantaged states (LLGDS) as a group growing in size and importance in the Conference. It included four EEC members (Belgium, the FRG, Luxembourg and the Netherlands). It had strongly expressed the view that Articles 58 and 59 of Part II of the RSNT, on LLGDS rights in the EEZ, were not satisfactory. It had sufficient members to be capable, if fully united, of blocking adoption of a convention. No instructions were sought. (EEC Commission documents hinted that the four EEC LLGDS members had indicated they would not join in a blocking move.)

The Government by decision dated 13 August approved the proposals for instructions, with amendments, as indicated above, in response to the observations of the Minister for Finance.

DELEGATION

Brian Nason of the Mission in New York took over the environment topic from Patrick Craddock. Otherwise the delegation was the same as for the Fourth Session.

GENERAL

Meetings of interest groups and other consultations *en marge* continued. The groups included the Margineers (of which Ireland was now Co-Chairman with Canada) and the coastal states group (CSG), now comprising 85 members, including Ireland. Although Ireland was the only EEC state invited to join, several other Western coastal states were also members at this stage. The delegation continued to be active in interest groups on delimitation and MSR. The Arab Group emerged as more cohesive and more active, particularly in opposing extended continental shelf jurisdiction. The EEC member states held many coordination and cooperation meetings. The regional groups met, including the Western European and Others Group (WEOG) on procedural matters such as the venue and duration of the next session. The Evensen Group was less active than at previous sessions, partly because Minister Evensen was busy as acting President (see below).

Progress was slow, due at least in part to Group of 77 (G-77) procrastination in the First Committee, inspired by several considerations, including dissatisfaction with the changes incorporated into the ISBA regime in the RSNT. These were generally perceived as having moved too far towards the position of the industrialised states. There was some inconclusive off-stage discussion of consolidation/formalisation of the RSNT.

PLENARY

At the beginning of the session the President proposed formally, as a new procedure, that the Committees should concentrate on key issues, suggesting a list that the Committees could modify or expand as they thought fit. This proposal was on the understanding that a further revision of the RSNT would not be undertaken at the session. No mention was made of indicative voting or of formalisation of the RSNT. The President indicated his intention to have his PSD drafts discussed in informal meetings of the Plenary and, in the light of those discussions, to revise the drafts with a view to bringing them to the same stage of advancement as the RSNT, in which they would be included as Part IV. He left over the question of dealing with the document regarding a preamble and final clauses submitted by the secretariat (A/Conf.62/L.13), while indicating that provisional application of the convention would fall within those clauses. As the President had to absent himself to attend a session of the UN Conference on Trade and Development for some weeks, he proposed that Minister Evensen (Norway), a senior Vice-President, should be acting President in his absence. These proposals, made first in the General Committee, were accepted by the Plenary.

SECOND COMMITTEE

The Second Committee held no formal meetings, conducting its business in negotiating groups, consultative groups and informal Committee meetings. Within the Plenary guidelines the Committee identified priority issues and established negotiating groups to deal with them. These groups were open-ended, but included a special membership of volunteer delegations that were expected to take special responsibility to advance progress. At a certain stage in the work of most of these groups, the Committee Chairman convened a smaller consultative group (30 or so delegations) on the issue, with a view to seeking compromise formulae that might be agreed by the Committee. The invitees were representatives of interest groups and some neutrals. The negotiating and consultative groups were usually Chaired by the Committee Chairman, but occasionally by acting Chairmen. The Committee Chairman set out the results of these deliberations in his report to Plenary.

The priority issues identified were (i) the legal status of the EEZ and the respective rights in it of the coastal state and other states; (ii) land-locked states' rights of access to the sea and related rights of transit; (iii) revenue sharing in respect of exploitation of the area of the continental shelf beyond 200 miles; and (iv) definition of the outer edge of the continental margin. Later two further issues were identified: (v) straits and (vi) delimitation between neighbouring states. These issues were assigned to five negotiating groups, (iii) and (iv) being assigned to one group. The Irish delegation was a volunteer in the negotiating groups on (iii) and (iv) and on (vi) and an invitee to the consultative group that followed in each case. It was a participant also in the other negotiating groups.

Informal meetings of the Second Committee were held near the end of the session to consider the other issues. At these meetings there were some proposals to identify other specific priority issues for special treatment but none were adopted. Likewise, a Soviet Union proposal to amend Article 55 on anadromous species evoked no support in the Committee. In EEC consultations Denmark commented favourably on the Soviet Union proposal, but the other EEC members rejected it. In his report the Chairman indicated that some issues (for example archipelagos) were the subject of promising separate consultations between interested delegations. He mentioned that on several unidentified issues (presumably including anadromous species) that the proposals made were substantially the same as earlier proposals, and that they continued to attract little support. He also pointed out that more than 50 RSNT Part II articles had not drawn any comment, with the implication that they commanded broad support—an indication of at least some progress in reducing the number of contentious issues.

Exclusive economic zone and fisheries

In the negotiating group on (i—the EEZ) the existing differences persisted between those who saw the EEZ as a zone of national jurisdiction similar to the territorial sea, those who saw it as high seas except in regard to rights to resources, and the LLGDS who basically resisted the EEZ concept. The EEC and its members maintained their Fourth Session amendments, which were designed, firstly, to preserve most high seas freedoms (navigation etc.) in the EEZ and to limit coastal state fisheries controls. The clashes between CSG members and the LLGDS continued also in the context of LLGDS' efforts to expand their fishing rights beyond those provided in Article 58. This part of the issue was transferred to an unofficial group of 21 delegations, comprising ten from each side with Ambassador Satya Nandan (Fiji—Committee Rapporteur) as Chairman, as a consequence of which the Committee Chairman did not refer the matter to a consultative group. This group of 21 did not reach agreement, but Ambassador Nandan produced draft provisions on his own responsibility in an attempt to reach a compromise. These caused some concern among some of the EEC members insofar as the LLGDS fishing rights proposed were not confined to the surplus of the total allowable catch (TAC) over the coastal state's harvesting capacity. The Committee Chairman did not mention these drafts in his report. A consultative group was established for the status of the EEZ. The Committee Chairman reported that the group had not reached agreement, but had come close with an approach based on the view he had expressed in his introduction to the RSNT. He reiterated this view that the EEZ must be *sui generis*, aligned neither to the territorial sea nor the high seas, but with establishment of residual (effectively high seas) rights for states other than the coastal state—as was essayed in the RSNT, Article 46 and others.

Continental shelf

In the negotiating group on (iii) and (iv)—the continental shelf, including revenue sharing—the Irish delegate explained the Margineers' formulae for determination of the outer edge of the margin. This was done bearing in mind the Committee Chairman's view, expressed in his introduction to the RSNT, that these formulae were of such a technical nature as to require examination by experts. The Irish delegate also replied to queries raised by several delegations, some of which were only superficially technical. In the ensuing consultative group the practicality of these formulae seemed to be gaining acceptance, although there were hints at a possibility of presentation of another formula. In addition, some delegations, including the Arab Group (presumably influenced, at least in part, by the oil producers among its members), reiterated their opposition to any extension of jurisdiction beyond 200 miles. The LLGDS sought to secure for themselves rights of exploitation in any extended area. The discussions also tended to emphasise that revenue sharing would be an essential element of a package deal on the issue of extended jurisdiction. There was considerable controversy about rates, and the mooted possibility of their variability in the light of experience of exploitation. There was general but not unanimous support for the Margineers' overall position by CSG members. The Margineers, in their own consultations, concerned with tactical considerations, concentrated on the details of a revenue-sharing scheme. The Irish delegation was cautious on the subject in the light of its instructions, and only at a late stage overtly indicated conditional acceptance. With this indication only Australia among the Margineers remained opposed in principle, but it was reconsidering its position. At one stage support seemed to be growing around a scheme of revenue sharing in respect of production beyond the 200-mile limit (a) based on gross revenue; (b) with rates progressing annually from 1 per cent to 5 per cent after an initial five-year levy-free grace period; (c) with some relief from payments by developing countries; (d) with the benefits going to developing states, especially land-locked developing states; and (e) with a role for the (ISBA) authority in distribution.

The proposed boundary commission did not figure in the discussions.

In his report, the Committee Chairman expressed the view that acceptance of coastal state continental shelf jurisdiction beyond 200 miles would be an essential ingredient in a package deal on the Second Committee items.

Delimitation

The negotiating group on (vi)—delimitation—was established only in the sixth week of the session. The Irish delegation was among the volunteer members. The role of the median line was the main focus of discussion. An amendment proposed by Canada sought greater emphasis on that role, while Spain sought to reassert its role as an interim measure (as in the 1958 convention). The Spanish proposal derived some credibility from the fact that the RSNT provision on interim measures was not very practical. A Portuguese oral alternative proposal to provide that there should be no change of rights in the disputed area pending settlement of the dispute drew some favourable attention from both sides, but was not elaborated. In the negotiating group debate the Irish delegation promoted its amendment, to eliminate any specific reference to the median line, on the basis of the principles identified in the International Court of Justice judgement in the North Sea cases, and rejected claims that state practice indicated a different approach. The supporters of a dominant median line role attacked equitable principles as a criterion on the ground that it was too vague a concept. The trend of the debate pointed to a narrowing of the majority in the support for the position of Ireland and its allies. There was also a push for addition of compulsory settlement provisions on which Ireland and its allies did not have a group position (see below regarding PSD discussions). No significant change emerged in the consultative group (in which the Irish delegation was among the invitees) although the tone of the exchanges was more conciliatory. The Committee Chairman in his report described the main provision (Paragraph 1 of RSNT Articles 62 and 71) as the most likely compromise on criteria, and hoped that an acceptable compromise draft on interim measures might emerge. From the point of view of the Irish delegation there had been no significant loss or gain. The increase in support for the opposing position was probably due to improved organisation and lobbying on the part of the delegations promoting it. Although unwelcome from the Irish point of view, it still left the opponents in a minority. The outlook on the interim measures called for alertness but was not a cause for serious alarm.

Land-locked states and straits

The Irish delegation also attended the negotiating groups on (ii) access and transit rights for land-locked states and (v) on straits. It was not a volunteer delegate in either group nor was it an invitee to either of the consultative group that emerged. The delegate's limited size meant that its attendance bowed to its more pressing concerns. Suggestions in regard to land-locked states' rights of access to the sea seemed to be gathering support until rejected at a late stage. The Committee Chairman in his report expressed disappointment at the negative outcome to this promising situation. On straits the bordering states sought changes to the RSNT that they felt were necessary to achieve a balance between their rights and the rights of users. The discussions were inconclusive. The Committee Chairman reported that consultations were ongoing between the interested parties and that he hoped they would result in an acceptable conclusion.

THIRD COMMITTEE

Priority issues identified in the Committee, which were negotiated in informal meetings, included aspects of the MSR regime and of the provisions on preservation of the environment.

Marine scientific research

A compromise text on an MSR regime for the territorial sea, which gave the coastal state exclusive control was conditionally agreed. In negotiations on MSR within the EEZ and on the continental shelf (in which the Irish delegation was a participant), deadlock on the details of a consent regime persisted. In an effort to overcome this, the Committee Chairman convened a consultative group of fifteen heads of delegations (not including the Irish delegation). To this group he presented a text that would broaden the right of the coastal state to refuse consent in certain circumstances, but this was not agreed. The Committee Chairman in his report said that amendments proposed to the RSNT had not been widely supported, but that consensus on a regime for MSR in the EEZ and on the continental shelf seemed to be emerging. The sensitive question of military research was not raised in the discussions.

Environment

Negotiations in informal meetings concentrated on the rights of the coastal state to make and enforce laws to prevent vessel-source pollution. These issues were transferred to a negotiating group, chaired by Jose Vallarta (Mexico), of which Ireland was a member. A most serious issue was the extent of the coastal state's right to make and enforce laws for its territorial sea on design, construction, manning and equipment of vessels. The EEC-9 were among those who opposed allowing coastal state legislation imposing national standards more stringent than international standards, on the grounds that there would be no safeguard against these being excessive. No progress was made and the Committee Chairman reported that this was the key outstanding issue. On the other hand, there were indications that the demand of maritime states that coastal state regulations in regard to pollution within the EEZ and the continental shelf should conform to international rules would be accepted by coastal states, but only in return for wider coastal state powers of enforcement. There seemed to be some movement towards acceptance of coastal state powers of prosecution, without flag state priority, for violations causing serious pollution. The only real progress achieved was consensus on a text on preservation of special areas within the EEZ. This text would permit application of national standards in such areas, subject to a role for international organisations, such as the International Maritime Consultative Organisation, in their determination.

Transfer of technology

Negotiations on TOT, both in informal Committee meetings and in a negotiating group chaired by Mr Cornel Metternich (the FRG), were unproductive. Differences between the G-77 and the industrialised states continued, particularly in regard to a role for the ISBA authority. This presumably was what prompted the Committee Chairman's suggestion in his report that coordination of the work in this area in the First and Third Committees would be helpful. An amendment to include specifically countries other than developing countries among potential TOT beneficiaries, consolidating a trend at the Fourth Session, was not opposed. This was obviously welcome to Ireland.

FIRST COMMITTEE

International seabed area

The First Committee was faced with a very difficult situation. There was a general perception that the RSNT on the ISBA regime, prepared by its Chairman, did not accurately reflect the discussions at the Fourth Session and had moved too far towards the position of the industrialised countries. In a formal meeting of the Committee the G-77 rejected the RSNT as a basis of discussion, leading to a long procedural debate. The outcome was the establishment of a workshop open to all delegations with two Co-Chairmen, one from each side (a reflection of the loss of confidence of the G-77 in the Committee Bureau). There was some difficulty in choosing the Co-Chairmen, but eventually Dr S.P. Jhigota (India) and Mr Hans Sondaal (the Netherlands) were appointed.

The workshop decided to address the system of exploitation first (as preferred by the industrialised countries) rather than the authority institutions (as preferred by the G-77). The basis of discussion was the RSNT and an alternative G-77 text. The G-77 objected to the RSNT provisions giving states and others parity of access to the ISBA with the authority. Rather the authority should have preferred access and engage in exploitation through a viable enterprise. A statement by the EEC-9 accepting the establishment of the enterprise made it clear that this was on condition of guaranteed access for other entities on reasonable terms. A negotiating group of 26 delegations (but open to all others) was set up under the Co-Chairmen. Discussion on criteria for access and the extent of authority discretion in granting access ensued, but no agreement was reached. The US Secretary of State, Mr Henry Kissinger, on a visit to the Conference, made a statement to a meeting of heads of delegations indicating three points on which the US would agree if linked to reasonable access: (i) that the enterprise should be so financed as to enable it to begin exploitation at the same time, or virtually the same time, as others; (ii) that the necessary technology would be transferred to it; and (iii) that the convention should include a provision for review of the system of exploration and exploitation 25 years after its entry into force. The statement was lacking in detail and the G-77 requested further elaboration. It failed to have the impact on the negotiations that the US had expected, and no significant progress was made.

The issue of the authority institutions was not reached in the discussions.

Clearly the system of exploitation was the most difficult issue. It was anticipated that settlement of this question would greatly facilitate agreement on other issues. Interestingly, in the last week of the session, a number of African states having association status with the EEC approached the heads of delegation of the EEC members with a proposal for a meeting in Brussels, to clarify certain aspects of the issue of exploitation.

PLENARY

Peaceful settlement of disputes

The President's revised text on PSD (A/Conf.62/WP.9/Rev.1) presented at the end of the Fourth Session was considered article by article in informal meetings of Plenary, mainly chaired by Minister Evensen in the President's absence. The most important controversial issues were (i) choice of forum, including the residual procedure, i.e. the forum having jurisdiction where the disputants' choices did not include a common forum, and (ii) exceptions from the compulsory PSD procedures, both automatic and optional.

The Latin American countries and most other members of the CSG (but not Ireland, Australia or Portugal *inter alios*) opposed a compulsory system, unless it included a new special law of the sea tribunal as a forum and excepted disputes arising in regard to marine zones of national jurisdiction. The Eastern European Group favoured a wide choice of fora, including such a new tribunal, although their own preference was for special procedures, and they opposed any possibility of a state being forced to appear before any forum against its will (presumably as a residual procedure). The main preoccupation of the WEOG, of which Ireland was Chairman at the session, was to procure a compulsory system. France and the UK were vehemently against establishment of a tribunal, but the others of the EEC-9 would accept it if necessary to secure a compulsory system. All of the EEC-9 advocated arbitration as the residual forum, but again only France and the UK were insistent. Likewise all of the EEC-9 were opposed to any exceptions, but recognised this as unachievable and strove to limit any exception in regard to zones of national jurisdiction. The Irish delegate's statements in Plenary followed these lines, particularly in advocating arbitration as the residual forum and opposing exception of disputes arising in regard to the EEZ. Among the optional exceptions in the text was one in regard to delimitation disputes conditional on acceptance of a regional or third-party procedure with binding effect—the Irish statements did not advert to it. The discussions moved on to the annexes dealing with the various procedures and with a draft statute for a tribunal.

After the session the President prepared a revised text (WP.9/Rev. 2), which was given the same status as the RSNT and included in it as Part IV. The main changes made were (i) the exemption of disputes arising in respect of exercise of sovereign rights or jurisdiction from binding procedures was limited in that it did not extend to a) disputes in regard to residual rights (i.e. preserved high seas freedoms); b) disputes in regard to MSR; c) disputes about contravention of international standards on preservation of the environment; or d) disputes about manifest failure to comply with convention obligations in regard to fisheries (Article 17); and (ii) arbitration was established as the residual procedure (Article 9(5)). These changes represented significant movement towards Irish preferences in this area.

Preamble and final clauses

The drafts on a preamble and final clauses were not reached, hence there was again no opportunity to present the 'Community clause' designed to (i) enable the EEC to become a party to the future convention and (ii) ensure that reciprocal exclusive rights between member states arising from EEC membership would have priority over rights for third parties under the convention. Pursuant to the decision of the EEC Council of Ministers to seek such a clause, the delegations of the EEC members and its Commission discussed in coordination meetings both the text of the clause and the procedure to be followed. France and Ireland opposed a commission proposal to amend the text to refer specifically to the EEC, but it was eventually agreed that such an amendment should be submitted as an alternative. When it became clear that there would be no Conference consideration of the final clauses at the session, the Netherlands EEC Presidency sent a letter to the Conference President. This explained the nature and functions of the EEC; referred to the transfers of competences by the members to the EEC, including competences in areas to be covered by the future convention; indicated the EEC's capacity to become a party to international agreements; pointed out the need for the EEC to become a party to the future convention to enable the EEC members to implement it in the areas where competences had been, or would in future be, transferred; and set out the drafts prepared in the EEC to that end.

On the final day of the session, 17 September, Plenary adopted a proposal, presented to the General Committee the previous day, to hold another session in Geneva beginning 23 May 1977. The Attorney General, attending again as special representative of the Government, spoke for the Irish Vice-Presidency in the General Committee debate on this question. He expressed concern at the lack of progress, particularly in regard to the ISBA regime and proposed intersessional meetings as a remedy. The Conference President encouraged this idea in Plenary. He also suggested that (i) the first three weeks of the next session should concentrate on First Committee issues; (ii) all Committees should work during the following three weeks; and (iii) the President and Committee Chairmen should, in the light of that work, produce an informal composite negotiating text. This would bring together in a single text all the subjects covered in the three parts of the RSNT, together with the revised PSD text to be produced after the current session.

CONCLUSION

Not only did the Fifth Session fall far short of the unrealistic role foreseen for it by the US Secretary of State in the spring, but it was generally regarded as the least successful session thus far. Its limited progress cast doubts on the wisdom of having such a short interval between sessions. In addition some Western delegates began to speak offstage of converting UNCLOS III into a perpetual conference on the lines of the UN Conference on Trade and Development. In that scenario it would meet annually to attempt to steer law of the sea developments but without adopting any international legal instrument. The implication of a free-for-all approach to the ISBA did not commend this rather extreme idea to the G-77. The Irish delegation was likewise unimpressed, if not for quite the same reasons. Yet fears of loss of patience and dangerous unilateral action were exacerbated.

In the Second Committee nothing concrete emerged. Indeed an Irish delegate commented that the extremely hard work of the delegation on its items of interest throughout the session had not yielded as much as a change of a comma. While this was literally true, it owed much to the nature of the session, including the acceptance at the beginning that a further revision of the RSNT would not be undertaken. The Committee Chairman in his report indicated that he saw indications of eventual solutions to the outstanding issues. There was a similar lack of overt progress in the Third Committee, but the Chairman's report was optimistic. He felt that discussions pointed towards agreement based on the acceptance of most of the RSNT, a progression that he believed would be greatly assisted by settlement of certain issues in other Committees. The individual interests of importance to Ireland were covered by the Second and Third Committees. The prognosis on these in the delegation report was that there were good prospects that broadly acceptable, if not always ideal, solutions would be adopted.

There was negligible progress in the First Committee, despite the Kissinger statement suggesting US concessions, which did not have the intended impact. The possibility of failure here, with its potential for undermining the Conference as a whole, was a matter of serious concern to countries that were anxious for adoption of a convention. These, of course, included Ireland, which, like many others, had an additional incentive in its prospects of procuring acceptable solutions in the areas of its important interests. That the US shared these concerns, even if not for precisely the same reasons, was clearly apparent from the published commentary on the Fourth and Fifth Sessions by one of its senior delegates. This deplored the prospect of solutions on so many important issues being sabotaged by failure of successful negotiation of the ISBA regime.

The death of Mao Tse Tung, Chairman of the Central Committee of the Communist Party of China, was the subject of a day-long meeting of Plenary on 13 September to pay tribute to his memory. The tributes were led by the Conference President and the UN Secretary-General through his Special Representative. The Chairmen of all the regional groups spoke, including Ambassador Cremin for the WEOG. The others who made statements were the spokesmen of the G-77, the Arab Group, the Nordics, the Organisation of African Unity (OAU), the Association of South Eastern Asian States, the EEC and the US. Some other delegations also spoke individually, including France and the UK. The Chinese delegation responded appropriately.

Chapter IX

SIXTH SESSION

The Sixth Session was held at the United Nations headquarters in New York for eight weeks, from 23 May to 15 July 1977.

PREPARATIONS

The Conference President having suggested that there should be intersessional consultations on the ISBA regime, an Evensen Group meeting convened in March in Geneva to consider the topic. About 85 delegations attended, but unfortunately not the most hardline of the Group of 77 (G-77). The new US head of delegation, Mr Elliott Richardson, reconfirmed US willingness to accept start-up financing of the enterprise and a future review of the system of exploitation. No clear results emerged, but Minister Evensen issued a report in which he included some drafts covering *inter alia* the question of a review and provision for protection of producers of land-based minerals. Also, in response to the request received at the end of the Fifth Session, the EEC organised a seminar for its associated African states on exploitation of the area, particularly technical and financing aspects. The attendance was disappointing, but papers were widely circulated and may have increased G-77 understanding of the practical difficulties involved in seabed exploitation.

The EEC members continued their efforts at coordination and cooperation. Among the matters arising was a commission proposal that a common position should be adopted in regard to membership of the authority organs, in the EEC context. The proposed position would be to the effect that while membership of the authority assembly would be for the member states, the commission should represent the EEC on the council. This commission suggestion came at a time when it was far from clear how membership of the council (at least) would be determined and what system of voting would apply. Moreover, the competence of the EEC covered at most only a very limited part of the matters to be dealt with in the ISBA regime. In addition, the logic of the idea would be difficult to explain to the other participants in the Conference. Only Denmark supported the proposal, the major industrialised countries opposed it and the majority, including Ireland, advocated leaving the question until the relevant ISBA provisions became more predictable (an Irish position for which specific authority from the Minister for Foreign Affairs was obtained). The promotion of the 'Community clause' was also considered.

In Dublin the Inter-Departmental Committee (IDC) met as usual for ongoing assessment of developments.

INSTRUCTIONS

Following meetings of the IDC to review the developments at the Fifth Session and the usual consultations with other departments, the Minister for Foreign Affairs made a submission to the Government on 12 May 1977 in regard to the delegation's instructions. It was proposed *simpliciter* that the existing instructions on the territorial sea and contiguous zone, the high seas, straits, archipelagos and TOT were adequate and should be confirmed. Effective confirmation of instructions on the EEZ and fisheries including anadromous species (salmon), the continental shelf, delimitation and regime of islands, preservation of the environment, peaceful settlement of disputes (PSD) and the preamble and final clauses, including the 'Community clause', was also suggested. Details of the situation at the Conference were given in regard to each of these topics. The only (and slight) additions proposed to the existing instructions concerned MSR and the ISBA regime.

Exclusive economic zone and fisheries

On the EEZ it was reported that a clear majority (excluding the landlocked and geographically disadvantaged states (LLGDS)—but perhaps only for tactical reasons) accepted the establishment of a 200-mile EEZ, although differences regarding the details persisted. Indeed several states, including Ireland and some other EEC members, the US, the Soviet Union and Japan, had already unilaterally declared, or were about to declare, such zones, at least for fisheries. The LLGDS cohesion was undermined by variations in their interests in regard to fishing rights, which became more obvious with the progress of negotiations. On anadromous species it was commented that the RSNT provision established the primacy of the state of origin and was probably the best achievable. A reopening of the issue might result in omission of any provision.

Continental shelf

On the continental shelf the state of consideration of the three outstanding unresolved issues was outlined—precise identification of the outer edge of the margin, a boundary commission and revenue sharing. In regard to revenue sharing the detailed recommendation was to the effect that only provisions that would not inhibit production or be inequitable to the shelf state should be accepted.

Regime of islands and delimitation

On regime of islands and delimitation it was considered that the delegation should continue to seek further improvement of the RSNT provisions, although this was unlikely to be achieved and the provisions were adequate.

Environment

On preservation of the environment, satisfaction was expressed that the RSNT provisions on dumping and vessel-source pollution accorded with Irish policy. Effective confirmation of existing instructions, including the objective of a reasonable balance between respective enforcement rights of the flag state, the port state and the coastal state, was suggested and, consistent with these instructions, authority to support the RSNT. On MSR likewise there was reference with satisfaction to the fact that significant reflection of the Irish contribution to the ISNT had been carried forward into the RSNT. It was proposed that specific authority to support compulsory and binding PSD in this field be added to the instructions.

International seabed area

In regard to the negotiations on the ISBA regime concern was expressed at the vulnerability of the Conference as a whole to failure in this field. Irish policy strongly favoured adoption of a convention. Moreover, the RSNT provisions on Irish vital interests were in most instances already generally satisfactory and in the other instances tending in that direction. Accordingly, collapse of the Conference would be a serious setback. It was suggested therefore that the delegation should be concerned to support proposals in regard to the ISBA that were likely to lead to an acceptable compromise. In an overview of the state of negotiations the system of exploitation was identified as the main issue. This issue had many components matched by proposals, in some cases competing, including (i) establishment of an international authority to supervise/control the ISBA; (ii) the structure of the authority, the membership of its organs and their decision-making procedures; (iii) the authority's power to exploit directly; (iv) non-discriminatory access for other entities; (v) reservation of mining sites for the authority; (vi) establishment of an enterprise as the operative exploitation arm of the authority and making it viable through financing and transfer of the relevant technology; (vii) the extent of the authority's discretion in granting exploitation licences to other entities; and (viii) the authority's power to take measures to prevent unreasonable damage to producers of competing land-based minerals, for example through control of production and participation in international commodity agreements. Support for the US-proposed provision for future review of the system of exploitation was recommended. Otherwise the spelling out of instructions was mostly the same as previously. However, recommendations to partly revise instructions on financing of the authority and the enterprise, and of compensation to land-based producers, responded to the concern of the Minister for Finance to avoid adverse economic and financial implications for Ireland. Thus, support for financing of the authority from its own revenues except for an initial specified limited period was recommended. Financing of the enterprise through mandatory contributions by contracting states should be resisted, unless necessary for a successful outcome. In the latter event, only contributions limited in time and amount, and levied on the basis of ability to pay and potential for economic gain from exploitation, should be accepted. Likewise, if compensation for land-based producers became a necessary element, every effort should be made to minimise payments by Ireland. The EEC Commission proposal that membership of the authority should fall to the EEC, represented by the Commission, rather than to member states was not mentioned.

Peaceful settlement of disputes

In regard to PSD, satisfaction was indicated that the main thrust of the provisions of the earliest draft had been carried through the two revisions and, together with some desirable amendments, incorporated in the RSNT. Thus the RSNT established an obligation to deal with a dispute by negotiation followed by (non-binding) conciliation and, if these were unsuccessful, to submit the dispute to compulsory and binding procedures. It included a choice of binding fora—the International Court of Justice (ICJ), a new law of the sea tribunal, arbitration and, for particular parts of the convention, special procedures (similar to arbitration), including unspecified special procedures for the ISBA regime. Three changes, regarded as improvements from the Irish point of view, had been made in the course of the revisions. These were (a) making arbitration the residual procedure; (b) significant limitation of permissible exemptions, particularly in regard to exercise of sovereign rights and jurisdiction; and (c) mitigation of the financial implications of the establishment of the proposed law of the sea tribunal. There was mention in the submission of the fact that ICJ jurisdiction extended only to states, and that it would not, therefore, be available to the EEC.

Preamble and final clauses

In regard to the texts on the preamble and final clauses, which had yet to be discussed at the Conference, the preamble was described as unlikely to pose difficulties. Attention was again drawn to the possibility that problems could arise from provisions in the final clauses for provisional application and reservations. The need to have the 'Community clause' included was also mentioned.

The Government approved the proposed instructions by decision dated 26 May.

Delegation

Mr Costello had ceased to be Attorney General, having been appointed a judge of the High Court, and there was no visit to the session from a special representative of the Government. His successor as Attorney General was Mr John Kelly, who previously, as Minister of State in the Department of Foreign Affairs, had taken a direct interest in the Conference, and was personally involved in preparations for the Fourth Session. Matthew Russell, a senior officer in the Attorney General's Office, joined the delegation and attended the session for a period. The writer was appointed as Ambassador to Denmark early in 1977, and formally took up duty at the end of April. However, a temporary absence from the posting was arranged to enable attendance at the session. Piers Gardiner was the sole delegate from the Geological Survey of Ireland (GSI) in the absence of Keith Robinson. Isolda Moylan, from the Mission in New York, took over responsibility for the environment topic.

General

Interest groups on the various issues resumed their consultations at the session. The Irish delegation participated in the interest group on islands and delimitation, in the Margineers regarding the continental shelf and in the coastal states group (CSG) in regard to the EEZ. The

EEC meetings included a first examination of the Conference Secretariat's document on final clauses in preparation for a likely discussion in Plenary. Not surprisingly, it was felt that such a discussion would be a necessary step if drafts were to be included in the proposed informal composite negotiating text (ICNT).

PLENARY

It was agreed at the first meeting of Plenary that the first two to three weeks of the session should be devoted almost exclusively to First Committee issues, as had been suggested by the Conference President at the end of the Fifth Session. In the following two to three weeks all issues would be addressed. It was also agreed that at the end of this second period an ICNT would be drawn up, dealing in a single document with the entire range of issues covered in Parts I to IV of the RSNT. This text would be prepared, in the light of the preceding deliberations, by the President jointly with the Chairmen of the Main Committees, in consultation with the Chairman of the drafting group and the Rapporteur-General—a group described as the Collegium. It was hoped that the ICNT, also a negotiating document like the RSNT, would provide the basis for the adoption by consensus of the future convention. In the event the ICNT appeared only after the session. It was clear from the accompanying memorandum that the views of the respective Committee Chairmen prevailed in their areas of responsibility. The ICNT included some compromise proposals agreed in negotiating groups, but not on main issues. It did not incorporate any significant advance on First Committee issues, disappointingly so in the light of signs of emerging agreement in some areas. The texts on final clauses drafted by the secretariat were included, although they had not been considered by the Conference.

SECOND COMMITTEE

In accordance with the agreed procedural arrangements the Committee did not meet until the fourth week of the session. It decided to continue with the negotiating and consultative groups on the priority issues and to consider in informal Committee meetings any other issues raised.

Exclusive economic zone

Regarding the EEZ, the EEC delegations' position remained roughly that of maintaining support for the amendments on high seas rights and limitation of coastal state fishery controls as proposed at the Fourth Session. The commission, in the person of Eamonn Gallagher, the director-general of the new EEC Fisheries Directorate (and a former official of the Department of Foreign Affairs), urged a more cohesive attitude. He argued *inter alia* that the EEC was effectively a coastal state and should take a coastal state line. His argument relied on the element of the EEC common fisheries policy that provided for common access by each member state to the fisheries of all member states. This was still a source of controversy among the members. Thus his argument, while EEC friendly, was problematical for both members with an anti-coastal state attitude and those with extensive fishery waters, if for opposite reasons. Not surprisingly, the Commission line did not achieve an EEC position as suggested. The question of the respective rights of the coastal state and other states was again referred by the Committee to the consultative group set up at the Fifth Session, but no progress was made. The deliberations moved to an informal group chaired by Ambassador Jorge Castañeda, head of the Mexican delegation. Following the deliberations in his group he prepared compromise texts on this and other issues on which the participants agreed. They included (a) a slightly more moderate description of the jurisdiction, rights and duties of the coastal state in the EEZ, as compared with that in the RSNT; (b) a slightly more elaborate description of the rights of other states in the EEZ; and (c) related changes in the provisions on the high seas. The texts were subsequently incorporated in the ICNT. The status of Ambassador Castañeda, who was also a prominent leader of the CSG, undoubtedly facilitated this compromise. It moved slightly towards EEC, including Irish, concerns to maintain non-resource-related high-seas rights in the EEZ. The Nandan-chaired group of 21, set up at the Fifth Session, resumed consideration of the issue of fishing rights for the LLGDS in the EEZ of other states. There was some indication of progress at a late stage, but no agreement on any change to be included in the ICNT.

Fisheries

Some slight changes to the fisheries provisions not relevant to Irish interests were agreed. In an informal meeting of the Committee late in the session the Soviet Union made a new proposal on anadromous species that was in some, but not in all, respects favourable to the state of origin. However, it was rejected by the other interests, including Denmark. The Irish delegation, regarding the proposal as of doubtful benefit and fearful that a new disagreement might result in the omission of any provision, acquiesced in EEC opposition to it. The ICNT did not incorporate any change.

Continental shelf

The issues of definition of the outer limit and revenue sharing were again referred to the consultative group set up at the Fifth Session, and the Irish delegation was very active both inside and outside this group. The Margineers prepared a revised proposal on revenue sharing. However, as some Margineers, including Ireland, still had reservations on this proposal (also including US opposition to its exemption for developing countries) it was submitted anonymously, but linked to acceptance of the definition proposal. It reiterated a grace period of five years, with levies on gross production after that period rising yearly from 1 per cent to a maximum of 5 per cent. The (ISBA) authority would have a role in distribution of the proceeds and in deciding on exemptions, but not in assessment. This proposal seemed broadly acceptable in the consultative group, but higher rates and a preferential reference to LLGDS on distribution of the revenue were nevertheless proposed. An Irish suggestion, within the Margineers, that it should be possible to have a reduction in the rates, or even an exemption, if exploitation was rendered uneconomic, was resisted by the other Margineers. They feared any move in that direction could open the way for an assessment role for the authority—an eventuality that none of them, or Ireland, would welcome. The LLGDS continued to oppose the definition proposal, probably for tactical reasons based on the perception of at least some of them of not having received adequate concessions on fishing rights in the EEZ of other states. The Margineers' limits proposals were also attacked by others, notably the Soviet Union and Japan. Colombia suggested a secretariat comparative study of the results of the various limits proposals and the Margineers, after initial hesitation, agreed. The proposals to be covered were 200-mile distance, 500-metre-depth criterion, the Hedberg and Gardiner alternative formulae contained in the Irish amendment, and also the true outer limits of the margin unaffected by any of these proposals.

In EEC cooperation meetings agreement was reached to support extended jurisdiction, but with only the UK (a Margineer) and France prepared to endorse the Irish amendment. Denmark felt the amendment could be detrimental to their interests on the Rockall Plateau. However, the Irish delegation was dismayed at an FRG proposal, made in the Second Committee, to drop the Gardiner formula from the Irish amendment. In a subsequent EEC meeting it was suggested this action may have been due to some internal delegation confusion, an explanation that was not borne out when the FRG repeated the proposal at a subsequent session. The LLGDS declared, late in the session, that a Conference declaration requiring equal treatment for their companies in applying for exploitation licences would meet their demands for mineral exploitation rights on the shelf of other states. For the Margineers this was a welcome development.

The delegation and the other Margineers were disappointed when the ICNT incorporated essentially their (anonymously presented) revenue-sharing proposal, including their rates, but did not incorporate their limits proposal, to which they had sought to link it. This separation was despite an approach to the Second Committee Chairman by four Margineer heads of delegation, including Ireland's Ambassador Cremin. The President's memo accompanying the ICNT did, however, acknowledge the need for a precise definition of limits, and the pending secretariat study of the effects of the various proposals probably determined a wait-and-see attitude.

Delimitation

Delimitation of zones between neighbouring states was again referred to the consultative group set up at the Fifth Session. Discussions revolved mainly around the RSNT without any meeting of minds between the opposing interest groups. The Chairman had identified interim measures as a key element, and Ireland proposed that a moratorium in the disputed area might be an acceptable compromise on this issue. Belgium, a neutral, made a similar proposal, whereas Spain, with others of the opposing group, proposed an amendment making the median line the interim measure, unless other measures were agreed. Ireland and others also proposed an amendment to Paragraph 1 (criteria) of the RSNT articles that would delete the reference to the median line. The opposition conversely proposed an amendment asserting a central role for the median line as in the 1958 convention. Variations on Paragraph 2 (PSD) were also proposed. The whole RSNT text was retained in the ICNT unchanged. A feature of the negotiation was the improved organisation of those opposed to the position of Ireland and its allies (although into an extreme position), mainly through the efforts of the UK delegation. Among delegates that became more active on the issue were Poland and Canada, respectively on the side of Ireland and of its opponents.

Regime of islands

The Committee Chairman resisted requests to refer the regime of islands to a negotiating group, and thus it was one of many subjects dealt with in informal meetings of the Committee. The Irish and other like-minded delegations proposed a new paragraph to the RSNT article that would deprive all islands in certain offshore locations of an EEZ and continental shelf. This was naturally opposed by the other interest group but also by the Pacific island states led by New Zealand. The reaction of the latter was moderated by private assurances from Ireland and others that priority for satisfactory delimitation provisions over the regime of islands provisions was the objective. Thus, by arrangement, Ireland and Papua New Guinea (one of Ireland's allies on the topic) proposed a compromise in the form of a cross-reference in the regime of islands provision establishing such priority. The opposing delegations on delimitation sought an amendment giving all islands an EEZ and a continental shelf. The RSNT provision was carried into the ICNT unchanged.

Territorial sea and contiguous zone

There was no discussion of the territorial sea or the contiguous zone and the impliedly acceptable RSNT provisions were carried into the ICNT. Some slight changes to the RSNT provisions on straits and archipelagos, agreed between the most interested parties, were also incorporated into the ICNT.

The RSNT Article 136 entitled 'Transitional Provision' (in regard to territories whose people did not have full independence) was carried into the ICNT but placed separately after all the other articles and even the *testimonium*. Thus it was clearly separated from the regime of islands, where it had originated, and removed from the remit of the Second Committee.

THIRD COMMITTEE

Environment

When work on the Committee topics began in the fourth week, negotiations on preservation of the marine environment were conducted in informal meetings chaired by Jose Vallarta of Mexico, who had presided over negotiating groups and informal meetings at previous sessions. First addressed were the various aspects of issues in regard to vessel-source pollution in the EEZ including (i) the powers of enforcement of the coastal state and the port state; (ii) legislative powers of the coastal state in regard to control of pollution; and (iii) institution of proceedings. In regard to (i) there was some clarification of the respective enforcement powers of the flag state, coastal state and port state, with limitations on port state right of prosecution and elaboration of provisions for transfer by it to the flag state of proceedings already commenced. In regard to (ii) it was generally accepted that coastal-state legislation must conform to internationally accepted norms. Coverage of ship design, construction, manning and equipment in such legislation was strongly opposed (by the EEC members *inter alios*) against unsuccessful efforts by the US, Canada and others to permit legislation to cover these features of ships, at least in the territorial sea. Regarding (iii) priority for prosecution by the flag state (as in the RSNT) gathered support and was carried into the ICNT, but this priority would not apply to civil, as distinct from penal, proceedings. Clarification of procedures, including notification of the flag state when one of its vessels was prosecuted by another state, also signalled progress. Regarding another topic, French efforts to have a definition of dumping (in the 'use of terms' provision) that included incineration were successful, a significant progression. The ICNT differed from the RSNT in reflecting these advances. They were all improvements from the Irish point of view, which favoured a balance between measures to preserve the environment and maintenance of freedom of navigation.

Marine scientific research

The key issue in regard to MSR was the proposed requirement of coastal-state consent for research within its EEZ or continental shelf, as contained in the RSNT, which was opposed by research states. Negotiations proceeded at first in informal Committee meetings and later in a small group, which included the Irish delegate. When no progress was made a group of delegates (again including the Irish delegate) from like-minded states produced a text that included a requirement to accept PSD where consent was denied. This text was opposed by the G-77, who regarded such compulsory PSD (and also 'tacit' consent—as in the RSNT) as dilution of the consent principle, whereas researching states still opposed that principle. A second attempt at a compromise draft providing a qualified consent regime was rejected by the more extreme G-77 members. The language of the ICNT provisions was more elaborate than the RSNT in spelling out the nature of valid research and in indicating positively the obligation to grant consent, but also in slightly strengthening the reasons for denial. Compulsory PSD in regard to denial of consent was not included. The Castañeda proposals on the EEZ (see above) at least improved the prospects of agreement on this topic.

Transfer of technology

With the RSNT as the basis of discussions on TOT, the G-77 were concerned about the monopoly positions of the multinational companies and advocated a general role for the (ISBA) international authority. There was, however, no agreement on this. The industrialised countries were anxious to protect patent rights, and preferred to deal with the issues in existing UN and other international bodies already engaged generally on TOT arrangements. The RSNT text was generally regarded as reasonably balanced between the two interests and was largely maintained in the ICNT. The role of the international authority was confined to TOT in regard to the exploitation of the ISBA, and the protection for the rights of owners of technology was preserved.

FIRST COMMITTEE

International seabed area

As decided, the session concentrated in the early weeks on the ISBA regime and the usual controversial issues, namely (i) system of exploitation; (ii) powers, functions, composition and decision-making procedures of the authority organs; (iii) conditions for contractors; and (iv) resource policy including protection of land-based producers. These issues were not only interlinked but also tended to overlap. There were some signs of progress at the preceding intersessional meeting, at the informal Committee meetings at the session, both chaired by Minister Evensen, and in some small negotiating groups. In regard to (i), while there was general acceptance of direct exploitation by states or their sponsored entities, there was no such acceptance of an automatic right as against authority discretion or the latter's role in negotiating contracts, including financial terms (iii). There seemed to be progress on division of functions between the authority assembly and its council (ii), elaborating on the understanding that the former would determine policy and the latter would make decisions in accordance with policy. Regarding (iv) the industrialised countries were sceptical of the need to protect producers of land-based minerals through stabilisation of world markets and international commodity agreements and/or compensation. They thus continued opposition to authority functions of limiting production in the ISBA or participating in commodity agreements. More positively other issues seemed soluble, for example viability of the enterprise through financing and transfer of the necessary technology, anti-monopoly measures and acceptable PSD provisions.

Ireland was not prominent in these negotiations but participated actively in the ongoing EEC deliberations. Its position, as in instructions, included support for a strong authority to protect the interest of mankind as a whole and developing countries in particular, in conformity with the UN General Assembly Declaration of Principles. It saw industrialised state participation as necessary to provide the financing and the technology required to enable exploitation of the ISBA by both the enterprise and states or state-sponsored entities, and thereby to ensure both the necessary supply of minerals to all consumers and the revenue to help developing countries. Those members of the EEC having seabed mining capacity sought limitations on authority powers unacceptable to Ireland and to some other members. Thus a common position of the EEC-9 on this was not feasible. However, the Irish delegation felt that, although the texts tabled informally by the Chairman tended to favour the demands of developing countries at the expense of the views of industrialised countries, the former nevertheless had responded negatively. Unusually the delegation (in the person of the head of delegation, Ambassador Cremin) made a statement in the Committee. While reiterating the salient points of the Irish policy position (closer to that of the G-77), it urged the need for incentives and guarantees included in earlier texts to attract investment and technology essential for exploitation of the area. The making of the statement must have surprised both of the opposing sides.

There was expectation that the ICNT would include at least some of the promising compromise texts, and disappointment when it did not do so. While reversing the RSNT's trend of favouring the position of the industrialised states, it made no gesture towards them of including compromise texts that the G-77 seemed ready to accept. In fact it provided that there should be reversion to a unitary system of exploitation (by the authority only) after 25 years in the absence of agreement to the contrary—not only an unacceptable proposition for the industrialised countries, but also an ironic distortion of the US review proposal. Some perceived this outcome as due to the Committee Chairman's non-involvement in the informal negotiations. If the G-77 were grievously disappointed with the RSNT after the Fourth Session the industrialised countries were equally disappointed with the ICNT.

PLENARY

Peaceful settlement of disputes

The PSD texts (as incorporated into the RSNT at the end of the Fifth Session) were considered in informal meetings of the Plenary. The main issues were (i) choice of procedure; (ii) interim measures; (iii) release of detained vessels; and (iv) automatic and optional exemptions from application of binding procedures. Regarding (i) the G-77 seemed prepared to accept that arbitration would apply where the parties did not share a common choice, and Western countries were willing in return to accept establishment of a special law of the sea tribunal. The Eastern

European Group, who were willing to accept only special procedures, maintained, in addition, that resort to these procedures should be confined to situations where technical issues were at stake. The CSG sought amendment of the RSNT in regard to (iv) to exempt exercise of sovereign rights and jurisdiction (in coastal state marine zones) totally from application of binding procedures. The EEC-9 could accept exemption of disputes regarding living resources but were divided on exemption in regard to MSR. Large states were insistent on an optional exemption for military activities.

The ICNT preserved the RSNT provisions on choice of procedure (including both the establishment of a special law of the sea tribunal and making arbitration the residual procedure). It made the tribunal the residual procedure in regard to release of vessels. Exhaustion of local remedies as a precondition for reference to PSD procedures was provided. The provisions on exemptions from applicability of compulsory and binding procedures to disputes arising in respect of sovereign rights and jurisdiction were redrafted. (Ireland, almost alone, had opposed proposals in the CSG to exclude totally their application to exercise of coastal state rights, etc., in the EEZ.) As changed they excluded compulsory application of binding procedures in regard to discretionary decisions of coastal states in the exercise of rights in regard to living resources or MSR. This redraft, although different in form, was clearly influenced by the Castañeda texts on rights in the EEZ (see above). Optional exceptions to compulsory application of binding procedures included (as previously) sea boundary disputes (only where other compulsory and binding procedures were available) and military activities. Law enforcement activities arising from rights under the convention were added to these exceptions. Disputes arising regarding the ISBA would be referred to a seabed chamber of the proposed tribunal, whose judges would be selected by the assembly of the authority—a provision about which some of the EEC members had doubts. If the authority was not a party to the dispute, it could be referred to arbitration by the respondent. The ICNT on PSD was broadly acceptable to Ireland.

Preamble and final clauses

Despite the President's declared intentions, consideration of the drafts of the preamble and final clauses was again not reached. The document (A/Conf.62/L.13), prepared by the secretariat for the Fifth Session, included texts only on non-controversial elements. It also listed the controversial elements and identified the problems they posed. Among these was provisional application, and reference was made to the article on that subject in the ISBA regime. Reference was also made to the Transitional Provision (on non-independent territories) currently attached to RSNT Part II. The UK Presidency of the EEC reminded the Conference President by letter of the need for a 'Community clause', as indicated by the Netherlands Presidency letter at the Fifth Session. Texts of final clauses set out in the Secretariat document (only on non-controversial elements, i.e. ratification, accession and entry into force) were incorporated into the ICNT by the Collegium as was a text of a preamble (despite neither having been considered in the Conference), and also the Transitional Provision transferred from Part II of the RSNT to the end of the ICNT (see above). The provisional application article included in the ISBA regime in the RSNT was not carried over, either there or in the final clauses.

In EEC meetings the 'Community clause' was discussed also in the context of the PSD provisions, to which amendments, for example regarding the choice of procedure, might be required to accommodate the EEC as a party. There was also concern that third countries should not be in doubt as to the division of competences between the EEC and its members, and to ensure that no convention forum could adjudicate on this question. Measures to avoid conflict between the European Court of Justice and such a forum, in case of a dispute between EEC members, would also have to be considered. The Commission was required to produce a paper on these problems. Separately the Commission again proposed that the draft clause should be amended to name the EEC, and also to provide that the term 'state', when used in the convention, would include an entity that became a party under the clause. The member states were doubtful about both ideas, the implications of which had not been fully explored. Collateral consequences of the second idea would impinge on membership of the ISBA authority organs. Thus it was not unrelated to the Commission proposal previously made in regard to EEC membership in the organs.

The final plenary meeting on 15 July was a subdued affair at which only essential business was conducted, due to a power blackout in Manhattan throughout the previous day (see below). That event was also blamed for the failure of the ICNT to appear on the last day as intended. In fact it did not appear for several further days. Plenary recommended a Seventh Session to be held in Geneva from 28 March 1978 for seven or eight weeks, and the General Assembly accepted the recommendation in due course.

CONCLUSION

The Irish delegation was pleased at the emergence of the ICNT as a further step towards a successful outcome, and that progress had been made at the session on several issues. This was particularly the case within the mandates of the Second and Third Committees, overtly in many instances and less openly in some. Unfortunately this was not the case in regard to the First Committee work on the ISBA regime. Apparent progress at the intersessional meeting and during the early weeks of the session was not carried into the ICNT and might even have been lost. Failure to agree on the regime was still a threat to success of the Conference as a whole.

The blackout occurred on the evening of 13 July, and in mid-town Manhattan, which includes the UN headquarters and the hotels in which most of the delegates were accommodated, it lasted for approximately 24 hours. The full implications included not only lack of light but of the power needed for water supply, for lifts in high-rise buildings, for food storage, for restaurant and other services, for some transport services, for communications etc. The writer was fortunate to leave a reception in an apartment building in upper Manhattan just in time to escape being trapped in the lift. The lights went out there as he boarded a taxi and they went out block by block as the taxi proceeded down Second Avenue. In the hotel, access to his room (on the nineteenth floor) was possible only by climbing the internal, totally dark, stairway, so dark that during daylight on 14 July he and another Irish delegate passed one another unrecognised. On that day (14 July) the UN building was closed. Unable to contact colleagues the author spent most of the day sitting in a park, blissfully unaware that Ambassador Cremin was struggling with the communications failure. It presented considerable difficulties to his efforts to inform his EEC colleagues that an EEC heads of delegation dinner he was to host that evening had to be cancelled. Overwhelming feelings of relief greeted the restoration of power in the late evening of 14 July. Yet some inconveniences remained, including the author's failure to recover clothes from a laundry before leaving New York. They had obviously shared the same fate as the ICNT!

Chapter X

SEVENTH SESSION

With the consent of the United Nations General Assembly the Seventh Session was held in two parts, at the Palais des Nations (UN Office) in Geneva for eight weeks, from 28 March to 19 May 1978, and at the UN headquarters in New York for four weeks, from 21 August to 15 September 1978. A resumption of the Seventh Session was preferred to calling a new session with a view to ensuring avoidance of a general debate, which was not unusual at the opening of a session.

PREPARATIONS

The report of an arbitration tribunal established to adjudicate on delimitation of the continental shelf between the UK and France in the English Channel appeared in late 1977. This case differed from the North Sea cases in at least two significant particulars—(i) the litigants were both party to the 1958 Convention on the Continental Shelf, although France had entered a reservation detracting from the role of the equidistance method as in the delimitation provision, and (ii) the tribunal was mandated to specify the line of division. In carrying out that task the tribunal employed different methods of division in different areas, invoking both the 1958 convention provision (including the reference to special circumstances and the French reservation) and the criteria identified by the International Court of Justice (ICJ) in the North Sea cases. It expressed the view that there would be little if any significant difference in the practical results whichever of these two rules were applied. The tribunal, again unlike the ICJ, had to address specifically the effect of offshore islands in delimitation. In employing the equidistance method in the region of the Channel Islands the tribunal decided that, because of their closeness to the French coast, application of equidistance *simpliciter* would substantially diminish the space accruing to France and would produce an inequitable result. It determined that only a twelve-mile zone should accrue to these islands. Moreover, it also concluded that avoidance of distortion in the division required that only half effect should be given to other islands (of which each of the parties owned some) in determining the dividing line. This result strengthened the position of Ireland and its allies on delimitation, most particularly in the endorsement of the priority of equity over the employment of the equidistant method of division. It also favoured their position on regime of islands. Turkey felt that the decision justified an amendment of the informal composite negotiating text (ICNT) provision on that topic.

After the Sixth Session the ICNT provisions on the international seabed area (ISBA) regime were the subject of trenchant public criticism by the US head of delegation. He complained that they had not been openly prepared, commented unfavourably on their departures from the texts prepared by Minister Evensen following the meetings he had chaired, and described the ICNT texts as unacceptable to the US.

Informal consultations for two days in December 1977 and an inter-sessional meeting for two weeks in February 1978 were held in New York under the chairmanship of the President. The Irish delegation was represented by Ambassador Cremin and Geraldine Skinner. The topics dealt with were mainly the ISBA regime and land-locked and geographically disadvantaged states' rights in the exclusive economic zones (EEZs) of other states. The agenda was much wider but only limited substantive issues received close attention. Regarding the ISBA there was some progress on the financial arrangements, aided by a UN Secretariat study, and on production limitation, on the basis of a report by technical experts. No progress was made regarding LLGDS rights. There was also a brief discussion of Conference procedures for the Seventh Session, on the basis of an informal paper by the President that suggested negotiating groups on hard-core issues. The President prepared reports on these exchanges. Discussions were also held *en marge* on an emerging problem regarding the Conference Presidency (see below).

The EEC continued meetings to seek coordination of positions and cooperation among the members and, particularly, to prepare for promotion of the 'Community clause'. In Dublin the Inter-Departmental Committee (IDC) met to review developments and to consider the desirability of confirming or adapting policy.

INSTRUCTIONS

Following deliberations in the IDC and the usual consultations with other interested departments, the Minister for Foreign Affairs made the customary submission to Government, dated 23 March 1978, concerning the delegation's instructions. Support for the ICNT provisions was proposed for territorial seas, contiguous zone, high seas, straits and archipelagos, which enjoyed general acceptance.

Exclusive economic zone and continental shelf

More specific attention was given to the still unresolved issue of LLGDS rights, with a recommendation to seek to prevent LLGDS access to EEC fishery waters. Similarly an instruction to prevent LLGDS access to Ireland's continental shelf was suggested. Delegation acceptance of revenue sharing was to be conditional on adoption of satisfactory shelf definition and outer limit provisions, i.e. provisions that would give Ireland jurisdiction over the relevant part of the Rockall Plateau. If the best provisions that could be achieved were ambivalent on this question, the Departments of Industry and Commerce and Foreign Affairs should consult to decide if revenue sharing could be accepted. In any event every effort should be made to keep revenue-sharing rates as low as possible and any role for the (ISBA) international authority in assessment should be opposed.

Delimitation and regime of islands

It was recommended that existing instructions to seek to improve the ICNT should be confirmed, but that the delegation should be free to accept an adequate package if more suitable provisions did not prove feasible.

Environment and marine scientific research

Confirmation of existing instructions was suggested, with the addition of opposition to any role for the (ISBA) international authority in TOT other than as in the ICNT (where its role was confined to ISBA-related technology).

International seabed area

The submission referred to the issues addressed at the Sixth Session, at which there had been indications of agreements in principle on some matters between the G-77 and the industrialised countries (which included several EEC members), although these were not adequately reflected in the ICNT. The dissatisfaction of the industrialised countries at this outcome was demonstrated in the subsequent strong statement by the US head of delegation. However, a full meeting of minds on important details in all of these issues had yet to emerge. Failure in this sphere and consequent failure of the Conference was still a possibility.

Ireland's basic position in favour of a strong authority and measures to protect producers of land-based minerals was mentioned and confirmation of existing instructions was suggested, including the instruction to support proposals (not inconsistent with the basic position) likely to lead to agreement.

Peaceful settlement of disputes, preamble and final clauses

Confirmation of existing instructions *simpliciter* was proposed in regard to peaceful settlement of disputes (PSD) (which maintained opposition to exclusion of exercise of coastal state rights in the EEZ from compulsory and binding procedures). On the preamble and final clauses (yet to be discussed at the Conference) attention was again drawn to the potential dangers to the package nature of the convention in articles on provisional application and on reservations. Moreover special difficulties would arise in applying provisional application in respect of the ISBA. Accordingly, the submission sought confirmation of existing instructions (i) to support a carefully structured provisional application article (although the ICNT, unlike the revised single negotiating text (RSNT), had no such article) and (ii) to oppose permission of excessive reservations. The need for inclusion of a 'Community clause' was mentioned, as well as the consequential complications (for example, regarding information on and recognition of EEC areas of competence, choice of PSD fora, and avoidance of conflicts of jurisdiction), some of which would be exacerbated if the draft already submitted were amended to include specific reference to the EEC, as the EEC Commission had lately proposed. As these complications were still under examination, the instruction proposed, not surprisingly, was simply to support a clause that would protect the rights of the EEC and the members. Concern was expressed at the difficulties in the way of achieving general acceptance of the clause among Conference participants, particularly in the light of the complications.

It is clear from the submission that suggestions for instructions had become more specific in several areas, and that adaptation of some instructions was geared towards accepting the best feasible but adequate results rather than holding out for more desirable but unachievable provisions. This of course reflected a perception that the Conference was approaching the crucial phase in achieving a consensus package.

The Government, in a decision of 11 April, adopted the instructions proposed in the submission.

DELEGATION

The Department of Foreign Affairs decided that the author should continue as a member of the delegation, at least temporarily, combining this assignment with his responsibilities as accredited Ambassador. Brendan Finucane was present only briefly at the first part of the session and departed to take up an appointment with the newly established National Board of Science and Technology (NBST), after which he was no longer available for the delegation. No delegate dedicated to MSR attended the second part. Margaret Cawley, from the economic division in the Department of Foreign Affairs, took over the environment topic and Justin Dillon, from the Department's legal division, joined mainly for the ISBA regime.

GENERAL

Interest group meetings continued during the session. The Irish delegation participated in groups on the continental shelf (the Margineers), anadromous species, delimitation and regime of islands and coastal state rights (the coastal states group (CSG)). The EEC members continued to hold meetings during and between the two parts of the session. The Evensen Group was not active during the session.

PLENARY

The Conference was faced with an unwelcome problem at the beginning of the session—its President, Ambassador Amerasinghe, was omitted from the credentials of the Sri Lanka delegation following a change of government there, and his appointment as Permanent Representative (PR) to the UN had been terminated. This situation raised questions as to whether, being no longer an accredited state representative, he could continue as President. Although this development had been known for some weeks and had been the subject of informal exchanges, a long, intermittent (lasting more than two weeks) procedural debate in Plenary ensued and the substantive Conference work came to a halt. The Latin American and Caribbean (regional) Group (LAC) characteristically took the legal stance (with logical argument) that he had to withdraw; the Asians (his own regional group) and Africans supported his wish to continue; the Western European and Others Group (WEOG), concerned mainly at the potential for damage to the Conference, and the Eastern European Group (EE) took no position.

Sri Lanka was not against Amerasinghe's remaining in office. The UN legal counsel was reported as holding that, as he had been properly elected, he would remain in office unless he resigned or was removed, although some adjustment of the rules of procedure might be required.

It was broadly agreed that the Presidency should in any case remain within the Asian Group, although there were some indications of a different view among the LACs. Eventually Nepal proposed that Ambassador Amerasinghe should continue in office unless a decision was taken by consensus that he should not do so. Ironically, in view of its content, this proposal was put to a vote and carried by 75 votes for to eighteen against, with thirteen abstentions, 31 non-participants and 21 absent. WEOG and EEC delegations were split in the vote. The Irish delegation did not participate, feeling that the matter was not one that should be decided by a vote. After the vote several LAC delegations withdrew temporarily from the Conference in protest. The President's continuance was not further challenged, although some delegates from the LAC Group pointedly refrained for some time from addressing him at meetings as President.

The President, having thus retained his office, sought in Plenary to get down to work expeditiously to make up for lost time, and was facilitated by a good atmosphere among delegations despite the preceding controversy. Plenary selected seven outstanding core issues, and decided that concentration should focus on these, with a negotiating group established for each issue. The first three of the seven issues were within the mandate of the First Committee and the remaining four within the mandate of the Second Committee. They were (1) system of exploration and exploitation of the ISBA and resource policy; (2) financial arrangements for the international authority, the enterprise and contractors; (3) organs of the international authority, their composition, powers and functions; (4) LLGDS rights of access to living resources in the EEZ in the same region or sub-region; (5) applicability of PSD procedures in respect of exercise of sovereign rights of a coastal state in its EEZ; (6) definition of the outer limits of the continental shelf and revenue sharing; (7) delimitation of boundaries of marine zones between opposite and adjacent states. Negotiating Groups 1 to 7 were set up to deal with these issues respectively. There was some controversy as to whether the negotiating groups should report to Plenary or to the appropriate Committees, raising questions about the continuing roles of the Committees and their Chairmen in regard to these issues. This problem was defused by the decision calling for reporting to both the President and the appropriate Committee Chairman. It was recognised that other specific matters (including regime of islands, some Third Committee matters and the preamble and final clauses) could also be discussed in their appropriate fora. It was decided to deal with the pre-amble and final clauses in Plenary rather than to set up a fourth committee. It was proposed to set a timetable with a view to completion of negotiations and production of a draft convention at the session. This would be achieved through two stages. The first would be revision of the ICNT by the Collegium, through incorporation of provisions found, from widespread and substantive support in a Plenary debate, to offer substantially improved prospects of consensus. The second stage would be examination of the ICNT as so revised. This proposal drew opposition and in fact revision of the ICNT at the Geneva meeting proved impossible. This led to a proposal for resumption of the session in New York for four weeks from 21 August. The proposal was carried on a vote by a narrow margin (51 to 46 with many absten-tions). Unconvinced of the usefulness of the proposal but unwilling to deny a majority wish, the Irish delegation abstained. In the event revi-sion of the ICNT was not achieved at the New York meeting either.

A schedule of work on the core issues for the first two working weeks in Geneva was adopted. Direct Irish interests were involved in the four Second Committee issues and the delegation had a leading role in regard to issues 6 (continental shelf) and 7 (delimitation). Thus while it participated in all the negotiating groups it was obviously most active in Groups 6 and 7.

SECOND COMMITTEE

Exclusive economic zone

Ambassador Satya Nandan (who had chaired the G-21 on this subject at the Sixth Session) presided over Negotiating Group 4 (rights of LLGDS in the EEZ) and submitted a proposal, and a subsequent amended version, the latter of which he described in his report to the Committee in Geneva as offering substantially improved prospects of consensus (the formula for justifying revision if endorsed in Plenary debate). Compared with the ICNT it had more elaborate provisions on access. It provided for priority treatment for LLGDS, as compared with other countries, in distribution of the fisheries surplus (the excess of the total allowable catch (TAC) over the coastal state's harvesting capacity). It included geographically disadvantaged states as well as land-locked states and distinguished between developed and developing states, and gave greater rights to the latter of each of these duos, includ-ing rights not necessarily confined to the surplus. It was supported by many, including Denmark as EEC spokesman, both in the negotiating group and the Second Committee. EEC support was based on the presumption that there would be no EEC surplus and the fact that the LLGDS in its region were developed states only having rights in regard to the surplus. In the Committee, Ireland and the other Margineers and some CSG members expressly linked acceptance of these proposals to similar acceptance of the Irish continental shelf amendments. In New York there was still LLGDS opposition, even if muted. The Committee Chairman concluded that this was still a hard-core issue and that more negotiation on it was needed.

Ambassador Constantin Stavropoulos (Greece) was Chairman of Negotiating Group 5 (applicability of compulsory PSD in regard to exercise of coastal state sovereign rights in the EEZ), and he convened a small consultative group of fifteen (in fact seventeen) comprising five (in fact seven) from the CSG, five from their opponents and five 'neutrals'. At Geneva this group sent forward a draft to the negotiating group that provided for compulsory conciliation where an allegation was made of (i) abuse of power by the coastal state in non-compliance with conservation obligations; (ii) failure to determine the TAC and/or its harvesting capacity; or (iii) refusal to allocate a surplus. In New York meetings of the negotiating group there was wide support for the draft despite some reservations. The Second Committee Chairman concluded that Negotiating Group 5 had successfully fulfilled its mandate but that other relevant PSD questions were still outstanding.

Continental shelf

Negotiating Group 6 (outer continental shelf limits and revenue sharing), chaired by the Second Committee Chairman himself, deferred work until the UN Secretariat study of the effects of the various limits proposals and accompanying map came to hand. The study affirmed the applicability of the formulae in the Irish amendment and that they involved compromise on coastal-state claims. According to the Irish delegation's assessment the study discredited the viability of the 500-metre isobath criterion proposed by the Soviet Union, a view implicitly endorsed by the Soviet abandonment of this criterion. The study, however, indicated that the data on which it was based was in some respects inadequate. It was also shown to include errors that undermined its persuasiveness. Privately, the Soviet Union proposed jurisdiction to the edge of the margin (to be determined scientifically or by the Hedberg formula) but not beyond 250 to 300 nautical miles, without any boundary commission supervision. In the negotiating group both the Soviet Union proposal (margin edge but not beyond 300 miles) and the Irish amendment were tabled. The Soviet proposal was supported only by the EE. The Irish delegate criticised it as an inappropriate, inequitable and unacceptable method of dealing with a natural feature, and also noted that it would place under national jurisdiction 20 per cent more of the margins worldwide than would be the case under the Irish amendment. He rejected a suggestion by Hungary to amalgamate the two proposals. The LLGDS criticised the 60-mile distance in the Hedberg formula as permitting extension beyond the edge of the margin in some places. Denmark, more fundamentally, criticised the definition as elaborated in Paragraph 2. Counter-proposals were made, for a simple 200-mile limit by the LLGDS, the Arabs (who were more insistent at this session) and Japan; and for simply the whole margin by Sri Lanka (anticipating a need for special treatment of the exceptional geological circumstances in the Bay of Bengal). A proposal by Austria (a leading LLGDS), made privately to the Margineers and the Soviet Union, comprised the Irish amendment with reduced distances in the Hedberg formula, higher revenue-sharing rates, a Conference resolution indicating opportunities for licensing of LLGDS companies for exploration and improved access for LLGDS to EEZ fisheries. (When the last element emerged from Negotiating Group 4 the LLGDS rejected any link.) Indonesia also proposed a package to the Irish delegation involving acceptance of the Irish amendment and some changes to other features, including higher revenue-sharing rates and a boundary commission with a verification or stronger role. Although they disagreed with elements of the proposal, the Margineers encouraged Indonesia to consult on it with others. Having done so, Indonesia decided the time was not opportune to submit the proposal openly.

The Soviet Union proposed another study with larger-scale maps, this time by the Intergovernmental Oceanographic Commission of UNESCO (IOC), which would also cover the latest Soviet proposal (margin edge but not beyond 300 miles). Despite the Margineers' opposition to what they regarded as a delaying tactic, it was decided the secretariat and the IOC should examine the feasibility of a study and of a larger-scale map also showing the 300-mile limit. The IOC reported for the New York meeting, pointing to the difficulty of basing a study on the inadequate data available, the difficulties and expense that would be involved in accumulating adequate data, and the length of time that would entail. It indicated some difficulties in applying all proposals but particularly in applying the Soviet proposal (margin edge but not beyond 300 miles). It was unable even to add a depiction of the latter to the existing map. An unexpected problem arose for the Margineers when the map suggested that the formulae in the Irish amendment, in contrast to the Soviet proposal, would not give India an area in the Bay of Bengal having major resource potential. This problem was resolved when the map producers acknowledged that this perception was due to an error in the map, but at the cost of further loss of credibility for the study.

The three main proposals remained on the table, with the Irish amendment gaining some support among delegations, including those of China, Mauritius and the Seychelles. Irish statements in the negotiating group emphasised the scientific soundness, practicability and compromise nature of the amendment (in contrast to the Soviet Union proposal) and that acceptance of satisfactory provisions on identification of limits was necessary before any negotiation of revenue sharing. A Soviet Union suggestion that lapse of time and increase of knowledge would lead to wider claims under the Irish formulae was countered by a proposal for a time limit within which coastal states must establish limits.

There was little discussion of revenue sharing, but there were some proposals both for reduction or even abolition of the grace period and increase of the rates as set out in the ICNT. More radically, Nepal proposed the establishment of a common heritage fund to which coastal states would contribute from production from non-living resources of the (whole) continental shelf. There would be no grace period in respect of these contributions and rates would begin at 15 per cent and advance to 30 per cent. This very extreme proposal did not gather any significant support, but it tended to raise expectations for higher levels of revenue sharing.

The (Group and Committee) Chairman reported that general agreement had not been reached and reiterated his earlier opinion that the basis for a solution rested on a combination of provisions on limits and revenue sharing.

During this session of difficult negotiations the Margineers' fragile unity was preserved in the face of several divisive developments. These included the Indian concern regarding the Bay of Bengal and the fact that the Soviet Union proposal would not be acceptable for some Margineers but would be for others. Differences of view among them on the establishment of a boundary commission, or on its powers and functions, and on acceptance of revenue sharing or of the rates or of exemptions for developing countries were further difficulties. The chairmanship, shared by Ireland and Canada, did well to hold the group together.

Delimitation

Negotiating Group 7 (on delimitation of marine boundaries) was chaired by Judge Eero Manner of Finland. Each of the opposing groups sought to substitute for the ICNT text the draft it had submitted informally at the Sixth Session (tabled in the negotiating group as working documents NG 7/10 on the Irish side and NG 7/2 on the opposition side). In the debates each side adhered closely to its existing position. Towards the end of April Chairman Manner tabled a redraft of the ICNT article, including Paragraph 1 setting out the criteria for delimitation, as a working document. He subsequently indicated his conclusion that his redraft had elements that with some slight amendments could be a basis for resolution of the issue. This conclusion ignored the express rejection of the redraft, particularly Paragraph 1, by the co-sponsors of document NG 7/10 (including Ireland), because it did not maintain the dominance of equitable principles among the criteria. They accordingly objected strongly to his conclusion. In reaction they set up an informal group (which became known as the group of 29 (G-29)) with the Irish delegate as chairman and main spokesman. This group sought, in a deputation to the Conference President, in a meeting of Plenary and in a stormy informal meeting with the President and US and Soviet Union delegates, to have the issue returned to the Committee. Under pressure the group agreed to continue deliberations in Negotiating Group 7, on condition that these would be conducted only on the basis of the ICNT and the drafts tabled by the opposing sides, i.e. not on the basis of Judge Manner's draft.

When Negotiating Group 7 resumed it first addressed the ICNT Paragraph 1. The G-29 received express support from the Soviet Union for the first time (despite the latter's failure to persuade the group to incorporate opposition to compulsory PSD in its position). Madagascar (one of the G-29) proposed, as a compromise, to add to the text of that group's document NG 7/10 a reference to the median line as one method of delimitation that could be used where appropriate, and the group consented. An Irish statement on 8 May *inter alia* supported the Madagascar proposal and confronted the claim that equitable principles as a criterion was too vague. Nineteen of the speakers supported document NG 7/10 while fourteen supported document NG 7/2. Chairman Manner convened two meetings of six delegations, three from each side (including Ireland), on Paragraph 1 and also met separately with each of these trios. It was accepted that the paragraph should have four ingredients, i.e. agreement, equitable principles, equidistance and special or relevant circumstances. While this represented some progress, helped by the Madagascar proposal, the problem resided in the interrelationship of the ingredients. Ireland explained that equitable principles must have priority, and that the Madagascar compromise was as far as the G-29 could go in accepting equidistance as an ingredient. A succession of informal drafts by the Chairman followed. These were all rejected by the G-29 as not in conformity with that position (which was of course unacceptable to the opposing group). These drafts evolved, with a gradually decreasing role for the median line, so that the final one was close to the ICNT text. Although this was still rejected by the G-29, as the ICNT had been, on account of the nature of its reference to the median line, the group was pleased that, without espousing the ICNT, it had moved the Chairman towards it. Chairman Manner reported to the Second Committee at the end of the Geneva meeting that he had not found it possible to find a text with wide approval—a long way from his conclusion early in the session (see above).

Negotiating Group 7 continued at the New York meeting and considered all three elements of the provision, with PSD first, and interim arrangements and Paragraph 1 (criteria for delimitation) following in that order. The separate consideration facilitated the G-29 in maintaining its solidarity, which covered only Paragraph 1, while they had differences on the other two elements. The group's position on Paragraph 1 was to accept the four elements, with agreement on the basis of equitable principles predominant, equidistance in the form of the Madagascar compromise and a reference to islands in the context of special or relevant circumstances. Irish statements on 15 August and 8 September made all these points. This was of course rejected again by the opposing group, but outside support for the G-29 came again from the Soviet Union, from the Netherlands more clearly than previously and, for the first time, from China, Mozambique, Maldives Islands and (land-locked) Burundi. On the other side there was new support from Indonesia and Costa Rica. There were 23 speakers in favour of document NG 7/10 (the G-29 proposal) and fifteen in favour of document NG 7/2 (the opposing group's proposal). Counting co-sponsors and other supporting speakers on both sides the statistics favoured the G-29 by 39 to 26. Nigeria (one of the G-29) suggested the ICNT text as a viable compromise.

Document NG 7/10 was ambivalent on PSD because of differences in the G-29. The Soviet Union was strongly opposed to any compulsory and binding PSD provision. Amendments to the ICNT by the Soviet Union, Bulgaria (an EE 'neutral') and Argentina (one of the G-29), tabled at the Geneva meeting, excluded compulsory and binding procedures. Some G-29 members supported these and other members, together with the co-sponsors of document NG 7/2, opposed them. Ireland favoured PSD procedures but the delegation, aware that its geographical neighbours were similarly inclined and conscious of its position as Chairman of the G-29, maintained silence on the topic. Professor Louis Sohn of the US delegation, an expert on PSD procedures, conducted discussions in a restricted group of fifteen (not including Ireland), following which he tabled a paper in the negotiating group with fifteen alternatives, none of which had commanded consensus in the restricted group. He revised the paper for the New York meeting. A list of delimitation settlements already reached was requested by some of those opposed to compulsory procedures, obviously with the intention of establishing that the vast majority of these were reached without resort to such procedures. There was no meeting of minds on the issue.

On interim measures (to apply pending settlement of a delimitation dispute) the ICNT was not very convincing in basing them on a regard for the criteria (in Paragraph 1) that by definition would not have yet led to settlement. It was nevertheless an improvement, from the Irish point of view, on the RSNT, which would have applied the median line pending settlement. However, as the G-29 common positions on this element extended only to opposition to the median line, document NG 7/10 reproduced the ICNT text. In Geneva, Papua New Guinea repeated the proposal of a moratorium and Norway and Surinam made suggestions with some promising features. Positive responses to these by the Irish delegate and others prompted the Negotiating Group Chairman to report at the end of the Geneva meeting that a compromise seemed attainable. However, in New York the emphasis returned to support of, and opposition to, the median line as an interim measure. Ireland supported a moratorium limited to activities in the disputed area in the absence of other agreed arrangements. No progress was achieved.

At the end of the session the Chairman of Negotiating Group 7 reported that there was a lack of consensus on all three elements of the provision, although there was broad agreement on some aspects within each of the three. In response to a direct Irish representation he mentioned the proposal for a specific reference to islands in the context of the circumstances criterion. The Irish delegation was very active on this issue throughout the session, and at the end was satisfied that a serious loss of ground threatened in the early stages had been averted through the considerable efforts of the delegation and its G-29 allies. However, a solution seemed no nearer and further major efforts would obviously be required to protect Ireland's interest.

The Second Committee, meeting informally in both Geneva and New York, took up items other than core issues on the basis of the ICNT. The agreed working procedure was that any proposal for amendment of the ICNT that met with significant objections would not warrant a change. Amendments were proposed to 50 ICNT articles and five new articles were suggested.

Exclusive economic zone and anadromous species

Notable among these amendments was a Soviet Union proposal aimed at ensuring preservation of high-seas freedoms in the EEZ, apparently reflecting dissatisfaction with the ICNT treatment of this topic although the latter seemed generally acceptable. However, there was agreement among all interested parties to an amendment to the article on anadromous species (salmon). This would reduce the consultation obligations of the state of origin in regard to conservation measures and increase the consultation obligations of other states in regard to their exercise of exploitation rights. It represented a move towards Irish interests.

Regime of islands

Turkey and nine other co-sponsors submitted an amendment during the Geneva meeting that was discussed in New York. As an exception from other islands, the ICNT excluded rocks unable to sustain human habitation or economic life from generating EEZ or continental shelf jurisdiction. Japan sought deletion of this exception whereas Turkey proposed adding islets to the exception. The latter, encouraged by the decision of the Anglo-French arbitration, also proposed to distinguish islands in a delimitation situation from others, and that application of equitable principles should determine what marine spaces accrued to islands in that situation. Ireland was not among the ten co-sponsors of the first element of the Turkish amendment because of an understanding, dating from the Fourth Session, with New Zealand and the South Pacific island states. In the debate the Irish delegate did, however, support the Turkish and oppose the Japanese amendment. He also again advocated a suitable cross reference to the delimitation articles as an alternative to the second element in the Turkish amendment. Other G-29 members and Iceland also supported the Turkish amendment, while indicating they were not seeking to limit the claims of island or archipelagic states to adequate marine zones. The Turkish amendment was opposed by the South Pacific island states, which claimed the ICNT provision was a compromise and that attempts to change it would oblige them to support the Japanese amendment. G-29 members Venezuela and France (presumably reflecting its diversity of interests in regard to islands world wide) supported Japan. Most of the co-sponsors of NG 7/2 also of course opposed the Turkish amendment and supported Japan, although Canada, Denmark, Malta, Spain and Sweden of that group rejected both amendments. At the end the Irish delegate again mentioned the cross-reference proposal and suggested that this, together with an appropriate reference to islands in the delimitation provisions, would facilitate retention of the regime of islands provision as it was in the ICNT. (The Irish delegate had made the same suggestion in the discussions on delimitation in Negotiating Group 7). The delegations of Ireland, Nicaragua and Turkey, aware that the Chairman did not intend to suggest any amendment to the ICNT provision, made a direct presentation to him, in the course of which they persuaded him, with some difficulty, to refer in his report to the importance attached by some delegations to the relationship between the regime of islands and delimitation provisions.

As to several other issues raised, the Chairman merely listed them in his report to Plenary at the end of the session.

THIRD COMMITTEE

The Third Committee, with none of the core issues in its mandate, discussed aspects of preservation of the environment and MSR, mainly in informal meetings.

Environment

The meetings on the environment, chaired again by Jose Vallarta (Mexico), were influenced by the very recent wreck of the oil tanker *Amoco Cadiz* on the coast of Brittany, which had caused serious pollution. France and others sought amendments to strengthen the coastal state's powers of prevention, amendments that were opposed by the maritime powers and some developing states. However, agreement was reached on some of the proposals. The Committee report at the end of the Geneva meeting listed among provisions agreed and to be included in due course in a revision of the ICNT (i) a requirement on states to promote routing systems to minimise the threat of vessel-source polluting accidents; (ii) an addition to the cooperation measures obliging notification of coastal states threatened by a polluting accident; and (iii) new measures to protect fragile ecosystems. The report also listed proposals on which discussion was ongoing in search of consensus and proposals where no agreement had been reached, both of which were re-addressed at the New York meeting. Further agreement was reached in New York on (iv) a French proposal to strengthen coastal-state powers of intervention outside its territorial sea to protect its coastline against pollution from a marine casualty, together with a definition of the term 'marine casualty' and (v) clarification of the conditions for inspection of a foreign vessel. Among proposals still under consideration at the end of the session were some aimed at further strengthening the enforcement powers of the coastal state and the port state.

Marine scientific research

There was a general perception that the ICNT comprised a delicately balanced package produced by lengthy negotiation and that further 'improvement' was unlikely. Only the US demurred specifically, maintaining that the ICNT was overly restrictive on researchers. It insisted on re-opening discussions in New York, where it submitted a series of amendments. Some were of a drafting or clarifying nature and attracted wide, but mild, support. Substantive amendments were met with vehement opposition from the CSG and the Group of 77 (G-77). These groups also threatened to seek amendments in the opposite direction. Researching states among the EEC members were sympathetic to the US amendments, but regarded attempts to incorporate them in the existing package as unrealistic at that stage. The amendments included some that would modify the MSR regime on the continental shelf beyond 200 miles so as to erode the coastal-state consent regime. Ireland and France rejected that proposal, thus preventing any EEC-9 position in its support. Collaterally, the author was the object of somewhat intemperate lobbying by a senior US delegate. The delegate indicated continuation of US support for extended continental shelf jurisdiction (clearly an important Irish interest) could be dependent on the prospects for success of its MSR aims. He urged immediate change of Irish MSR instructions, or departure from them by the Irish delegation, to lend support to those US aims, thus encouraging continued US support for extended jurisdiction. He was politely, but firmly, informed that standing Irish instructions could not be departed from, and that they could not be reconsidered until after the session. At the stage of reconsideration the US views would be made known to the Government.

The Committee Chairman reported factually on the exchanges at the informal meetings and expressed the view that there was overwhelming support for retention of the ICNT texts. Nevertheless, the US was not unduly discouraged.

Transfer of technology

The only discussions on TOT were in the context of ISBA technology.

FIRST COMMITTEE

International seabed area

The work on the ISBA was pursued in Negotiating Groups 1, 2 and 3 dealing respectively with Conference core issues 1, 2 and 3.

(i) Negotiating Group 1 (system of exploration and exploitation), chaired by Ambassador Frank Njenga (Kenya), comprised a nucleus of

50 delegations including six from the EEC (but not Ireland). However, it was widely attended and no distinction was made between the nucleus and others. Three topics in particular were addressed.

While parallel exploitation (directly by the authority and by states or their entities) and the need for a subsequent review of the system were both agreed, there were outstanding issues about the details of implementation of this parallel method, and about the mandate for review and the consequences if it failed. A two-sites approach was mooted for the former—an applicant for a licence would submit two sites and the authority could retain its choice site and grant a licence for the other. A moratorium on further contracts was suggested by the G-77 as a solution if the review failed.

(ii) On the role of the authority the EEC-9 made a moderate common statement, indicating a general willingness to negotiate and also to compromise on transfer of seabed mining technology. The problems included the authority's discretion in awarding mining contracts, whether a transfer of technology would be a condition for a contract, whether developing countries as well as the Enterprise should be beneficiaries under TOT and whether PSD procedures would apply.

(iii) Discussion of limitation of production was facilitated by a sub-group of technical experts. Industrialised countries preferred a system of compensation for developing land-based producers. Canada (a developed country and major land-based producer) and the US submitted jointly a compromise proposal on limitation that was rejected by the seabed miners among EEC members.

In Geneva the Chairman prepared a draft taking account of the exchanges, which was accepted as a basis for negotiation. At the New York meeting a listing by the EEC-9 of matters requiring further negotiation was supported by the US, albeit in more moderate terms. The G-77, however, reacted strongly, stating that if there was to be a re-opening of matters it could not be confined to that list. The discussions in fact concentrated on the authority's discretion in the granting of contracts and the contractors' TOT obligations. There was disagreement among EEC members on several matters, including the prevention of a dominant position among seabed miners. The Chairman produced a revised version of his Geneva draft. When this was criticised by both sides he concluded that further negotiation would be necessary.

In Negotiating Group 2 (financing of the authority and the enterprise and financing conditions in mining contracts), chaired by

Ambassador Tommy Koh (Singapore), the topics included whether payments for early support of the Enterprise should be compulsory or voluntary, the authority's source of revenue and (not unrelated to that) financial terms for mining contracts. Texts produced by a group of financial experts were discussed in Geneva and revised by the Chairman in the light of these discussions. Of the three topics, financing of the authority was the least difficult and financial terms of mining contracts the most controversial. The revised texts were considered in New York. Alternative G-77 proposals on financial terms of contracts were rejected by the industrialised countries as inconsistent with the international code of commercial practice. Proposals were also made by the EEC-9 and by Norway. A Netherlands proposal (a more flexible version of that of the EEC-9 and supported by them) was also promising. The Chairman produced a revision of his draft that was based on the Norwegian proposal with adaptations to make it more acceptable to the G-77. It was unacceptable to the seabed miners, including those in the EEC. Little attention was paid at this stage to financing of the authority and the enterprise.

Negotiating Group 3 (powers, functions, composition and decision-making procedures of organs of the authority), chaired by the First Committee Chairman, Ambassador Engo, had a very difficult mandate, particularly in regard to composition of and voting in the council. Composition questions raised included representation of interests and the possibility of permanent membership. The ICNT provisions on relationship between the assembly (with policy-making function) and the council (with executive function in implementing policy) seemed acceptable in principle, but the seabed miners were concerned about how it would work in practice. It was urged that subsidiary organs be kept to a minimum.

PLENARY

Peaceful settlement of disputes, preamble and final clauses

Plenary held no discussion on the ICNT articles on PSD. It did, however, hold a few informal meetings in New York to discuss for the first time the preamble and final clauses, although some delegations regarded this as premature in the light the large number of substantive issues still outstanding. A general debate was held in which the main emphasis was on participation in the future convention. This enabled the EEC, through its Danish Presidency, to raise in Conference discussions for the first time the need for the 'Community clause'. Similarly New Zealand sought a right of participation for the Trust Territories of the Pacific Islands, which it claimed had competences in matters to be covered by the convention. The Palestine Liberation Organization (PLO), the representative of the Palestinian people, which had observer status at the Conference, likewise requested the right of participation. The reaction to the Danish statement on the clause was not positive except for a few of the LAC members. Clearly participation would become a highly politicised issue. Other potentially difficult issues, for example reservations, provisional application, relationship between the future convention and other conventions, and entry into force, were not reached.

DRAFTING COMMITTEE

The Drafting Committee commenced its work with informal meetings at both parts of the session. It dealt with internal references in the ICNT and prepared a list of terms needing harmonisation. In New York it set up six language groups, corresponding to the official UN languages, to start preparations for the different language versions of the convention.

PLENARY

At a late stage of the session the apparent imminence of US legislation authorising deep seabed mining and pending similar legislation in other industrialised countries became a source of controversy, and led to exchanges in both the General Committee and Plenary. Drafts of such legislation had been before the US Congress for some time, but in autumn of 1977 the administration had indicated that it no longer objected to the legislation proceeding. The G-77 expressed concern at this development, and denied that high seas freedoms provided a basis for such legislation. They invoked the 1970 UN General Assembly Declaration of Principles that provided that the deep seabed, together with its resources, was the common heritage of mankind. They maintained that, in contrast to traditional exploitation of for example living resources of the seas, exploitation of seabed resources was excluded by the Declaration from high-seas freedoms. Accordingly, unilateral exploitation would be a violation of international law, and the intended legislation would constitute an obstacle to negotiations and to the emergence of a convention. The US in reply claimed that high-seas freedoms did extend to exploitation of the deep seabed. Advances in research into the ISBA and relevant technology, together with the disappointing lack of progress on the question at the Conference, were undermining existing US restraint in the matter. The US hoped for adoption of a convention before exploitation began on the basis of the legislation that was in any case fully compatible with the aims of the

Conference. The US was supported by the Federal Republic of Germany (the FRG), Belgium, France, Italy, the Netherlands and the UK of the EEC members and by Japan. The Soviet Union, China, Australia, New Zealand and Norway (speaking also for Sweden and Finland) called for restraint on the part of the industrialised countries. In the event no legislation was enacted during that year but the potential for conflict remained.

The Conference decided to recommend holding an Eighth Session in Geneva for six weeks from 19 March 1979 with the objective of conclusion of informal negotiations and revision of the ICNT. The possibility was also mentioned of formalising the revised ICNT, which would lead to formal negotiations, hopefully culminating in the adoption of a convention. Accordingly, the Conference requested authority also to hold further meetings in 1979, if deemed desirable. The UN General Assembly agreed to these proposals in due course.

CONCLUSION

Although revision of the ICNT had not been achieved at the Seventh Session, drafts had been formulated in several areas that were available for such revision in the future. This was a matter of general satisfaction to the Irish delegation although it was dissatisfied with progress on at least two of its main direct interests—continental shelf outer limits and delimitation of maritime zones between neighbouring states.

Chapter XI

EIGHTH SESSION

The Eighth Session was held, firstly, in Geneva for six weeks, from 19 March to 27 April 1979, and resumed in New York for six weeks, from 19 July to 24 August 1979. Ireland held the Presidency of the EEC in the second half of 1979, including the period of the New York meeting.

PREPARATIONS

An intersessional meeting was held in Geneva for three weeks from 23 January 1979. It focused on aspects of the international seabed area (ISBA) regime; the disputes settlement procedures aspect of delimitation and also some touching on the criteria and interim arrangements elements; and the continental shelf. Tentative agreements reached, particularly on the ISBA regime, lacked authority due to poor representation of African countries. There were, however, material exchanges between the Margineers and the Soviet Union on the continental shelf limits (see below). Meanwhile EEC consultations continued and in Dublin the Inter-Departmental Committee (IDC) met as usual to consider the implications of developments.

INSTRUCTIONS

Following the IDC deliberations and consultation of other interested departments, the Minister for Foreign Affairs again made a submission to the Government, dated 13 March, proposing instructions for the delegation for the Eighth Session. For the most part confirmation of existing instructions was suggested with addenda in some cases. However, there was greater emphasis on the need for flexibility to facilitate pursuit of the vital national interests, in the context of developments and at what was obviously perceived as a decisive stage of the Conference.

Exclusive economic zone and anadromous species

There was more specific identification of what was acceptable as land-locked and geographically disadvantaged states (LLGDS) rights as a step towards consensus, i.e. access, particularly for developing countries, to only the surplus of living resources (fish) in their region, but no right of access to non-living resources (minerals). On anadromous species (salmon) there was reference to the text agreed at the Seventh Session as appropriate for incorporation in the anticipated revision of the informal composite negotiating text (ICNT).

Continental shelf

On the continental shelf a boundary commission could be accepted, if its task was only a technical one of certifying the correctness of application of the formulae by a coastal state in identification of the outer limits. Regarding the Irish amendment, the opposition was assessed and its varying motivations explored. Bargaining was certainly the purpose of the LLGDS (mostly for fishing rights) and probably of the Arabs (for more onerous revenue sharing), while the Soviet Union had strategic concerns with which at least one Margineer (US) partly empathised. In parallel with those concerns, the Soviet Union and the US were seeking a dual regime regarding artificial islands and marine scientific research (MSR) respectively on the shelf, with no, or at least reduced, coastal state control of these elements outside the EEZ. It was estimated that the Irish amendment had not gathered enough support to defeat a combination of its opponents in a vote requiring a two-thirds majority, or even to have the amendment incorporated into a revised ICNT. In the light of these circumstances and of intersessional exchanges with the Soviet Union (see below), broad confirmation of existing instructions was suggested, but with added authority to support the ICNT together with the Irish amendment, even in modified form, provided it enabled Irish jurisdiction on the Rockall Plateau. Regarding revenue sharing, specific opposition to reduction of the five-year grace period was proposed together with greater flexibility on rates (some Margineers were already willing to accept higher figures). Acquiescence in higher rates, but not much higher than in the ICNT, was suggested if it proved necessary to secure acceptance of extended jurisdiction.

Delimitation

Endorsement of existing instructions was proposed but with flexibility to accept the ICNT text or any other package adequate for Irish purposes. This took account of the ICNT's priority for equitable principles in the criteria for division (although there was also the slightly undesirable specific mention of the median line), and also of the welcome omission of the median line as an interim measure. The danger of erosion of these factors was evidenced by the drafts of the Negotiating Group Chairman, particularly at the early stages of the Seventh Session.

Regime of islands

Authority to accept the ICNT was proposed, on the basis that it was the best likely to be available, in view of the concerns of the South Pacific island states added to the opposition of the delimitation protagonists. Although a cross-reference to the delimitation provision would be welcome, failure to achieve it should not prevent acceptance of the ICNT provision.

Marine scientific research

On MSR reference was made to the US position as indicated at the Seventh Session. It was submitted that greater freedom for research, but only non-resource-related research, on the continental shelf beyond 200 miles could be conceded, if it would facilitate acceptance of coastal-state jurisdiction to that area. This was based on an expectation that the Soviet Union and, more particularly, the US would insist on such freedom. Otherwise the ICNT that was broadly on the lines promoted by Ireland should be supported.

Transfer of technology

Confirmation of the existing instructions was proposed, i.e. to favour a voluntary rather than compulsory regime, and not to accept a role for the (ISBA) international authority other than in respect of ISBA technology.

Environment

Confirmation of existing instructions was suggested, together with support for the amendments strengthening the rights and powers of the coastal state to protect its coast from pollution. These amendments included both those agreed at the Seventh Session for incorporation in a revision of the ICNT and others still under consideration.

International seabed area

Flexibility for the delegation in implementing existing instructions was suggested. It should continue to support *inter alia* an anti-monopoly clause, protection of land-based producers and a future review by a conference (rather than by the assembly) of the system of exploitation. It should also support the most generally acceptable method of granting of contracts by the authority, and a new move to 'trim' the convention provisions by leaving some of the detail to be worked out by the authority. Overall support for proposals likely to lead to consensus and not inconsistent with the instructions was again advocated.

Peaceful settlement of disputes

Again confirmation of existing instructions on peaceful settlement of disputes (PSD) was proposed with specific mention of support for mooted special procedures in regard to disputes arising from issues in regard to fisheries, MSR and protection of the environment (including vessel-source pollution in particular).

Preamble and final clauses

The preamble was not adverted to in the submission. The final clauses were dealt with in a request for confirmation of existing instructions, particularly regarding promotion of the 'Community clause' that was likely to be further complicated by requests made at the Seventh Session for rights of participation for other entities. Support for the widest possible participation by all entities exercising competences relevant to the convention was proposed. The potential problems in regard to provisional application and reservations were again mentioned.

The Government accepted these instruction recommendations.

DELEGATION

Several changes were made in the delegation at this stage. By prior arrangement Ambassador Cremin retired from the delegation after the Geneva meeting. Ambassador Kennan, then accredited to Greece, joined the delegation at the Geneva meeting as a deputy head and took over as head of delegation in New York. His experience of the EEC greatly facilitated the delegation's efficient management of the duties of the EEC Presidency. Seamus Mallon did not attend again after the Geneva meeting, at which it had become clear that the negotiation of fisheries issues had been effectively completed (even if formal agreement awaited completion of the convention package), and that attendance of a delegate dedicated to fisheries issues would no longer be required. Geraldine Skinner relinquished her direct responsibility for the First Committee and concentrated on the Plenary work on PSD and final clauses (including participation), as well as providing backup in regard to Second Committee matters. Justin Dillon continued to service the First Committee. Piers Gardiner did not continue as a delegate and was replaced by Ray Keary, also from the Geological Survey of Ireland (GSI), at the first part of the session, although sadly a family bereavement forced his early departure. David Naylor, deputy director of the GSI, attended at the second part of the session and at the Ninth Session. Brendan Finucane was no longer available and there was no delegate designated to MSR at the first part of the session. Declan Lyons, a very junior officer from the National Board of Science and Technology (NBST), came to the New York meeting belatedly, but he was recalled in a fortnight. The result was that the delegation was unable to pay more than occasional attention to the negotiations on this topic, particularly in New York, where the responsibilities of the EEC Presidency stretched resources. In these straitened circumstances the delegation had no alternative but to request the Italian delegation to take on the EEC Presidency duties in regard to MSR. For the Irish EEC Presidency at the New York meeting the delegation had an extra member, Colm O'Floinn, Third Secretary in the Department of Foreign Affairs, who had particular responsibility for liaison and logistical arrangements in the Presidency context and helped out generally. Matthew Russell from the Office of the Attorney General again attended for part of the session.

GENERAL

Interest groups continued to meet, including the Margineers (on the continental shelf) and the group of 29 (on delimitation), in both of which the Irish delegation was Chairman and principal spokesman. The EEC member states also continued their coordination and cooperation meetings, with the Irish delegation holding the Presidency for six months from 1 July, a period that included the New York meeting.

PLENARY

A procedural debate was avoided when it was agreed that the seven negotiating groups on core issues established at the Seventh Session should resume their work immediately, and that from the third week MSR and environment issues would be taken up. Among other issues mentioned for consideration were regime of islands (in the Second Committee) and the preamble and final clauses (in Plenary). The objective of revision of the ICNT was adopted, with a view to its for-malisation and, consequently, to future procedure by way of formal deliberation and formal proposals for amendment. In the event only a partial revision was achieved after the Geneva meeting (resulting in

ICNT Rev. 1), the revision proposals having been submitted to Plenary in the final days of that meeting. Despite indications of further progress at the New York meeting (except notably on the delimitation question, a vital issue for Ireland) no further revision was undertaken there. Formalisation of the text was not essayed.

SECOND COMMITTEE

Exclusive economic zone

In Negotiating Group 4 (on rights of the LLGDS in the EEZ), the LLGDS sought to re-open the texts that the group Chairman, Satya Nandan, had submitted in his report at the Seventh Session as fit for inclusion in a revision of the ICNT. The coastal states group (CSG) strongly resisted re-opening. In fact the negotiating group met only once. At the end of the Geneva meeting its Chairman reported that there was majority support for incorporation of the texts in the revision, and this was done. The negotiating group did not meet in New York but, in a meeting of the Second Committee, Romania proposed rights for LLGDS in the EEZ of another region if there was a scarcity of fish in their own region. This was opposed by the CSG and also by the EEC through its Irish spokesman.

Anadromous species

The text on anadromous species agreed at the Seventh Session was also incorporated in the ICNT Rev. 1.

Peaceful settlement of disputes

Negotiating Group 5 (on applicability of PSD regarding exercise of coastal state rights in the EEZ), did not meet, the Chairman of the Second Committee having decided that it had successfully fulfilled its mandate at the Seventh Session. The drafts that had commanded wide support at that session were incorporated in the revision of the ICNT at the end of the Geneva meeting.

Continental shelf

On the outer continental shelf limits the Soviet Union had had bilateral discussions with the UK (a Margineer) after the Seventh Session, and subsequent discussions with the Margineers *en marge* of the Geneva intersessional meeting. In the bilateral exchanges the Soviet Union indicated flexibility on overriding distance limits, suggesting alternative limits of 100 miles beyond the EEZ or 60 miles beyond the 2500-metre isobath. The Margineers remained unresponsive, reluctant to abandon the Irish amendment with its rationale based on natural prolongation as recognised in existing law, and also fearful of loss of significant areas of jurisdiction through application of the Soviet limits. The first of these concerns was addressed in the intersessional exchanges, when the Soviet Union indicated acceptance of the prolongation basis determined in accordance with the Irish amendment (including both the Hedberg and Gardiner formulae), but with no extension beyond the proposed Soviet limits. It hinted at increasing its distance proposals to 150 and 100 miles respectively. The Margineers were still reluctant, not least because they were unable to assess the effects of the limits on their areas of jurisdiction. The Irish assessment was that the isobath alternative cut-off with 100-miles distance would result in no reduction or, at worst, no significant reduction in the area Ireland would enjoy under unrestricted application of the Irish amendment and the Gardiner formula, and that retention of the prolongation basis would enable extension on to the Rockall Plateau, which was a vital interest. Some other Margineers, notably Argentina, Australia, Canada and New Zealand might need a widening of the 150-mile limit (beyond the EEZ) to meet their concerns, a widening that the Soviet Union was not ready to concede. At the intersessional meeting Mexico (a leader of the CSG) and Singapore (a prominent LLGDS member) privately indicated support for the Soviet compromise. This increased the pressure on the Margineers to accept it, but also held out the prospect of virtual consensus. The Margineers Group, faced with different effects of the Soviet proposals on their respective interests, were in serious danger of break-up. As the group comprised the core of support for the Irish amendment, its breakup would have disastrous potential for the viability of that amendment. The Margineers succeeded in deferring an open discussion on the Soviet ideas at the intersessional meeting, winning time to prepare for the session. It was in this context that the revised Irish instructions had been framed.

At the Geneva part of the session the Soviet Union worked energetically inside and outside Negotiating Group 6 (on outer limits and revenue sharing) to add its (narrower) cut-offs to the Irish amendment. Argentina, Australia, Canada and New Zealand, among the Margineers, feared that both of these cut-offs would deprive them of significant areas of jurisdiction. The inflexibility of the Soviet Union on the distances and of the Margineers in rejecting a dual regime regarding artificial islands and MSR (i.e. differing according to whether they were inside or outside the EEZ) resulted in a stalemate. The Soviet Union mounted a public exhibition (in the lobby of the UN building)

of maps designed to demonstrate that the Gardiner and Hedberg formulae were technically impractical (despite the conclusions of the two
independent studies at the Seventh Session). The exhibition was criticised by Ireland, as Margineers spokesman, in Negotiating Group 6,
both on its merits and as an inappropriate action while intensive negotiations were being pursued. When the Soviet proposal was tabled it
nevertheless included the essentials of the Irish amendment, adding the
narrower of the Soviet cut-offs. It also provided for exclusion of underwater ridges from jurisdiction, for raising the revenue ceiling to 7 per
cent and for the dual regime in regard to artificial islands and MSR.
Denmark, supported by the Scandinavians (except Norway, dissuaded
by its fellow Margineers), proposed a change to the Irish amendment
designed to ensure that jurisdiction over the Rockall Plateau would
accrue totally to the Faeroes Islands. Sri Lanka sought exemption from
application of both the Irish formulae and the Soviet cut-offs, on the
grounds of their disproportionately limiting effect in the exceptional
geological circumstances of the Bay of Bengal.

On revenue sharing both the grace period and the rates were
opposed by the LLGDS. Various proposals for change were made, but
none drew much overt support. The pre-existing lack of cohesion in
the Margineers on that issue still survived. Norway and the UK (and
Ireland, although not overtly) were prepared to accept higher rates, if
necessary. Argentina, India and Uruguay concentrated on exemption
from revenue sharing for developing countries, which would make the
detail irrelevant for them. Others, particularly Australia, were still resist-
ing any revenue sharing, at least overtly.

The Margineers and the Soviet Union engaged in consultations on
the boundary commission, as a result of which a Soviet proposal, which
would give the commission's conclusions only validating effect, was
agreed between them.

After consultation with the interested parties the Chairman presented a package to the Irish delegation that would include: the Irish
amendment; the wider Soviet cut-offs; a boundary commission as in
the Soviet proposal; revenue sharing after a five-year grace period with
rates beginning at 1 per cent and increasing by 1 per cent annually to
a maximum of 7 per cent. In addition, the package covered the artificial
islands issue by application to the (whole) shelf of a clause, taken from
the 1958 convention, giving coastal states exclusive rights to construct
them on the shelf, subject to their not interfering with recognised navigation sea-lanes; and it excluded the consent regime for MSR on the
shelf outside the EEZ, even for resource-related research. The Irish delegation indicated the package would probably be acceptable as a revision

except the MSR provision, which would be vehemently opposed. The Chairman submitted this package to Negotiating Group 6, omitting the MSR issue as a problem to be resolved elsewhere (i.e. in the Third Committee). There were footnotes, which referred to the Sri Lanka concerns and ocean ridges as problems for further consideration. The Margineers accepted the package, and the debate in the negotiating group showed a majority in favour of the proposed revision together with LLGDS acquiescence. It was incorporated in the revision of the ICNT at the end of the Geneva meeting. Ireland and the other Margineers were gratified that the Irish amendment had at last been incorporated into the Conference text, even if with some modification and some slight loss of ground in regard to revenue sharing and possibly in regard to the proposed dual regime.

Optimism at this outcome was found not to be totally justified early in the New York resumption of the session, as proposals affecting all three elements were pursued. On the definition the previously submitted Danish proposal drew scant attention but a new Chinese amendment raised fears of a re-opening. However, the most serious development arose from the apparent Soviet Union concern that the isobath cut-off provision could be abused by resort to an isobath on the seaward edge of an ocean ridge. Pursuit of this concern became a vehicle for negating that cut-off (and achieving the original Soviet objective of a simple distance cut-off) by provision for excluding measurement not only from oceanic ridges but also from genuine continental ridges. This could detrimentally affect *inter alia* Ireland's claim across the Rockall Trough. The Margineers sought to counter this by adding a listing of shelf features not to be covered in the exclusion, although some Margineers were not convinced that this would be adequate. The proposed addition was opposed by the Soviet Union. A Japanese proposal distinguishing ridges of oceanic crust was helpful, but suggestions by Singapore, Indonesia and the Federal Republic of Germany (the FRG) that the isobath cut-off should be dropped compounded Margineer, including specifically Irish, difficulties. Discussion was deferred when the Chairman indicated that further amendment of ICNT Rev. 1 would not be feasible at the session.

Some LLGDS attacked the ICNT Rev. 1 provision on revenue sharing as inadequate. Existing radical proposals were invoked, including a revised version of the Nepal proposal for a common heritage fund. New proposals were made by the Netherlands and Sri Lanka that would omit the grace period and raise rates. These were all opposed by the Margineers, particularly Australia (still overtly against any revenue sharing), as excessive and economically unrealistic. However, the

LLGDS opposition was less effective than previously, its cohesion having been eroded by the Geneva revision on fishing rights. Separately, the US sought to modify the exemption for developing countries from revenue-sharing obligation.

Singapore suggested that the decisions of the Commission on the Limits of the Continental Shelf (boundary commission) should be binding on the coastal state. The Soviet Union and the Margineers consulted on a counter-suggestion but deferred action when it emerged that no text revision would be undertaken.

Chairman Aguilar's report was confined to a factual account of the exchanges.

Delimitation

The prior intersessional meeting in Geneva (chaired by Negotiating Group Chairman Judge Manner) made little progress on any of the elements of delimitation of maritime boundaries, even on the settlement of disputes element on which it mainly concentrated. In regard to criteria, the main development was the suggestion by the Chairman of a 'non-hierarchical' approach, i.e. enumerating the elements while avoiding a hierarchical order—thus effectively eliminating the ICNT priority for equitable principles. At a meeting of the G-29 at the beginning of the session it was reported that meetings of the African and Islamic Groups had resulted in increased support for the group's proposal (document NG 7/10) and that some progress had been made also among the Eastern European (EE) and Latin American and Caribbean (LAC) Groups. The members favoured keeping the Madagascar amendment on hold and preferably moving to a smaller consultative group to expedite negotiations. However, Negotiating Group 7 resumed and its Chairman continued to seek variation of the ICNT in a direction making it more favourable to the co-sponsors of document NG 7/2 (opponents of the G-29), particularly by setting out the criteria in non-hierarchical form. There were also some suggestions that variations in criteria would be appropriate as between the EEZ and the continental shelf and between opposite and adjacent states—particularly by Israel. The Chairman's non-hierarchical approach evoked the usual favourable response from the co-sponsors of document NG 7/2, many claiming that employment of the median line subject to special circumstances guaranteed equity. The G-29 argued against departure from the existing law as identified by the International Court of Justice (ICJ). A clear majority (including the US, the Soviet Union, China, Cuba, Hungary and Viet Nam) supported the G-29 in its opposition to the Chairman's idea. However, this did not deter him and, when in a later debate a slight majority of speakers favoured the document NG 7/2 proposal (due to temporary passivity of G-29 members), he was encouraged in his approach. Some 'neutrals' prepared a draft on the same lines and the Mexican delegation consulted on it with three delegations from the G-29 (including the Irish delegation). The Irish delegation alone was consulted on a later but very similar version. In both consultations the unacceptability to the group of the draft was explained, principally because it did not preserve the priority of the equitable principles criterion—the term did not even appear in the first draft, which spoke merely of an equitable solution. The group was dismayed when Mexico tabled the second draft unchanged as a proposed compromise in Negotiating Group 7. In the debate the G-29 members rejected it out of hand. The Irish delegate, as chief spokesman, recorded that no account had been taken of the group's concerns as explained in both consultations. His statement indicated that any proposal that failed to reflect the current state of international law on the topic, or that sought to exclude the primary rule on delimitation, was unacceptable. It characterised the Mexican draft as a median line provision and inconsistent with current international law. It also discredited an attempt, by the Greek delegate, to promote the role of the median line by reference to statistics of delimitation settlements already concluded. He claimed that in the majority of these the median line had been used. The Irish statement pointed out *inter alia* that the less complicated cases, in which employment of the median line was in conformity with equitable principles, would obviously be the easiest and the first to be settled. The most important of the statistics cited was the number of cases in which it had not been employed. Moreover, there was a considerable number of cases in which settlement had not been reached despite the availability of the median-line method.

A subsequent Mexico–Peru proposal (document NG 7/36), tabled after consultations with (but without the support of) the Irish delegation, was less unacceptable to the G-29. In that draft the dilution of the role of equitable principles, as compared with the earlier Mexican draft, was slight. It was cautiously greeted by the G-29 as a basis for negotiation although requiring amendment, but the co-sponsors of document NG 7/2 criticised and/or rejected it. The Soviet Union proposed an amendment that improved it from the point of view of the G-29. The Chairman held separate consultations on this draft with the Irish delegate and the Spanish delegate (spokesman for the co-sponsors of document NG 7/2), but these were inconclusive. Surprisingly, a revised version tabled by Mexico and Peru, while taking account of some Irish suggestions, changed the thrust of the draft by altering the sequence of the criteria. It was rejected by the two opposing groups and both drafts were angrily withdrawn by the proposers. The Chairman in his report at the end of the Geneva meeting doubted that a viable text on criteria was possible. Nevertheless he again promoted the idea of a 'non-hierarchical' text but suggested, as a basis for compromise, a draft that was similar to the penultimate Mexico-Peru draft (document NG 7/36, regarded by the G-29 as promising) and not non-hierarchical. However, his changes included a controversial reference to equidistance as a rule rather than just a method, an innovation that was unacceptable to the G-29.

Although the need for an interim measures provision was questioned at the intersessional meeting, the supporters of document NG 7/2 insisted at the session that the median line should be provided as the interim measure. The G-29 could accept an interim measures provision, but not one providing for the median line. The moratorium as suggested by Ireland did not attract support. India (a co-sponsor of document NG 7/2), Iraq and Morocco (members of the G-29) proposed a text that did not refer to either the median line or a moratorium, but encouraged the parties to refrain from aggravating or prejudicial unilateral action. This gathered some support and the Chairman, after consultation, proposed a text (document NG 7/38) on the same lines. In his report at the end of the Geneva meeting he put it forward as a possible basis for compromise.

At the intersessional meeting the discussions on PSD in regard to delimitation (text for inclusion in the PSD, Part IV, of the ICNT) were based on multiple alternative models submitted by Professor Sohn (US) at the Seventh Session, and a new paper by Ambassador Shabtai Rosenne (Israel). It became clear that compulsory and binding PSD procedures, as implicit in the ICNT, were unacceptable to a majority, despite support from a significant minority. At the Geneva part of the session, despite extensive work in a consultative group chaired by Professor Sohn, to which he submitted three further papers and Ambassador Rosenne submitted another, no advance was made. The Chairman's report at the end of that meeting put forward a text (NG 7/41), based on the new papers. It provided for (i) an optional exemption in regard to delimitation disputes from the convention's binding PSD procedures, (ii) without condition of applicability of other binding procedures, (iii) on condition of reference of disputes arising after entry into force of the convention to non-binding convention conciliation procedures (reflecting the Soviet Union position); and (iv) an ambivalent reference to acceptance of binding procedures if a solution was not achieved through the conciliation procedure. The Irish delegate was not active in these deliberations.

Judge Manner's report indicated that he could not suggest that any proposal for amendment of Articles 74/83 commanded sufficient support to improve the prospect of consensus. He suggested that continuation of negotiations could lead to a solution. The Second Committee debate on the report revealed nothing new in the positions of delegations. The Second Committee Chairman concluded that the basic elements of the report were accepted. Revision of the ICNT at the end of the Geneva meeting did not include any changes to the delimitation provisions.

At the resumption in New York the co-sponsors of document NG 7/2 sought to deal with the three elements (criteria, interim measures and settlement of disputes) as interdependent ingredients of a package, presumably hoping to achieve a change on criteria in return for the apparently inevitable failure to secure compulsory and binding settlement of disputes procedures. The G-29 felt that the best prospects of an acceptable compromise on Paragraph 1 (criteria) rested with the ICNT, with possibly some input from a combination of document NG 7/36 (proposed by Mexico and Peru at Geneva) and a Soviet Union-proposed amendment to it. However, the group decided to be cautious about this. In Negotiating Group 7 the Irish delegate reiterated the G-29 position that the equitable principles criterion must be dominant and must have priority over any particular delimitation method. Accordingly, a 'non-hierarchical' text was not a feasible solution. The responses from the opposing group were more muted than previously. Neither group mentioned the draft in the Negotiating Group Chairman's Geneva report. The Chairman held separate meetings with the two groups and a combined meeting with the Irish and Spanish delegates. The Spanish delegate, surprisingly, indicated a willingness to accept the ICJ judgement as a basis for the criteria. In subsequent direct exchanges with the Irish delegate he expressed an anxiety about exaggerated interpretation of the term 'equitable principles'. A Spanish draft put forward as meeting both of these points provided for agreement in accordance with equitable principles (as in the ICJ judgement and the ICNT), contained an enigmatic reference to the equality of states and mentioned the median line in a manner that did not make clear that its use would be subservient to equitable principles. Spain rejected an Irish suggestion of an amendment to the median line reference to clarify this subservience, and the effort was abandoned. The Chairman indicated his intention of including in his report a version of the Spanish draft but with amendments towards the Irish suggestion. This drew protests, mainly from the co-sponsors of document NG 7/2. He did not include this text in his report but he circulated it as a negotiating group document (NG 7/44). His report, at last, conceded that a non-hierarchical text could not be the basis for consensus, but it surprisingly mentioned equality of states as an additional ingredient. He was more optimistic than previously about the prospects of compromise on criteria, to which he felt his document NG 7/44 could contribute. From the Irish point of view some welcome changes in his thinking had been achieved.

The text in the Negotiating Group Chairman's Geneva report on interim measures (NG 7/38) was the basis for the New York discussions. Surprisingly, there was little criticism by the co-sponsors of document NG 7/2 in regard to the omission of mention of the median line. There was controversy about the requirement (supported by Ireland among others) to refrain from aggravating the situation—as distinct from hampering agreement—on the grounds that it amounted to a moratorium. Successive revised versions, which omitted or amended that requirement, failed to facilitate agreement in two small consultative groups convened by the Chairman. The Chairman in his report described the most recent version as promising. It omitted the requirement not to aggravate the situation but retained the requirement not to hamper or jeopardise a final agreement.

On PSD all the alternative models, the Chairman's text (document NG 7/41) from the Geneva meeting and a further US proposal were considered in New York. Different views continued to be expressed, with the Soviet Union maintaining its adamant opposition to compulsory binding procedures. After consultations the Chairman produced a revision of his text. The changes were merely elaborations or redrafting of the previous text. The revised version drew the same objections as previously. The Chairman's report nevertheless described this approach as the most realistic basis for a solution.

Ireland, the only speaker on Chairman Manner's report in the Second Committee, pointed out that the criteria text mentioned in the report (document NG 7/44) had not been discussed in Negotiating Group 7, and did not express any view on its content.

At the end of the session the Committee Chairman, at the behest of the US, called together ten delegations (including the US and Ireland). The US proposed a provision in the delimitation articles enabling any state to make an interpretative declaration in regard to the criteria paragraph. A state availing of this facility would not have to accept any other interpretation. All the other nine delegations rejected this surprising proposal, including Ireland (which had advised the US against the venture in advance). Nevertheless, it was referred to in a subsequent article on the session by one of the US delegates in terms that suggested it could contribute to a solution.

Regime of islands

Among the topics discussed in informal Second Committee meetings was regime of islands. The proposal made by Turkey and others at the Seventh Session for amendment of the ICNT was again debated. Ireland supported both objectives of the amendment, and again orally suggested a cross reference to the delimitation articles, as an alternative to the part of the amendment that dealt with islands in a delimitation situation. When Turkey and its fellow co-sponsors agreed to support the Irish proposal, without dropping their own, Ireland submitted a written version in the form of adding 'without prejudice to Articles 74 and 83.....' to Paragraph 2. Despite intensive lobbying the response was disappointing, particularly the lack of support from the South Pacific island states, with whom Ireland had an understanding about the article.

The Second Committee Chairman's report merely included the topic in a list of topics considered in the Committee on which he did not comment.

THIRD COMMITTEE

While none of the Third Committee topics figured among the seven core issues, it met informally to consider some of the matters within its mandate on which there were still differences.

Marine scientific research

Mr Elliot Richardson, US head of delegation, invited a large number of delegations to a series of meetings *en marge* of the Geneva part of the session, with a view to persuading them to support the US amendments proposed at the Seventh Session. The Irish delegation was among the invitees (mostly CSG and Group of 77 (G-77) delegations) and was among the large attendance, despite not having at the relevant time a delegate specifically dedicated to MSR. A recurring Richardson theme at these meetings was the danger of an alliance in the US between mining corporations dissatisfied with the emerging ISBA regime and research institutes similarly dissatisfied with the MSR texts. Such an alliance, of what were described as stubborn and influential entities, could prevent the US from supporting the future convention. G-77 and CSG delegations were not receptive to the idea of the conciliatory role Richardson implied they should play, by accepting the US MSR amendments to avoid this danger. Ireland shared that point of view. For the G-77 it was crystallised in a sardonic suggestion, by the Brazilian delegate, that the US should explain to the relevant corporations and institutes that at UNCLOS III the US was dealing with stubborn and influential delegations that were firmly averse to the proposed changes. In the Committee the G-77, in particular, rejected the US amendments. At the end of the Geneva meeting the Committee Chairman reiterated his view that there was substantial support for the ICNT, but indicated that he would not oppose further negotiation in search of consensus. The revision carried out did not have any of the US amendments.

In New York there were exchanges outside the Committee on the main MSR controversial issues; i.e. the regime on the continental shelf beyond the EEZ (related to the continental shelf issues in Negotiating Group 6) and applicability of PSD procedures in regard to disputes. The Margineers deferred discussion on a new US draft on the former, due to a concern to preserve their fragile unity. In the Committee, although many delegations opposed re-opening of the issues, the US succeeded in having discussions of its drafts. The Chairman's report included proposed texts in which coastal state consent for MSR on the shelf beyond the EEZ would be implied, except in the case of resource-related research in areas designated by the coastal state. Moreover, these areas would only be those in which exploitation or exploration was occurring or about to occur. The Irish delegation's report was concerned that this text, with the seriously inadequate exception, would very likely be incorporated in the next revision. The proposed texts would also require compulsory reference to conciliation procedures in case of allegations of coastal state exercise of rights (other than refusal of consent for, or requiring cessation of, a project) in a manner incompatible with the provisions of the convention. The delegation, handicapped by the absence of a dedicated delegate for other than a short period, had been unable to arrange attendance at many of the Committee meetings. It also had to ask the delegation of Italy (the succeeding EEC Presidency) to manage EEC cooperation on the topic at a time when Italy, as well as the FRG and the Netherlands among EEC members, favoured the US position. In fact, the FRG was even more extreme than the US in wanting to re-open the provisions for the consent regime also in regard to the area inside 200 miles.

Transfer of technology

The Chairman indicated at the end of the Geneva meeting that the provisions had been discussed exhaustively and that the informal negotiations had been completed. Only one proposal for change, which commanded overwhelming support, was incorporated into the revision of the ICNT. This was the addition of a provision on establishment of national centres of marine science and technology. There was no meeting of the Committee on the topic in New York.

Environment

The proposals outstanding from the Seventh Session were discussed in Geneva. At the end of that meeting the Chairman identified a proposal, to amend the provision on responsibility for implementing obligations and liability for failure to do so, as qualifying for incorporation in the revision, and this proposal was incorporated. Likewise the amendments for strengthening the powers of the coastal state as agreed at the Seventh Session were incorporated. The Chairman concluded that with these amendments a desirable balance had been achieved and that negotiations had been completed. There was no meeting of the Committee on this topic in New York.

FIRST COMMITTEE

Some work on the ISBA regime was done in the January intersessional meeting, but the results lacked authority due to the limited representation at the meeting. At the session the three negotiating groups resumed their discussions, but at the end of the third week they had not achieved any significant advance. A small working group, the group of 21 (G-21), was established, comprising ten industrialised countries (including the US and six of the EEC-9), ten developing countries and China. Subsequently nineteen alternative members were also identified, for all members except the US and China, thus effectively enlarging the group (although it retained its name). It was chaired by the Chairman of the First Committee, and the Negotiating Group Chairmen were also involved. In addition a subgroup of legal experts was set up, with Mr Harry Wuensche (East Germany, the German Democratic Republic—the GDR) as Chairman, to deal with legal aspects of PSD in the context of the ISBA regime. At the Geneva meeting the G-21 produced texts on some of the issues that were incorporated in the revision. In New York the G-21 continued, and there were also more restricted negotiations, directly between specially interested delegations and with the Negotiating Group Chairmen. These exchanges produced further texts but no further revision was undertaken.

In Negotiating Group 1 (system of exploration and exploitation), despite G-77 resistance to any change, detailed procedural and substantive requirements for authority decisions and the nature of priority for the Enterprise (effectively elaboration of the parallel system) were examined. The issues of production limitation, review and TOT were also considered. Chairman Njenga prepared some compromise texts on requirements that responded mainly to industrialised countries' concerns. These were further considered in the G-21, which also discussed *inter alia* details of priority for the Enterprise and the review. It was accepted that the review would take place after an interval of between fifteen and twenty years. The consequences if the review failed were also addressed. In G-77 eyes these included a moratorium on contracts, an idea opposed by the industrialised countries. A further issue was the forum for review, a conference or the authority assembly. France again promoted an anti-monopoly clause, without support from any of its five EEC fellow members in the G-21, but the Soviet Union indicated an interest. The group made no progress on TOT, where the industrialised countries' position was that the obligation to transfer should not apply to technology available on the open market, or to processing technology. It was suggested by the Netherlands that joint ventures by the Enterprise and contractors might be helpful in the TOT context. Consideration of production limitation was assigned to a subgroup chaired by Satya Nandan and comprising delegations from land-based producers and consumers. The details of and availability of PSD procedures were discussed by the legal experts subgroup. Among issues covered in these discussions was an industrialised countries' preference for arbitration procedures (already established by the United Nations Commission on International Trade Law) rather than the proposed tribunal for the law of the sea, where the dispute concerned alleged failure to transfer technology. Some of the texts that emerged were incorporated into the revision of the ICNT but most were regarded as promising for further examination in New York.

In Negotiating Group 2 (financing of the authority and the Enterprise and financial terms of contractors) industrialised countries suggested that financing of the Enterprise should be through a combination of interest-free loans from state parties and commercial loans guaranteed by state parties. It was mooted that state loans should be on the same basis as UN scale of assessments for subscriptions, although it was not agreed whether all states, only states parties to the convention or only seabed mining states should be the lenders. Texts on all three of the group's subjects were incorporated in the revision of the ICNT at the end of the Geneva meeting, but these were neither comprehensive nor commanding consensus.

In Negotiating Group 3 (organs of the authority) the industrialised countries proposed that there should be a non-interference clause in regard to relations between the organs. On composition of the council there was no progress on numbers for the various categories. On voting, ideas of variations on two-third majority requirements, depending on the subjects, were explored, together with the possibility of a requirement for a greater majority in some cases. The texts incorporated in the revision of the ICNT concerned detail rather than significant substance, but several other texts were regarded as promising for further consideration in New York.

In New York work on issues across the mandates of the three negotiating groups was continued in the G-21 and in smaller *ad hoc* groups of interested delegations. While some progress was made this was not the case in regard to TOT, limitation of production, relations between the organs or composition of, and voting in, the council. A new element in the discussions on voting was a suggestion for a blocking minority. No further text revision was undertaken.

EEC cooperation in this field was not very successful due to significant divergences between national positions.

PLENARY

Final clauses

The final clauses texts on ratification, accession and entry into force, included in the secretariat paper (A/Conf.62/L.13), and the Transitional Provision, included in the ICNT, were also carried into Rev. 1 at the end of the Geneva meeting. The final clauses were considered in detail for the first time in informal meetings of Plenary at the New York meeting on the basis of the ICNT Rev. 1, and the secretariat paper that also covered more controversial elements without submitting drafts. These elements were identified at the start, including future amendment or revision of the convention, reservations, relationship to other Conventions, participation, transitional provisions, and establishment of a preparatory committee for the (ISBA) authority. These included the three issues mentioned in delegation instructions as of particular concern for Ireland—reservations, provisional application (as part of transitional provisions) and the 'Community clause' (in the context of participation). The non-controversial items were taken first and a group of legal experts, chaired by Minister Evensen, was set up to consider technical problems. The President prepared drafts on the basis of the group's deliberations. As no further revision of the ICNT was undertaken these were preserved for further consideration.

Participation and 'community clause'

In the informal meetings of Plenary the main controversial issues reached were participation and amendment or revision. The Irish delegate, as EEC Presidency, tabled and introduced in Plenary a draft 'Community clause' agreed in EEC coordination. The introducing statement explained that, in view of the transfer of competences to the EEC by its member states in areas to be covered by the convention, the member states would be unable to implement the Convention in these areas without the participation of the EEC as well. A draft in general terms was proposed that would (a) open the Convention for signature and approval, or accession, by certain types of international organisations that exercised powers in fields covered by it; (b) give them the same rights and obligations as state parties in the fields of their powers; and (c) enable their member states to grant each other mutual special treatment without having to extend it to other parties to the convention. The presentation was treated with a lack of comprehension and/or suspicion by most delegations, and met with straight, politically inspired, opposition from the Soviet Union and its EE allies. The Soviet Union had proposed a draft on participation by international organisations that did not meet EEC requirements, and was obviously intended to pre-empt the EEC proposal. It was clear that the EEC members were faced with a difficult task in achieving general acceptance of the clause. There were also proposals to enable participation by National Liberation Movements (NLMs) and by territories under UN trusteeship. The deliberations on amendment or revision were also incomplete. Further consideration of both of these issues was deferred. The discussion of provisional application revealed a general resistance to provisional application, either in stages or of part only of the convention. Moreover, in regard to total provisional application, the emphasis was on the difficulties, both legal and practical. The idea of a preparatory commission, which was not unrelated, emerged. The Transitional Provision (on countries not having full independence) was also discussed. The exchanges revealed differences between the G-77 and some Western countries (including the US and some EEC members) as to whether it was really transitional, whether it should be an integral part of the Convention and whether it was linked to participation. The President undertook to hold consultations with the interested parties.

Peaceful settlement of disputes and preamble

There was no separate discussion of PSD in Plenary at the session although special aspects of the topic arose in connection with some of the substantive issues in the Committee framework. The articles in Part IV were carried into ICNT Rev. 1 unchanged. There was no discussion of the preamble. The text on this topic was also carried unchanged into the ICNT Rev. 1.

The conflict about national legislation authorising deep seabed mining (now pending in the FRG as well as the US) was raised again by the G-77, both on the first day of the session in Geneva and its last day in New York. The arguments on both sides were the same as at the Seventh Session. During the New York meeting also, the CSG protested at press reports that the US had directed its ships and aircraft to enter waters immediately outside three miles in exercise of high-seas rights, action that the CSG described as inconsistent with good faith negotiation at the Conference. The US in its defence was ambivalent about the reports, and defended itself on the basis of existing high seas rights. It was supported by some other maritime countries. The Soviet Union expressed support for the CSG position, but specifically only in regard to waters out to a twelve-mile limit.

The Conference decided to recommend the convening of a ninth session in two five-week parts in 1980, from 3 March to 4 April in New York and from 28 July to 29 August in Geneva. The Plenary adopted the objective of completing the informal negotiations at the first part. This would be followed by formal discussions in Plenary, preparation of a further revision (ICNT Rev. 2) as a draft convention, formal consideration of the draft convention and of any formal proposals for amendments, all leading to adoption of a convention. In due course the UN General Assembly accepted this recommendation for the holding of the Ninth Session.

Conclusion

Considerable progress had been made at the Eighth Session, not least in the First Committee work on the ISBA regime. Several issues within the mandates of the Second and Third Committees had been effectively settled. The partial revision of the ICNT in Geneva was an undoubted advance. Although it was disappointing that further revision at the end of the session was not achieved, useful progress had been made also in New York. However, much important detail in regard to the ISBA regime was still outstanding and two of the Second Committee core issues were still unresolved. The outer limits of the continental shelf and delimitation of marine zones between neighbouring states were both vital issues for Ireland. Unexpected and disturbing problems had arisen in the former in New York, threatening to undermine the value of the incorporation of the Irish amendment in the ICNT Rev. 1 in Geneva. The delimitation issue remained intractable, and the delegation and its allies were at full stretch in seeking to preserve the ICNT provisions that were generally, if not totally, satisfactory. There were also some vital and sensitive unresolved questions in the PSD provisions and the final clauses. It seemed that the Conference was entering the endgame. The delegation would be faced with the difficult and delicate task of ensuring that a final surge for settlement of outstanding issues would not involve changes adversely affecting Ireland's interests.

A personal event affecting a member of the delegation again intruded. Ray Keary's mother died suddenly during the Geneva meeting and naturally he returned home immediately. This happened at a week-end, and his expeditious departure meant that his delegation colleagues did not have an opportunity to sympathise with him.

Chapter XII

NINTH SESSION

The Ninth Session of the Conference was held in two parts, at the United Nations headquarters in New York for five weeks, from 3 March to 4 April 1980, and at the Palais des Nations in Geneva for five weeks, from 28 July to 29 August 1980.

Preparations

The Irish delegation, as Chairman, convened two intersessional meetings of the Margineers, in Geneva in November 1979 and in New York in January 1980, with a view to preparing a text on the ridges problem (in the formula for shelf outer limits identification) for the Ninth Session. Both were attended by the author and Geraldine Skinner. Although not convinced by the Soviet Union insistence that there was a real problem, the Margineers felt that they would have to deal with it in a way that would protect their interests while avoiding the criticism, as at the Eighth Session, that their response to the Soviet position was an effort to extend their areas of shelf jurisdiction beyond what was permitted by the Irish formulae. All the Margineers except India attended both meetings. A text that had emanated from exchanges between the Soviet Union and the UK and the US was promising in that it specified that prolongation could be invoked in respect of ridges of a continental nature. However, it also provided that only the 350-mile cut-off (150 miles beyond the exclusive economic zone (EEZ)), and not the alternative cut-off of 100 miles beyond the 2500-metre isobath, could be applied to those ridges, with the exception of features ('plateaux, banks and spurs') proposed by the Margineers at the Eighth Session. The Margineers generally, and Ireland particularly, were dissatisfied with that provision and prepared their own draft based on an Australian proposal. This draft, while maintaining the existing informal composite negotiating text (ICNT) Rev. 1 exclusion of the deep ocean floor and its oceanic ridges from shelf jurisdiction, expressly included elevations ('such as plateaux, rises, banks and spurs') that were natural components of the margin, ensuring that jurisdiction on those features would be determined in accordance with the formulae in the Irish amendment and either of the alternative cut-offs. (For Irish interests application of the isobath cut-off was essential.) It was agreed by the nine Margineers present, including a reluctant UK, and the US, which was also pursuing its concerns otherwise. The Irish delegation kept the tenth Margineer, India, informed of the proceedings.

Evensen also convened, in Geneva in November, an informal meeting on final clauses to advance the work undertaken by the group of legal experts under his chairmanship at the resumed Seventh Session. There was a good attendance from the 40 invitees, including Ireland in the person of Geraldine Skinner. Amendment and reservations were among the topics discussed, but not participation or provisional application. Evensen subsequently produced texts, based on these discussions, for the consideration of the legal experts at the Ninth Session.

The EEC meetings continued intersessionally (under the Irish Presidency until the end of 1979). The Inter-Departmental Committee (IDC) also continued to meet.

INSTRUCTIONS

Following the IDC deliberations and consultation as usual with other interested departments, a submission on instructions was made by the Minister for Foreign Affairs to the Government on 26 February. It was much briefer than its predecessors, seeking confirmation of existing instructions on most issues. These included two unresolved issues of vital interest to Ireland, continental shelf and delimitation, as well as marine scientific research (MSR) where there was an anxiety in regard to the proposed text on MSR on the shelf outside the 200-mile zone. It suggested supplementary instructions on the EEZ and the international seabed area (ISBA) regime.

Exclusive economic zone and fisheries

Concern was expressed that the ICNT Rev. 1 provisions on land-locked and geographically disadvantaged states (LLGDS) access to fishing resources in the EEZ of neighbouring states was not confined in all circumstances to the surplus, a concern said to be shared by the UK and Denmark among our EEC partners. This was not consistent with the EEC reaction when the text, which was subsequently incorporated in the revision, emerged from Negotiating Group 4 at the Seventh Session. The EEC had concluded at that time that it would not be affected by

LLGDS rights because it would have no surplus, and had no developing land-locked neighbours who might have rights not confined to the surplus. Moreover, Denmark on behalf of the EEC, had welcomed the text in the negotiating group and the Second Committee at that stage. Looking back it seems that the concern could only have been based on a rather strained interpretation of the Rev. 1 text. It does not seem to have been based on anxiety that the Romanian amendment proposed at the end of the Eighth Session (that would give LLGDS access to the EEZ of another region if there was a scarcity of fish in their own region) might become irresistible. The submission also raised the possibility of seeking an amendment (presumably to Rev. 1) at the stage of formal amendment, although indicating that this would be unlikely to succeed and would probably be counter-productive.

International seabed area

On the ISBA regime, confirmation of support for a strong authority, for compulsory peaceful settlement of disputes (PSD) and for emerging consensus on the outstanding issues was again proposed. In addition a few of the issues were selected for supplementary instructions. Thus support was suggested for (i) provisions on production limitation that would not inhibit a supply of essential minerals at a fair price; (ii) initial financing of the Enterprise through state loans determined in accordance with the UN scale of (subscription) assessments; (iii) a voting system in the council that would protect the interests of minorities, including seabed miners; and (iv) future review of the system of exploration and exploitation to be carried out by a conference with a generally acceptable mandate. As it was not at all clear how the details of (ii) would work out it was proposed that the Department of Finance would be consulted before any proposal was supported (although the Irish position was unlikely to have much influence on the outcome).

Reference was made to the plan that the Conference should conclude at the Ninth Session, although it is clear that the delegation was again sceptical about the prospect of that being achieved.

The Government by decision dated 28 February adopted the instruction proposals.

DELEGATION

By prior arrangement, Ambassador Kennan left the delegation at the end of the Irish EEC Presidency and the author was appointed head of delegation for the Ninth Session. The delegation no longer included delegates dedicated to covering the EEZ, fisheries and anadromous species (salmon), preservation of the environment and transfer of technology (TOT) as these issues, like several others in the Second Committee, had effectively been settled. Because there was no formal agreement on any part pending agreement on the whole, it was necessary to keep a watching brief on these issues in case of an unexpected reopening or other development (for example in regard to LLGDS rights). Geraldine Skinner, then legal adviser in the Department of Foreign Affairs, continued to join in dealing with the Second Committee issues, also serviced the topics dealt with directly in Plenary (PSD and final clauses), and maintained a watching brief on the First Committee and on effectively settled issues in the Third Committee. Mr Aidan Mulloy, counsellor in the Mission in New York, looked after the servicing of the First Committee at the New York meeting, a task taken over by Philip McDonagh, First Secretary in the Mission in Geneva, at the resumed session. Thus Justin Dillon was no longer on the delegation. Assignment of Agnes Breathnach from the Department of the Taoiseach (to which the National Board of Science and Technology (NBST) was attached) to cover MSR restored the delegation's capacity to follow more closely, and to influence, the negotiations on this important topic. David Naylor from the Geological Survey of Ireland (GSI) continued as a vital delegate on the continental shelf issue. Matthew Russell from the Office of the Attorney General again attended for part of the session.

The Minister for Foreign Affairs, Mr Brian Lenihan, attended briefly at the Geneva part of the session as special representative of the Government. He had meetings with Conference President Amerasinghe, Conference Secretary-General Zuleta, Second Committee Chairman Aguilar and the heads of the US and the Soviet Union delegations as well as heads of other key delegations (see below).

GENERAL

Proceedings in the First and Second Committees and their negotiating groups were delayed by the late arrival at the session of the two Committee Chairmen. Interest groups took the opportunity to consult internally and, in some cases, with their opposing groups, during this time. The Irish delegation was engaged in internal consultations in the Margineers, the G-29 on delimitation and a group on MSR. The other nine Margineers were involved in efforts to allay Indian misgivings about the ridges text agreed by the other Margineers intersessionally. Meanwhile the US continued to pursue their concerns on this problem directly with the Soviet Union. EEC meetings dealt mainly with the 'Community clause', and with MSR on which the EEC-9 were seriously divided.

PLENARY

It was confirmed that the objective of the session was that the informal negotiations would be finished in New York. A plenary debate at the end of the meeting on the proposals for revision of the ICNT Rev. 1, and subsequent revision by the Collegium in the light of that debate, were also planned. In Geneva there would be a formal debate on the revised text leading to a Draft Convention and its subsequent adoption. In the event only a partial revision (Rev. 2) was effected after the Plenary debate at the end of the New York meeting. Some weeks elapsed before it was issued. Further revision was effected at the end of the Geneva meeting following a similar procedure. The Collegium, in conformity with the stated objective but to the dismay of many delegations, labelled this revised overall text as the Draft Convention (informal text), rather than just as Rev. 3. Ireland made statements in each of the Plenary debates on revision. In view of the nature of the debate and the time limitations imposed, the New York statement, made on 2 April, was confined mainly to dealing with matters of direct and vital interest. These were continental shelf jurisdiction, delimitation and regime of islands, MSR and the 'Community clause'. A brief endorsement of the other Second Committee Chairman's proposals for revision was also included. The Geneva statement, made on 26 August following effective settlement of some of those issues, was more expansive. It started with a warm welcome for the general progress made by the Conference and a hopeful view of the prospects of an early and successful conclusion, and went on to deal specifically with delimitation and the 'Community clause'.

At the beginning of the session the Group of 77 (G-77) again protested at seabed mining legislation that had now been enacted in the US and the Federal Republic of Germany (the FRG). The same arguments were made as before on both sides, with the US pointing out that their legislation would not come into force until 1 January 1988, allowing plenty of time for the proposed convention to enter into force in the meantime.

SECOND COMMITTEE

Exclusive economic zone and anadromous species
Although Negotiating Group 4 had been wound up, the LLGDS sought continuance of negotiation on their rights of access. In the Committee the amendment proposed by Romania at the Eighth Session, which would give LLGDS rights of access to the EEZ in another region if there

was a scarcity of fish in their own region, was pursued by many LLGDS. It was opposed again by coastal states, and by the EEC through its Italian Presidency. The EEC did not pursue its concerns about the ICNT Rev. 1 text on LLGDS rights of access. Argentina and Canada proposed coastal state rights, mainly for conservation, outside the EEZ for straddle fish stocks, i.e. stocks that were mainly inside the EEZ but extended beyond it. It was opposed by the EEC, rejecting in principle any extension of coastal state fisheries jurisdiction outside the EEZ. Neither the Romanian nor the Argentina/Canada proposal drew sufficient support to be proposed for incorporation in the revision. Argentina and Canada continued to pursue their proposal at the Geneva meeting and produced several progressively moderated amended versions of it. The last of these met with the approval of Ireland, Denmark and UK but not of other EEC members, so the EEC opposition was maintained. Eventually it was agreed that the EEC would not oppose that version but it was not then pursued by the sponsors. The only revision to the text on the EEZ or fisheries at the end of the New York meeting (ICNT Rev. 2) related to marine mammals and there was none at the end of the Geneva meeting (Rev. 3).

Continental shelf

On the definition of the outer limits of the continental shelf the Soviet Union was still seeking to cut off jurisdiction measured from continental ridges at 350 miles from the baselines without allowing application of the alternative cut-off of 100 miles from the 2500-metre isobath. The Arab Group was now willing to accept jurisdiction outside the EEZ but only on the basis of a simple distance limit. The LLGDS were unwilling to engage in discussions, possibly because they no longer had a united position on this issue. The Margineers meanwhile had slightly amended their intersessionally agreed text, changing the order and omitting the listing of features, to meet an Indian concern. This new text was presented to Chairman Aguilar on his arrival. At his request, a technical presentation was made to him to demonstrate that the Soviet Union ridges text would negate the isobath alternative cut-off, which was an essential part of the compromise reached and incorporated in the ICNT Rev. 1 at the Eighth Session. When Negotiating Group 6 met, the Soviet Union tabled their own ridges proposal, portraying it as a defence of the ISBA. The Arabs indicated their flexibility.

Chairman Aguilar met the Margineers and gave them a text on ridges received from the Soviet Union and described as previously agreed between the Soviet Union and the UK and the US—in fact the text that had been put before the Margineers by the UK and the US at their intersessional meeting, with which the Margineers were not fully satisfied. The Soviet Union had indicated to him that it would accept this text if it was unchanged and if there was no further discussion of other elements (presumably the boundary commission and revenue sharing). Chairman Aguilar advised the Margineers that this offer was their best basis for a solution and that they should respond to it by devising only minimum suggestions for changes to this text. After an initial demurrer, voiced by the Irish delegate, the Margineers agreed to examine the text and respond. They addressed particularly difficulties affecting Australia, New Zealand and the US, and also Irish concerns to maintain application of the isobath cut-off. The difficulties of the former two were met by adding rises and caps to the list of natural shelf components in the Soviet text (as in the Margineers text prepared at their intersessional meetings)—clarifying that the isobath cut-off would apply to them. The Irish geological expert felt that the Soviet text introduced unwelcome complications to the article but assessed that, with the Margineers' changes, the Irish concern for application of the isobath cut-off would also be adequately protected. The delegation, in the light of this technical assessment, accepted the amended text. The US difficulties could not be resolved by the Margineers but were pursued directly by the US with the Soviet Union. Any remaining Indian concerns were also pursued otherwise (see special arrangements for limits in the Bay of Bengal below). The Irish delegate presented the amended text to Chairman Aguilar as comprising the maximum concession to which the Margineers would not object. After some clarifications the Soviet Union accepted it.

In the meantime there were parallel exchanges between the Margineers and the Soviet Union on the draft annex on a Commission on the Limits of the Continental Shelf (boundary commission) that the latter had prepared at the Eighth Session. The Margineers supported this draft when the Soviet Union accepted their wishes for a longer period (ten years) within which the coastal state must make its application, and for a longer term of office (ten years) for the Commission members. A US suggestion to amend the shelf article so as to give the Commission recommendations more force was rejected by the other nine Margineers. The text was given to Chairman Aguilar and tabled in Negotiating Group 6 without sponsors. Poland proposed amending the article on the shelf so that the coastal state would have to identify its limits 'on the basis of' the Commission's recommendations rather than just 'taking account of' them, if the identification was to achieve binding status. This was supported by a number of delegations, including those of the US (not surprisingly), the Soviet Union and some LLGDS.

Suggestions of higher revenue-sharing rates were largely ignored.

After consultation with the various interested parties, Chairman Aguilar presented the Irish delegation with a compromise package. Its elements were (a) the Irish amendment as in ICNT Rev. 1; (b) the ridges text accepted by both the Soviet Union and the Margineers; (c) the Annex on the Commission as proposed by the Soviet Union (in agreement with the Margineers), but with only a five-year term of office for its members; (d) an amendment of the shelf article in regard to the Commission's recommendations as proposed by Poland; (e) revenue sharing as in ICNT Rev. 1. When he subsequently tabled this package in Negotiating Group 6 the Margineers acquiesced in it. Despite Arab Group objections and queries from other (mainly LLGDS) delegations, it was generally supported, and Chairman Aguilar decided to submit it to the Plenary as suitable for incorporation in the revision. Meanwhile the US, pursuing its own concerns with the Soviet Union, was considering making, with Soviet acceptance, an interpretative declaration in Plenary to cover application of the ridges text to features on the Chukchi Plateau off the coast of Alaska. Some Margineers, particularly Australia and New Zealand, were disturbed by this, and felt that it made it difficult for them not to do likewise in regard to features off their coasts. Margineer efforts to dissuade the US proved unsuccessful. The Irish delegation, as Margineer Chairman, forewarned Chairman Aguilar and the Soviet Union delegation that the possibility of further interpretative declarations by other Margineers could not be excluded. When Chairman Aguilar submitted the package in Plenary, it was described by the Irish delegate as acceptable to his delegation as a revision, if also accepted by the other parties. The package was largely supported by most of the Margineers, including the US, and also by some other coastal states, by the Soviet Union and by most Eastern European Group (EE) members. Only the US made an interpretative declaration. Argentina, Canada and the UK protested at the proposed amendment in regard to the boundary commission recommendations. Canada also objected to the revenue-sharing rates. The EE diluted its support by disagreeing with the amendments of the Soviet Union ridges proposal added by the Margineers. The package was subsequently incorporated in the ICNT Rev 2. (Surprisingly, the Polish amendment in regard to the Commission's recommendations was not included— an apparent oversight rectified later in Rev. 3) The Irish delegation reaction was one of relief that the definition was finally incorporated in the Conference text in a formulation that despite the unwelcome complications that had accrued to it, would preserve Irish continental shelf jurisdiction interests.

At the Geneva part of the session it was accepted that Negotiating Group 6 had completed its work. Chairman Aguilar's statement in the General Committee that all the Second Committee issues had been settled, except delimitation between neighbouring states, was not disputed. However, he did have to resist pressure, mainly from the Arab Group, for further discussion of the shelf issue in the Committee. He did not submit any Committee Chairman's report to Plenary, where the Arab Group sought to re-open the issue, unsuccessfully. Meanwhile, although the Sri Lanka problem was not covered in the New York package it was mentioned in the Committee Chairman's report there. It evoked sympathy both among the Margineers and in the Conference generally. The Soviet Union was willing to accept the Committee Chairman's suggestion to deal with it in a statement of understanding by the Conference President (in an annex to the Conference final act) as to how to apply the provisions in the Bay of Bengal, but only if it applied exclusively in regard to Sri Lanka. The Margineers were supportive of Indian claims that the statement should apply also regarding India. In consultations with Sri Lanka and India before the Geneva meeting the Soviet Union relented. At Geneva the Irish and Australian delegations assisted the Sri Lankan delegation in preparing a draft of the proposed statement of understanding, and counselled caution in regard to any attempt to amend the boundary commission annex in case it might lead to re-opening. The draft statement eventually proposed in the Committee, and subsequently in Plenary, by Sri Lanka, concentrated on special application of the convention provisions in the Bay of Bengal, and no proposal was made regarding the boundary commission annex. There was no opposition and virtually no reaction from other delegations.

Delimitation

At the beginning of the session the Chairman of Negotiating Group 7 (Judge Manner) on delimitation held separate meetings with the two interest groups and others. He told the Irish delegate that he intended to concentrate on the criteria element as there was majority support for the drafts for the other two elements, interim measures and settlement of disputes—in fact these two elements received little attention. In the meeting with the G-29 it was again explained to him that the group could not be expected to accept erosion of the current state of international law on criteria as identified by the International Court of Justice (ICJ) in the North Sea cases or restoration of the 1958 rule that the ICJ had characterised as not generally applicable. Thus no downgrading of the role of equitable principles or enhancement of the role

of the median line in comparison with their roles as set out in the judgement of the ICJ would be accepted by the group. He offered two
successive drafts, both of which the group rejected. The first was an
amendment of the ICNT Rev. 1 provision to move it closer to the 1958
rule. The second, which provided merely that delimitation should be
'in accordance with international law', was considered by the group to
be inadequate. He then offered a third draft that would add a reference
to international law to the ICNT provision. This was examined in the
group, but also rejected when the Chairman advanced an interpretation
of it inconsistent with the group's position. This draft received a mixed
reception in the opposing interest group. When Negotiating Group 7
met, the co-sponsors of document NG 7/2 opposed the ICNT provision and claimed interlinkage between the three elements. The G-29
rejected the Chairman's two drafts even as a basis for negotiations,
denied that there was any rationale for interlinkage of the elements and
opposed inclusion of any drafts in the Chairman's report. At the insistence of the Committee Chairman the report was read in the
Committee. However, in place of a debate on substance there was a
dispute as to the forum for further negotiations. The Committee was
favoured by the G-29 and Plenary by the opposing group. The report
described the ICNT Rev. 1 Paragraph 1 on criteria as not providing a
basis for consensus because of opposition by the sponsors of document
NG 7/2. Inconsistently, it offered as a basis for consensus a draft that
had not been discussed in the negotiating group, but was effectively
the same as the first draft rejected by the G-29. The report also covered
the other two elements (interim measures and settlement of disputes),
putting forward the drafts that had emerged at the Eighth Session. In
the Plenary debate on revision the sponsors of document NG 7/2 opted
for incorporation of the Manner drafts on all three elements in the revision and were supported by some neutrals and, disappointingly, by the
US and the Soviet Union. The G-29 opposed incorporation. The Irish
delegate's statement argued that the Manner draft on criteria did not
meet the Conference guidelines for revision, and that in fact only the
ICNT provision had been accepted by both sides as a basis for negotiation. Surprisingly, the Manner drafts were incorporated when the
revision (ICNT Rev. 2) emerged after the session, apparently due in
no small part to off-stage representations by the US and the Soviet
Union. A reservation by the Second Committee Chairman in regard
to this Collegium decision was added to the accompanying memorandum. News of the decision leaked before the document emerged and
several of the G-29, through their Permanent Representatives to the
UN (PRs), made protesting representations to the Conference

President (including the Irish acting PR, in moderate terms). Later these PRs collectively, despite Irish hesitations that it might be counterproductive, sent a letter to the President. This protested that the revision of the criteria provision was not in accordance with the guidelines for revision adopted by the Conference, and would hinder rather than help negotiations. On delivery of the letter by the Irish (acting) PR the President's reaction was negative in tone but devoid of substance. He mentioned a need for a new procedure. In July he had an inconclusive long-distance telephone conversation with the author on the question of procedure.

When the session resumed in Geneva, the G-29 met almost daily to consider how they could recover from the New York setback. Reactions of members were measured. The Irish and Turkish delegations privately agreed that the revised text was not so unfavourable that its deletion should be sought if amendment proved impossible. In this context they decided that they would endeavour to ensure that criticism of the revised text would avoid attributing an unfavourable interpretation to it. They also concluded that there would be at best, at such a late stage of the Conference, only one opportunity to improve the text, and that great care should be exercised in identifying, and availing of, that opportunity. A Turkish private request to the US for its assistance in seeking amendment was refused. Both the US and the Soviet Union lobbied the Irish delegate to steer the G-29 towards acceptance of the revision, arguing (i) that the text reflected the ICJ decision and (ii) that the controversy was jeopardising the success of the Conference with the likely consequence of loss of benefits for Ireland in other parts of the Draft Convention. The Irish delegate did not find either argument convincing and both interlocutors were politely put off. At the opening meeting of the Plenary the Irish delegate, despite warnings of being out of order by the President, succeeded in reading in full the letter delivered to the President in New York, as a preliminary to an explanation of the G-29 position. The delegate's request to have the letter circulated as a Conference document was, not surprisingly, abruptly refused. In an early subsequent bilateral meeting with the Irish delegate the President offered, helpfully, to have the letter reproduced in full in the summary record of the meeting. The opposing group, presumably pleased that the revised text was for them an improvement on its predecessor, feeling that it probably had the support of a majority at the Conference, including the US and Soviet Union, and fearing that they could only lose ground in any further negotiation, were reluctant to engage. Rejecting proposals of the President and the G-29 to continue negotiations in, respectively, a new negotiating group or the

Committee, they insisted on Negotiating Group 7. When the President said the group was *functus officii*, they suggested procedural discussions. Reversion to the Second Committee was also rejected by the President who, however, indicated that the status of the Rev. 1 provision was equal to that of the Rev. 2 provision. The members of the G-29 were conscious that the majority of Conference delegations uninvolved in the issue were concerned only that it should be resolved, and that this should be achieved through compromise, as with other issues. It would be difficult to convince them that, uniquely in this particular field affecting only bilateral problems that involved vital interests, a compromise provision in the convention inconsistent with the existing law would not be justifiable. The G-29 needed to have negotiations in some form to secure a change, and the Irish delegate engaged in wide representations to that end. Six delegates from the group (Irish, Argentinian, French, Libyan, Turkish and Venezuelan) coordinated efforts towards an informal negotiation. These efforts were greatly assisted by representations by the visiting special representative of the Government, the Minister for Foreign Affairs, Mr Brian Lenihan, who, in meetings with the President, the Second Committee Chairman, the US and the Soviet heads of delegation and others, emphasised the need for changes to the text on criteria (although, very competent and experienced lawyer that he was, he felt the existing text was tolerable for Ireland).

Eventually, after the President's proposal of a new group petered out, it was agreed that a limited number of delegations from both groups would meet under the joint chairmanship of the group coordinators (Irish and Spanish delegates) to exchange views on all aspects of the topic. The delegates selected from the G-29 (mainly by the Irish group Chairman with a view to combining prominent and capable interlocutors with worldwide representation) were those of Ireland, Algeria, Argentina, France, Libya, Madagascar, Morocco, Pakistan, Turkey and Venezuela. From the other group the delegates were those of Spain, Chile, Colombia, Denmark, Greece, Japan, Malta, Nigeria, the UK and Yugoslavia. The meetings were held daily for six working days from 12 to 19 August and attracted considerable attention from non-participating delegations, partly because there was at the time little other public activity at the Conference. Three meetings were devoted to criteria, one each to interim measures and settlement of disputes. The exchanges developed into question and answer sessions, with delegates on either side posing questions and responding at will. On the G-29 side one question posed concerned the significance attached by the other side to the reference in the criteria text to international law. The response was that it would prevent exaggerated interpretation of the term 'equitable principles'. A delegate from that group questioned the relevance of the ICJ decision, since it was provided in the ICJ Statute that its decisions were binding only on the parties to that particular case. The Irish delegate responded that the ICJ had in its decision identified the generally applicable principles of law binding on all, an identification that could hardly be questioned in view of the authority of its source. Acrimonious exchanges between the Greek and Turkish delegates were defused through exercise of restraint by the latter. On interim measures the Irish delegate supported the ICNT provision as the best available, and he did not comment on settlement of disputes. The exchanges on interim measures revealed that more substantive content suggested by each group was unacceptable to the other, and that the ICNT provision was the only viable solution. The co-sponsors of document NG 7/2 claimed that compulsory and binding settlement procedures were essential, and that the three elements were linked. The G-29 rejected the linkage, and some members individually rejected binding settlement procedures. At the sixth and final meeting the Irish delegate presented a summary report of the exchanges that had been generally approved by the Spanish delegate. Nevertheless, due to the unwillingness of the opposing group to give it to the Committee Chairman, a joint report was not adopted. The Irish delegate gave a written report both to the Committee Chairman and the Conference President. It was believed that the Spanish delegate reported orally to the President. The Irish perception was that the G-29 had had the better of the exchanges, at least in regard to the criteria element. However, the difficulty lay in profiting from that advantage, particularly as the opposing group again stalled on any follow-up. That group rejected a proposal for establishment of a group comprising fewer delegates from the two groups together with US and the Soviet Union delegates, with the last two to prepare a text on the basis of the discussions. The Irish and Spanish delegates met and compared drafts, following which an Irish compromise draft was prepared that both agreed to put to their groups. The draft included references to (a) international law, making it the basis for determining equitable principles and (b) the median line in the sense that it could be employed only where appropriate. Both references were intended to maintain the predominance of the equitable principles criterion while meeting the declared preoccupation of the opposing group that there should not be an exaggerated interpretation of equitable principles. There were alternatives in the wording of the reference to circumstances. Both delegates were hopeful that the draft would provide the basis for a solution. The Irish delegate had secured that both the US and the Soviet Union would support the draft if it were accepted by both groups, and had checked that it was acceptable also to Second Committee Chairman Aguilar. The G-29 was at first inclined to accept the draft, but the inclination eroded when Venezuela (Aguilar's delegation) firmly rejected part of it. In the other group the reaction was mixed (possibly to some extent because it was presented as an Irish rather than a joint proposal) and particularly by the UK. The effort thus failed. In the subsequent Plenary debate on revision the two sides repeated their positions on the New York revision. The Irish statement identified the text on delimitation criteria as the only part of Rev. 2 to which Ireland had to object. For the G-29 it again argued that the New York revision was not in accordance with the guidelines for revision and that, as the group had feared, it had proved to be a disincentive to negotiation. Even signs of grounds for agreement, which had eventually emerged from belated exchanges between the two groups, had been ignored by the supporters of the revision, whose reluctance to negotiate seriously was deplored. Nevertheless it was hoped that these grounds could be built on in the future to achieve consensus. The opposing group reasserted their view on linkage of the elements. Disappointingly the Soviet Union again supported the New York revision despite the events at Geneva, as did 'neutral' Peru. New Zealand for the first time supported the G-29 position, and did so in strong terms. The revision effected in Geneva did not include any change to the delimitation text. However, the President's accompanying memorandum (in response to private Irish representations) recorded that one of the interest groups strongly objected to the text on criteria and that the issue was unresolved. This was a slight mitigation of the status acquired by the text through its survival into the 'Draft Convention (Informal Text)' that was the result of the revision. Opinions in the Irish delegation as to whether any improvement could be achieved in the future were divided.

Regime of islands

The regime of islands was not discussed at all at the session. Delegates, including the Irish delegate, who had proposed amendments to the provision at earlier sessions (to make it more clearly consistent with their delimitation position) requested in their New York statements in Plenary that it be taken up again. They also worked at both meetings at preparing a letter on the subject to the President. They eventually decided that the time was not opportune and deferred action. These delegates also had some doubts about raising the issue in this manner against the wishes of the Committee Chairman, and were fearful that a failed attempt at amendment could detrimentally affect the interpretation of a provision that was actually lacking only in specificity. It was not mentioned by the Irish delegate in the Geneva Plenary statement.

THIRD COMMITTEE

Marine scientific research

The debates on MSR continued to be difficult in regard to the regime on the continental shelf beyond the EEZ. The US and the FRG, in particular, pushed strongly to change the text that the Committee Chairman had submitted at the Eighth Session. This text excluded from the coastal state consent regime the area outside 200 miles, except for resource-related research in areas designated by the coastal state, and in which exploitation or exploration operations were current or imminent. The change they sought would remove the exception for resource-related research, thus excluding the consent regime completely from the shelf area outside 200 miles. This change was strenuously opposed by coastal states group members, notably Brazil, Canada, Norway and Ireland, who conversely sought that the consent regime applicable within the 200-mile zone (to all research) should apply throughout the whole shelf. Argentina, Australia, New Zealand and the UK took the coastal state line but less strenuously and with varying objectives. The Irish delegate was among the most active throughout the negotiations. Successive drafts tabled by the Chairman moved gradually towards the coastal-state position. His final draft retained the two-tier regime as in his Eighth Session text, but with amendments so that (a) the coastal state could trigger the consent regime merely by designating at any time, and details of operations taking place or planned in designated areas would not be required; (b) its designation could not be called into question in PSD procedures (in Part IV); and (c) the provisions on MSR were stated to be without prejudice to coastal state rights over the continental shelf as set out in the convention. In addition, the provisions on the coastal state's right to suspend or terminate a research project were clarified in its favour. The provision (in Part IV on PSD) that decisions on suspension, termination and withholding of consent could be referred to conciliation only would be retained. Ireland, regarding this package as having preserved almost all of the substance of ICNT as carried into its Rev. 1 (despite presentation as a two-tier regime), supported it in the New York debate on revision. It was incorporated in ICNT Rev. 2. Between the New York and Geneva meetings, the Department of Industry and Commerce identified a drafting fault in the text that could lead to an interpretation detrimental to coastal-state interests. At the instigation of the Irish delegate, a clarifying drafting amendment was made in Geneva, on the basis of unanimous acceptance that was achieved only through weeks of intensive lobbying of interested delegations, mainly by the Irish delegation. It was incorporated in the revision from which the ICNT Rev. 3 emerged.

The Committee Chairman felt at the end of the session that negotiation on all its topics (MSR, preservation of the environment and TOT) had been completed but kept the Committee at the disposal of the Conference. All the relevant texts were carried through into the ICNT Rev. 3—Draft Convention (Informal Text).

FIRST COMMITTEE

International seabed area

A significant breakthrough was made on the ISBA regime at the session, leaving at its end only a relatively small number of difficult problems to be resolved. Among the matters on which progress was made were (i) financing of the first exploitation venture of the Enterprise; (ii) rules on decision-making in the council; (iii) production policy; (iv) transfer of seabed mining technology to the Enterprise and developing countries; (v) financial terms for contractors; and (vi) the review conference. The group of 21 (G-21) commenced the work but devolved the negotiations on individual items to smaller working groups. Consultations between the Committee Chairman and working group coordinators were effective particularly in regard to (iii), (iv) and (v) above. An almost complete set of provisions was incorporated into ICNT Rev. 2 at the end of the New York meeting although it was recognised that the provisions would require further negotiation in Geneva.

The revised provisions, particularly those covering (i) financing of the Enterprise's first exploitation venture and (v) financial terms for contractors, were discussed at meetings of the EEC-9 between the two parts of the session. Regarding (i), it had been agreed at the first part that financing would be through interest-free loans from (convention) contracting parties and commercial loans. Most members, including Ireland, favoured setting out in the convention the amount of the necessary investment rather than leaving it to a recommendation of the proposed preparatory commission (see below), but others opposed seeking this change. There was concern about the consequences if the potentially larger contributors did not ratify or delayed ratification. Yet a deferment of payment pending their ratification could give them a veto. Scaled payment was mooted. Regarding (v), some seabed miners wished to reduce the fees and charges. Most considered the existing levels as the best attainable, but two members insisted they were excessive and would prohibit investment. No common positions were reached.

Following negotiation at the Geneva part of the session a full range of texts emerged. The following matters *inter alia* were covered. All parties to the convention would contribute financially to the authority (and would be members of its assembly). On financing of the Enterprise, the latest provisions still left the amount, and criteria for its adjustment in the light of experience, to be determined by the preparatory commission. This solution was adopted to meet opposing concerns in the context of current inability to estimate reliably the amount that would be needed. The G-77 feared a convention provision might prove over-restrictive and prevent Enterprise exploitation, while the industrialised countries feared excessive obligations would discourage states from becoming parties. Contributions would be calculated on the same basis as state contributions to the UN, those of non-UN members and provisions for shortfall to be determined by the assembly of the authority by a decision to be reached by consensus. The solution had the advantage that a state ratifying after the preparatory commission had dealt with the matter would have a reasonable estimate of the costs involved. As to decisions in the council, these would be taken by two-thirds or three-quarters majority or consensus, according to the issue, and lists of the respective sets of issues were drawn up. If an unlisted issue arose it would be required to be assigned, by a consensus decision, to one of the lists. Half of the membership of the council would be filled by interest groups, for example investors, consumers, exporters, etc. As a consequence the Western industrialised countries would have a blocking minority on at least some issues, provoking an unsuccessful demand for a similar capacity for the EE. On production policy it was provided that nickel production (the most threatening to land-based producers) would not exceed a proportion of future increase in consumption. This provision was criticised by producers and consumers, both regarding it as imbalanced to their disadvantage. Likewise developing countries considered a vague provision for compensation or economic adjustment as inadequate. Contractors' fees were unchanged.

Despite some reservations these texts were incorporated into Rev. 3—Draft Convention (Informal Text). Clearly a very significant advance had been made and there was renewed optimism that agreement was within reach. The Irish delegation was satisfied with the texts and happy at the progress made.

PLENARY

Preamble

In informal plenary at the beginning of the session the convention draft preamble was discussed for the first time. Immediately a difference of approach emerged between industrialised states that favoured a brief, non-controversial preamble, and the G-77, which sought a longer version with many recitals, including references both to the NIEO (new international economic order, a UN General Assembly plan for assisting underdeveloped countries) and to the General Assembly Declaration on the ISBA as the common heritage of mankind. The President proposed a text longer than that in the ICNT Rev. 1. It included references to the Declaration and to the special needs of developing countries but not to the NIEO. This was generally acceptable and was incorporated in ICNT Rev. 2 in New York and carried through into the Draft Convention in Geneva. It was not discussed again at the Conference and was included in the convention as finally adopted.

Peaceful settlement of disputes

Much work at the session was carried out in a legal experts group, particularly in regard to First Committee matters; in exchanges between the groups on delimitation; and in the Third Committee on disputes arising in regard to MSR. Already a number of fora had been identified as potential instances for binding procedures according to choices of the parties, including the International Court of Justice (ICJ), the proposed International Tribunal for the Law of the Sea, arbitration tribunals and, for particular sectors, special procedures (similar to arbitration tribunals). Where necessary the details of these fora and procedures were set out in annexes. The main achievement at the Geneva meeting was the reorganisation of the provisions into three sections comprising, respectively, voluntary procedures, compulsory and binding procedures and limitations and exceptions to the latter. The reorganised text was incorporated into the Draft Convention. In fact there were no further deliberations on these provisions that were included in the convention as finally adopted by the Conference.

Final clauses

On final clauses the legal experts group, assisted by the efforts of the informal intersessional meeting, continued its work in New York, dealing with the mostly non-controversial issues for example ratification, relationship with other conventions, denunciation and, cursorily, entry into force. The group also dealt with two of the more controversial items, reservations and amendment. The ICNT Rev. 2 carried over the provisions from Rev. 1, while still leaving blanks on the number of ratifications/accessions necessary to bring the convention into force, and the interval between achievement of that number and entry into force. In Geneva there was a sense of urgency that final clauses should not lag behind, and most subjects were addressed in informal plenary, but not participation. Provisional application did not feature.

The text incorporated into the Draft Convention covered also signature, reservations and declarations, relationship of the convention with other treaties, amendment and denunciation, as well as developing the ratification/accession and entry into force provisions. The convention would be open for signature (subject to ratification) for 24 months from the opening date. It would enter into force twelve months after deposit of the 60th instrument of ratification/accession. Larger and smaller figures had been proposed, and a veto considered but rejected. For a country ratifying/acceding later, the convention would enter into force 30 days after its ratification/accession. No reservations would be permitted except where authorised in a substantive provision. This approach anticipated adoption of the convention as a package and preservation of the package, while enabling for example the delimitation problem to be settled by authorised reservation that would not affect the package ingredients. Declarations not affecting the legal effect of provisions (as in international law) would be permitted.

The provision on relationship with other treaties followed international law (as set out in the 1969 UN Vienna Convention on the Law of Treaties) after an argument as to whether it was necessary.

Three methods of amendment would be allowed, all subject to a minimum interval of ten years from entry into force. Amendment of provisions on activities in the ISBA would be adopted through approval of the council and the assembly of the authority, and would require ratification by three quarters of the convention parties. It would come into force for all convention parties twelve months after that required number was achieved. The council would be obliged to ensure that the mandate of the review conference on system of exploration and exploitation would not be bypassed. Amendments to other convention provisions would generally be adopted by a conference requested to be convened by a party to consider amendment proposals, provided that at least half of the parties consented to the request within twelve months. This conference would have the same decision-making procedures as UNCLOS III. The amendments would require ratification by 60 parties or two thirds of the parties (whichever was greater), before entry into force for ratifying parties 30 days after this number had been achieved. For these other provisions there would also be a simplified amendment procedure. A proposal for amendment through this procedure would be circulated to all parties. It would be deemed to be adopted if no party objected within twelve months. If there was an objection to the amendment or the procedure, the request would be deemed rejected. If the amendment were adopted it would be subject to the same entry into force procedures as an amendment adopted by a conference. This relatively complex set of amendment procedures was obviously devised to protect the convention package, and particularly the ISBA regime, against unravelling by a self-interested majority, while enabling adoption of changes that became widely acceptable in the light of experience of the practical application of convention provisions. These proposed final clauses were incorporated into the Draft Convention. They were supported by the Irish delegation as they met its concerns in this field.

Participation and the 'Community clause'

Of course a further concern for EEC members still survived within the difficult subject of participation, i.e. that of enabling participation by the EEC. Ireland and the other EEC members had continued their lobbying for inclusion of the 'Community clause', led by the Italian Presidency at the first part of the session and by the Netherlands at the second part. These two also engaged in private consultations with many delegations, including such key delegations as the US and Peru. The Netherlands, in a statement during the deliberations, indicated the EEC's willingness to elaborate its draft (as tabled at the Eighth Session by the Irish Presidency) to meet concerns encountered during lobbying and consultations. These elaborations would deal with (a) provision of information on transfer of competences; (b) prevention of increase in representation resulting from the EEC becoming a party; (c) the situation if the EEC were a party and some of the member states were not; (d) respective responsibilities of the EEC and/or its members for implementation and applicability of PSD procedures; and (e) reconciliation of EEC special treatment between its members with their convention obligations. Neither Rev. 2 of the ICNT nor the Draft Convention incorporated a 'Community clause'.

The Transitional Provision (on not fully independent states) was carried into ICNT Rev. 2 and subsequently into the Draft Convention unchanged and still appeared in an un-numbered article after all the other articles. It was dealt with in consultations by the President with interested parties. There was also a link of this issue with participation in the convention of entities lacking some of the characteristics of states.

DRAFTING COMMITTEE

Although formal drafting was effectively on hold pending the negotiating text reaching virtually final form, the Drafting Committee met informally during the session and for three weeks in June between the two parts of the session. It sought to harmonise the language and terminology of the various texts that had emanated from various sources within the Conference and also, with the assistance of the language groups, to achieve linguistic concordance between the six language versions. Some Drafting Committee texts were submitted to the Second and Third Committees during the session.

PLENARY

It was concluded that a further session would be needed at least to address the few issues still clearly outstanding, including delimitation; participation; some ISBA matters, including a mandate for a preparatory commission (to prepare for establishment of the ISBA authority and the new tribunal) and preparatory investment protection (i.e. of prior investment in seabed exploration) on which the US had made a proposal; and examination of the proposals of the Drafting Committee on the final text of the Draft Convention. It was intended that the text, as so finalised, would be given the status of a formal proposal to the Conference, with the consequence that further procedures, including any proposals for amendment, would be formal. A work programme for the session was drawn up accordingly. Adoption of the convention was anticipated at the end of this procedure, followed by a signature session in Caracas before the end of 1981. The Plenary accordingly recommended a session of six to seven weeks in New York from 9 March, 1981. It also recommended a seven-week meeting of the Drafting Committee before the session.

In the early days of the session the staff of the Irish Mission and the delegation members were shocked by the sudden death of Ambassador Paul Keating, the Irish Permanent Representative (PR) to the United

Nations. It was particularly shocking for Aidan Mulloy, his deputy at the Mission. The writer, as a headquarters Assistant-Secretary in the Department of Foreign Affairs during Paul Keating's term as Departmental Secretary-General, had become a close friend. On a practical level Aidan Mulloy's responsibilities increased as acting PR, making his duties as a member of the delegation much more of a burden. Nevertheless he coped admirably.

Chapter XIII

TENTH SESSION—FIRST PART

Contrary to expectations at the end of the Ninth Session, the Tenth Session was again held in two parts, the first part at United Nations headquarters in New York for seven weeks, from 9 March to 24 April 1981.

PREPARATIONS

The Inter-Departmental Committee (IDC) continued its meetings in Dublin, but less frequently in view of the advanced stage of the negotiations on issues of national interest, including effective settlement of most of them. The EEC meetings also continued (with ten members from 1 January 1981 when Greece became a member). The deliberations were confined almost entirely to the 'Community clause' and the international seabed area (ISBA) regime. On the 'Community clause' the EEC Commission was fearful that as framed it might not enable EEC participation in the proposed preparatory commission (which was intended to make preparations for establishment of the (ISBA) authority and the International Tribunal for the Law of the Sea).

In EEC consultations on the ISBA regime the issue of seabed mining transfer of technology (TOT) was controversial. The Commission and Belgium were concerned that that the obligations went much further than positions adopted in ongoing negotiations on TOT under the auspices of the UN Commission on Trade and Development (UNCTAD). They feared that any UNCLOS III concessions would be invoked in those negotiations. The others felt that TOT obligations to the Enterprise were part of the parallel system of exploitation and as such *sui generis*. However, most were incensed by the inclusion in the text of the 'Brazil clause', which imposed a TOT obligation towards developing countries exploiters that they did not regard as an essential part of the parallel system. Belgium and the Commission proposed objecting to both provisions and making the 'Brazil clause' a deal breaker. The situation was complicated by the fact that TOT was not within EEC competence, and there were conflicting views (even in Irish civil service circles) on the extent to which common EEC positions had been adopted in the UNCTAD negotiations. The Irish delegation consulted the Department of Foreign Affairs economic division, which in turn consulted the Department of Industry and Commerce. After some exchanges among these three they all accepted that (i) the general provisions on TOT in the Draft Convention were consistent with the positions taken by developed countries in the UNCTAD; (ii) the seabed mining TOT provisions were *sui generis* and were not relevant to the UNCTAD negotiations; (iii) insofar as they related to the Enterprise they were an essential part of the parallel system that was in turn a vital part of the Draft Convention compromise, and Ireland could accept them; and (iv) the 'Brazil clause' was not an essential part of the parallel system. Accordingly, Ireland could accept the provisions mentioned in (i) to (iii). It could join its EEC partners in opposing the 'Brazil clause' (as not being an essential part of the parallel system) but not to the extent of making it a deal breaker. (It could in fact be argued that the 'Brazil clause' was justified by the UN General Assembly Declaration of Principles, with its support for special benefits for developing countries from exploitation of the ISBA. Moreover the transfer required would be on commercial terms, the technology could be used only on the site for which it was given and it could not be transferred to a third party. In short, even the obligation under the 'Brazil clause' was not particularly onerous.) Production limitation, to protect land-based mineral producers, was also discussed in EEC consultations, but, in the context of Canadian efforts to enable it to be more restrictive, the discussions were inconclusive.

In November, the Conference Secretariat sent a letter to all participants seeking any available data relevant to its efforts to assess the funding necessary to enable the first Enterprise exploitation. Ireland had no relevant data to furnish.

Ireland and Turkey exchanged views on how to progress the negotiations on delimitation. Ireland also made representations in Moscow and Washington in regard to its concerns about the delimitation texts that, however, failed to elicit any offer of support.

INSTRUCTIONS

Following the usual consultation with IDC departments and other interested departments, the Minister for Foreign Affairs made a submission to the Government on 23 February. It indicated that such issues as the exclusive economic zone (EEZ), anadromous species (salmon), continental shelf jurisdiction beyond 200 miles, marine scientific research (MSR), preservation of the environment and even regime of islands had been effectively settled in terms acceptable to Ireland. On delimitation of marine zones the Department of Foreign Affairs delegates sought and obtained the approval of the Minister for Foreign Affairs (who had become familiar with the state of the negotiation during his visit to the second part of the Ninth Session) on detailed proposals for reaction to the revised text. In his submission to the Government this text was assessed as not really damaging to Irish interests, although less favourable on criteria for delimitation than its predecessor. It was suggested that the possibility of improvement of the criteria provision should be explored. However, this course should not be pursued if it were impracticable or risked unfavourable amendment, and the existing text should not be specifically opposed. (This suggestion was of course consistent with, but less detailed than, the more detailed proposal approved by the Minister).

International seabed area

The submission anticipated that the negotiations would be completed, and placed most emphasis on further consideration of production policy, financial contributions to the Enterprise and the mandate for the preparatory commission. There was no specific mention of seabed mining TOT, existing instructions being clearly adequate. The submission proposed confirmation of instructions to support proposals likely to lead to consensus provided they were not inconsistent with more detailed instructions.

Final clauses

Within the context of final clauses, specifically participation, the 'Community clause' was referred to, and naturally confirmation of existing instructions to promote and support it was proposed. The concern of the Arab states, in particular, to permit participation of liberation movements was also mentioned.

The Government by decision dated 27 February accepted the proposals.

DELEGATION

The delegation was further reduced in the light of the progress on issues, particularly those of direct national interest. Mr Micheál Ó Cinnéide, First Secretary in the consulate in New York, serviced the

First Committee. Effective settlement of the continental shelf limits and MSR issues relieved David Naylor and Agnes Breathnach from the burden of attendance. The writer was free to concentrate on the Second Committee where delimitation was the main concern. Geraldine Skinner covered the informal plenary and the Drafting Committee as well as assisting on the Second Committee. Thus Joseph Hayes also left the delegation. A watching brief was also kept on matters in the Third Committee.

GENERAL

Two significant pre-session events seriously affected the session. The Conference President, Ambassador Amerasinghe, died suddenly in December 1980. His death both deprived the Conference of his adroit leadership and posed the by no means simple problem of finding a generally acceptable and similarly equipped successor. Even more disturbing in the context of Conference progress was a US press release, only five days before the opening of the session. It indicated that the new Reagan Administration intended to review the Conference text, about which it had serious concerns, and would not be in a position to complete negotiations at the session. This short statement was issued in a low-key manner. US media, having investigated further, portrayed it as signalling dissatisfaction with the provisions on the ISBA regime, prompted by major corporations that had plans for deep seabed mining. The apparent perception was that the text did not adequately ensure access for US industries to seabed minerals on fair and reasonable terms. The new US Senate was also regarded as dissatisfied, and it was reported that the US Defense Department had withdrawn its previously strong support for the Conference text generally. This development immediately, and to the dismay of most participants, undermined the plan to complete negotiations at the session. The writer learned of it just before leaving Copenhagen on 5 March *en route* to New York. His early departure was in response to a request to attend, as coordinator of the G-29, at a pre-session informal meeting of the General Committee on 6 March. This meeting was intended to preview the prospects, and related planning, for completion of the negotiations at the session. Prior to the US announcement delimitation was regarded as the most obviously intractable substantive issue. At this meeting the author expressed the view that the delimitation negotiations could be completed provided they were seriously undertaken immediately, and was supported in this view, if less than enthusiastically, by the Spanish coordinator of the opposing group. Of much greater general interest to most at the meeting was the statement by the acting US head of delegation. He explained that the review by the Reagan Administration did not mean that they were refusing to continue negotiations, but only that they were unwilling to finalise negotiations or enhance the status of the text at the session. Unfortunately, this proved not to be a well-founded explanation. Over the weekend, before actual commencement of the session, the acting head of delegation and some other US delegates were relieved of their offices. The opening of the session featured a less forthcoming US attitude. A new head of delegation was immediately nominated but not officially appointed for some time.

At the informal meeting it was also reported that the Asian Group, despite lengthy consultations, had not yet reached any position on the appointment of a new Conference President. Lack of a President to provide leadership was a serious disadvantage, particularly in the light of the situation arising from the US stance.

Interest groups met as usual, particularly at the beginning of the session while Conference meetings were in abeyance, pending developments on the Presidency vacancy and the US stance. The Irish delegation participated in the G-29 on delimitation, the smaller group concerned about the regime of islands and the Margineers. The EEC members also met regularly at heads and delegates level to consider the developments, to seek common positions where possible and particularly to plan for promotion of the 'Community clause'.

PLENARY

The UN Secretary-General, as temporary Conference President, opened the session on 9 March. The Plenary adjourned immediately, on the sole grounds, at least overtly, that the Asian Group needed further time to select a candidate for President. Meanwhile the world press took up the news, and the *Financial Times* particularly speculated whether the US intended to bring the Conference to an end. As elsewhere, newspapers in Ireland focused on the situation. Discussions on the possibility of a common démarche to the US by the EEC members revealed a wide divergence of attitudes among them. This was highlighted by a Danish proposal, with Irish support, that the EEC-10 should indicate support for the existing text, a proposal that some partners would not support. The Western European and Others Group (WEOG) rejected the proposed holding of a meeting of the General Committee under the chairmanship of a Vice-President in the absence of a President, but later accepted convening of a meeting of Plenary, which in the event proved irrelevant. In the meantime there were two candidates for Presidency in the Asian Group, Ambassadors C.W. Pinto of Sri Lanka and Satya Nandan of Fiji, both prominent Conference personalities. A Conference vote loomed with the possibility of emergence of a Latin American candidate also, probably Second Committee Chairman Ambassador Aguilar of Venezuela. In the event, and fortunately for the Conference, the two named Asian candidates withdrew in favour of Ambassador T.T.B. Koh of Singapore. He was approved by the Asian Group—despite efforts against him by the Soviet Union, according to rumour. Ambassador Koh was elected President by acclamation at the Plenary meeting on 13 March. The first week of the session had been taken up with this problem. Tributes to the late President, Ambassador Amerasinghe, were paid in Plenary on 17 March.

On 17 March also the President proposed to Plenary a two-week programme of work based on the plan adopted at the end of the Ninth Session. It comprised (i) continuation of work by the Drafting Committee; (ii) consideration of Drafting Committee reports in informal plenary; (iii) examination by the First Committee of provisions in regard to the preparatory commission on the basis of a draft resolution prepared by the President and the Chairman of the First Committee; (iv) consideration, also in informal plenary, of participation (after consideration of the Drafting Committee reports); (v) consultation between the two interest groups on delimitation; and (vi) Second and Third Committee meetings on a few other (unspecified) topics. Preparatory investment protection (PIP) was not included, although it had been mentioned among the outstanding issues at the end of the Ninth Session. (The US withdrew the proposal it had submitted on the topic at that session). The meeting featured some, albeit low-key, criticism of the US stance, together with appeals that its planned review be completed quickly. The Netherlands EEC Presidency, speaking for the EEC and its members, sought to distance them from the US stance without being critical of it, and urged both continuation of the work from where it had been left off and its completion as soon as possible. This statement was agreed by the EEC members to avoid individual and probably conflicting statements. In fact they were fundamentally divided. Belgium, France, the Federal Republic of Germany (the FRG) and Italy tacitly welcomed the US action as affording an opportunity for changes to the ISBA regime, even at the risk of failure of the Conference; Denmark, Greece, Ireland and the UK were dismayed, viewing it as a threat to the emergence of a convention. The EEC statement also appealed for early completion of the US review and continuance of the negotiations. President Koh's attitude was that work should continue normally as planned, with a view to adoption of a convention before the end of the year. He expressed the hope (which he probably did not seriously entertain) that the review would be completed before the end of the session (i.e. the current meeting, as then intended). The newly nominated US head of delegation (Ambassador James Malone, who was believed to be among US officials who had always been sceptical about the desirability of a convention) defended the US action, indicated he could not say when the review would be completed and was generally negatively non-committal.

Meanwhile the Irish delegation in a meeting with US delegates (including the nominated head) learned that the review process had begun, that the review group did not include any former delegate or current delegate other than the new head, that some of the group were inimical to UNCLOS or any other UN process, and that all aspects would be considered in the review, including the desirability of having a convention. Thus there was no delegation position on any question of substance and it was not known when there would be. The Irish delegation expressed concern that delicate compromise settlements on many difficult issues, reached with great effort over many sessions, might be jeopardised. Ireland also made representations to the US, through the US Embassy in Dublin and the Irish Embassy in Washington, urging early completion of the review, without receiving any relieving assurance. The Taoiseach raised the matter at a European Council meeting without evoking any significant reaction.

A second two-week programme of work was adopted at a plenary meeting on 31 March. It mainly provided for continuance as earlier proposed, and specifically arranged for, *inter alia,* a meeting of informal plenary on participation, one meeting of the Second Committee and two consultation meetings between the interest groups on delimitation. The President regretted that there had as yet been no delimitation meetings, and privately the Collegium had urged settlement of the delimitation issue, not least because that would be a sign of progress at the Conference. There was still no indication as to when the US would be in a position to resume negotiation.

It was decided at the Plenary on 10 April that the meeting should continue for a seventh week until 24 April, but with only Drafting Committee meetings and no substantive negotiations during that last week.

SECOND COMMITTEE

Delimitation

The G-29, meeting in the early days of the session, were concerned to secure continuance of negotiations on delimitation. There was initial reluctance by the opposing group to engage. That group's Spanish coordinator privately explained this as due to a fear that, in view of the uncertain future of the Conference, any compromise reached might be re-opened later. It seemed likely that the group also felt that, in the event of a collapse of the Conference, it would suit them to have the Draft Convention text, even if contested, as the Conference text. This would be preferable, from its members' point of view, than a text that might be reached by agreement and that would therefore, by definition, be less favourable to them. There was a further difference in regard to which text should be the basis of consultations. The G-29 favoured the draft prepared at the end of the Ninth Session (actually by the Irish delegation after consultation with the Spanish coordinator of the opposing group), although some members had problems with part of it. The coordinators met to discuss possible procedures and that draft, *inter alia*. The opposing group was critical of several aspects of that draft and insisted on the Draft Convention text as a basis—which the G-29 regarded as having resulted from an invalid revision. At a private discussion on 24 March, involving also members of the opposing group, the Conference Secretary-General Zuleta, Ambassador Nandan and a senior US delegate, the Irish delegate described the current situation in the exchanges. He also referred to the serious twin, if opposite, dangers of, on the one hand, over-haste and, on the other, deferment of, or procrastination on, the issue. Zuleta undertook to seek to emphasise in the Conference framework that the issue was still outstanding. (Subsequently it was mentioned by the President in a press conference and was included in the work programme he proposed on 31 March.) Under pressure from the President and in accordance with an agreement between the coordinators, a basis was found on 27 March to resume consultation the next week. These would take place in the co-chaired assembly of 20 delegations that had discussed the issue at the Ninth Session, and each side would be free to refer to any text. Four meetings were held altogether, starting in the fourth week. Morocco tabled a useful text on criteria at the beginning that preserved the G-29 basic position while seeking to address the preoccupations of the opposing group. The discussion at first centred on the question of a reference to international law in the criteria provision. The G-29 agreed to accept such a reference provided it was clearly drafted to achieve a purpose acceptable to both sides i.e. in their view as a guide to interpretation of the term 'equitable principles'. The opposing group reacted inconsistently to this offer. In particular Denmark was anxious that the reference should also cover other ingredients, for example prolongation as mentioned in the International Court of Justice judgement. That group's members were reluctant to depart from the Draft Convention text, and expressly resisted early completion of the negotiations. After the second meeting the G-29 participants were frustrated at what they perceived as time-wasting by the opposition, and the group strongly favoured resort to the Second Committee Chairman and/or the President. Accordingly, the Irish delegate reported to the Committee Chairman and, with others of the G-29, called on the President on 9 April. They explained the rationale of their negotiating position, their consequent concerns about the formulation in the Draft Convention and doubts about the willingness of the opposing group to engage seriously in negotiations. This appeared to be understood and elicited a promise to urge realism on the opposing group. At the next meeting that group seemed to show some flexibility on the formulation of the reference to international law. Other aspects of the criteria provision were also discussed, featuring merely a repetition of previous exchanges. The President consulted separately with delegates from the two groups (including the Irish delegate) on the possibility of his intervening. The Irish delegate advised caution on any action unless it was clear that the opposing group was ready to settle. Otherwise any text proposed would be rejected by that group and thus lost for any future settlement attempt. No progress was made at the fourth meeting. The Co-Chairmen prepared separate reports when the Spanish coordinator refused to convey a joint report to the Committee Chairman as well as to the President. The Irish report recorded the hopes of the coordinators, based on their assessment of the exchanges, that a consensus text could be achieved. When the Committee Chairman's report (which did not cover delimitation) was debated in Plenary, the Irish delegate specifically rejected, on behalf of the G-29, a suggestion by the Soviet Union that the two groups were moving towards acceptance of the Draft Convention provision. Some other members of the group also made this point. Clearly a stalemate continued.

Regime of islands

As planned, the Committee held (four) informal meetings to enable discussions on other matters. Those delegations, including Ireland, that would have welcomed improvement of the provisions on regime of islands, prepared a letter to be sent to the President. This was intended to set out their concerns about the text and to seek an opportunity to have a thorough discussion on the topic. In the event it was decided not to press for consideration of the topic at that stage, but merely to signal their wish to have it discussed later. This was influenced by an expectation that a change could not be achieved at that time, whatever about prospects later. Accordingly, a letter was not sent. After some subsequent hesitations the topic was in fact mentioned (by Algeria), in Plenary rather than in the Committee.

Continental shelf and the exclusive economic zone

The Margineers, meeting early in the session, decided to oppose strongly any re-opening of the continental shelf issue. This proved not to be necessary, and in the Committee the Irish delegate merely spoke generally against re-opening any fundamental issue. The Nepal proposal for a common heritage fund had additional sponsors but no significant additional support. It was opposed by Peru on behalf of the coastal states group (CSG). A proposal by the UK, in the context of the continental shelf and the EEZ, to soften the obligation to remove completely abandoned installations, attracted growing support from other delegations, including the Irish delegation. According to this proposal, complete removal would be required only if necessary to ensure safety of navigation or preservation of the environment, or to avoid hampering exercise of fishing or other rights. The proposal on straddle stocks by Australia and Canada drew vehement opposition from the Soviet Union.

Straits

A proposal, having the support of about 50 states, that exercise by warships of the right of transit passage through straits should be subject to prior consent or at least notification, was unacceptable to the major maritime powers, particularly the superpowers. The Soviet Union was particularly vociferous in objecting.

The Chairman's report dated 6 April was brief, vague and extremely cautious. Nevertheless, it expressed the view that there was consensus on the overall package. He accepted that further discussion of a few items might be needed in the future. (While these were not identified it was clear that the UK proposal on installations was included and the UK delegate mentioned it in the Plenary debate.) Creation of any new working groups would not be appropriate. In the debate some delegations protested at his failure to acknowledge the alleged volume of support for their suggestions.

THIRD COMMITTEE

Only one informal meeting of the Committee was held. There was general acceptance of the Chairman's view that there was no need for further negotiation on the compromises reached (on MSR, TOT and preservation of the environment) as reflected in the Draft Convention.

FIRST COMMITTEE

Preparatory commission

Two formal meetings of the Committee heard many statements on the draft resolution on the preparatory commission (prepared by the President and the Chairman of the First Committee). These included one by the Netherlands, speaking for the EEC members, indicating general agreement with the draft. It was clear that negotiations would be needed to reconcile differences between the G-77 and the industrialised countries, and the matter was referred to the group of 21 (G-21). The US agreed to participate but not to make final decisions on the text. A G-77 proposal, that only convention signatories should be members of the commission and that final act signatories could be observers, was rejected by several large industrialised countries (although some of them subsequently accepted it). General agreement also seemed likely on a commission function to draft rules and regulations for the authority. Despite private consultations held by the President and the Committee Chairman, little progress was made on decision-making in or financing of the commission. A further formal Committee meeting discussed a UN Secretary-General's report on potential financial implications for parties to the convention, and concerns at the high estimated costs of the institutions were expressed.

Production limitation

Three African producers of land-based minerals, Zaire, Zambia and Zimbabwe, circulated documents on the topic. These indicated that production limitation based only on the supply of nickel would have disastrous consequences for their cobalt exports, on which their economies were very heavily dependent. At the request of the Committee Chairman, they were met by representatives of the EEC members. The latter responded negatively to the African proposals, and some of them were also critical of the Draft Convention provision. The Chairman concluded that broader consultations would be required.

Preparatory investment protection

A proposal by the UK to discuss PIP was rejected by the G-77 in view of the position of the US.

Seats of the Authority and of the Tribunal

The Committee also discussed for the first time the seat of the Authority for which there were three candidates, Jamaica, Malta and Fiji. The latter two unsuccessfully queried the Chairman's view that the topic was within the mandate of the Committee rather than Plenary. The discussion revealed strong support for Jamaica. The President held consultations with these candidates and the candidates for the seat of the International Tribunal for the Law of the Sea. He announced that all candidates had agreed that decisions on both seats would be dealt with in Plenary, in the third week of the resumed session.

DRAFTING COMMITTEE

The Committee had met intersessionally for several weeks and resumed work early in the session. It produced a report with successively appearing addenda containing recommendations on various parts of the text. The Irish delegation sent these immediately to Dublin seeking comments from the Departmental experts on the various topics (mostly delegates at earlier sessions) for its assistance in the discussions in informal plenary. Late in the session the Committee issued recommendations on some provisions of the ISBA regime. On some issues the Committee felt that proposals for change were substantive in nature and included these in a separate paper, which the delegation also sent to Dublin. It was not clear how, or even in which Conference body, it was proposed to deal with this paper.

PLENARY

Drafting Committee recommendations were considered in informal plenary beginning on 25 March. The Second and Third Committee Chairmen indicated that they had examined the recommendations in regard to the texts coming within their respective Committee mandates, and were satisfied they did not affect the substance. By 3 April all these recommendations had been processed. Some were returned to the Drafting Committee for further consideration and re-submission. Most other recommendations were adopted. The recommendations in relation to the First Committee (ISBA regime) were not reached.

Participation and the 'Community clause'

Negotiations on participation became more intense when the President held consultations with a number of delegations including the Netherlands (continuing to act for the EEC on the topic of the Community clause by arrangement with the UK Presidency) and the

Soviet Union. *En marge*, the EEC members engaged with the Soviet Union to respond to its concerns about the legal aspects of the 'Community clause'. In the fifth week the participation issue was examined in two informal meetings of plenary. The President identified the problematic issues of participation, respectively by entities not having all the attributes of states and by international organisations. The G-77 suggested that negotiations should be conducted on the basis of a mini-package, an idea that attracted both support (including that of the Soviet Union) and objections. The Netherlands introduced a redraft of the 'Community clause' (prepared in EEC coordination consultations) in more elaborate form. It sought to recognise the function of an organisation to implement the obligations of the convention in areas in regard to which competences had been transferred to it by its members, and to that end sought opening of the convention to participation by such organisation, through signature, etc. It also differed from the earlier draft in (a) seeking to deal with the objective of non-accrual of benefits by ensuring that a third party would not have any obligation, through a relevant organisation, to one of the organisation's member states not party to the convention; (b) providing that such organisation and its member states must on request give information of any relevant transfer of competences; and (c) making both such organisation and any relevant member state responsible in a dispute about implementation in the areas of transfer of competences. In its statement the Netherlands sought to reassure delegations having concerns on legal aspects (notably the Soviet Union). At the end of the debate the President undertook to hold further private consultations with the most interested delegations, which again included the Netherlands. In his report on 24 April (the final day) he suggested further consultations. The report's treatment of participation generally evoked objections from some delegations that were not satisfied their views had been adequately reflected, and the President agreed to consult with them and amend it accordingly.

Two meetings of plenary were required to reach a decision on a resumption of the session. The G-77, the African, Asian and Latin American and Caribbean (LAC) Groups and the Eastern European Group (EE) advocated a resumption lasting six weeks. The WEOG favoured a four-week meeting. The US preference was for no further meetings before 1982, as its review was not expected to be completed by autumn. They would agree to a three-week meeting in the autumn for consultations, but without negotiations or text formalisation. Clashes between the US and some of the G-77 ensued. It was eventually agreed that a resumption lasting four weeks would be held in Geneva from 3 August, with the possibility of a further week. It would be immediately preceded by a meeting of the Drafting Committee for five weeks from 29 June. The plenary so recommended to the UN General Assembly, which accepted the recommendation in due course.

CONCLUSION

It was extremely disappointing that the plan, which for once had not seemed overly optimistic, to conclude the negotiations at the session had to be abandoned. However, in the circumstances of the US stand-off, which had the potential to be fundamental, and of the need to elect a new Conference President, the Conference Bureau had done well to avoid a breakdown and to secure continuance of the negotiations, more or less on a business as usual basis. Nevertheless, progress on issues, not only the ISBA regime, was inevitably slowed by uncertainty about future developments. The threat of US withdrawal was not clearly averted, but its withdrawal had been made more difficult and less likely by the management of events. The US would be under pressure to re-engage, but some concessions to its interests in regard to the ISBA regime would clearly be required. For Ireland the adoption of a generally accepted convention continued to be a prime objective. Essentially its individual vital interests were adequately met by the Draft Convention. Even in regard to delimitation the text was not seriously inimical to its interests, and there were signs that some slight improvement might yet be achieved. In the resumption, further progress could only be sought on the few outstanding issues, other than the ISBA regime, so as to enable concentration on the latter when, hopefully, the US re-engaged.

Chapter XIV

TENTH SESSION—SECOND PART

The second part of the Tenth Session was held at the United Nations Office (Palais des Nations) in Geneva for four weeks, from 3 to 28 August 1981.

PREPARATIONS

The Inter-Departmental Committee (IDC) met between the two parts of the session, albeit briefly, as there was little to discuss as to policy, or even tactics, in the light of developments at the Conference. The EEC members met to discuss mainly the 'Community clause', and also developments in regard to the international seabed area (ISBA) regime, including the US stance. There was little hope of agreement on action on the latter as the members were fundamentally divided in their attitudes. However, there was broad agreement on the issues in regard to the preparatory commission and preparatory investment protection (PIP).

INSTRUCTIONS

In contrast with previous practice when there were two-part sessions, the Minister for Foreign Affairs made a fresh submission, dated 28 July 1981, to the Government on instructions for the second part of the session, after consultation as usual with other interested departments. This change was probably due to the fact that the US announcement of its review came after the Government decision on instructions before the session. In fact the submission indicated that no new or revised instructions were needed. It again listed the items of national interest on which provisions in the Draft Convention had been virtually agreed in terms acceptable to Ireland. It referred to the state of negotiations on delimitation, and assessed that the provision in the Draft Convention was not seriously inimical to Irish interests, but that improvement would be welcome. There was no mention of the regime of islands. It also described the situation with regard to the ISBA regime. It expected that the US review would not be completed in time to enable progress in Geneva, and anticipated the need for a further session the following year, when progress would again be dependent on the US attitude.

DELEGATION

The delegation comprised three members. The writer (head of delegation) was responsible for Second Committee matters, with assistance from Geraldine Skinner who primarily attended to informal plenary discussions. Philip McDonagh from the Mission in Geneva covered first Committee matters. A watching brief was still maintained on Third Committee issues and, in practice, there was considerable flexibility among the delegates on attendance at the various meetings.

GENERAL

As expected, the review not having been completed, the US delegation was not in a position to indicate what changes it would request, or even if it would support adoption of a convention. It was therefore unwilling to engage in negotiations, but desired consultations on matters of concern both to the US and to other delegations. It indicated that responses in such consultations would be fed into the review process. Pressed by the President, it agreed to make a comprehensive presentation of US concerns in Plenary on 5 August.

Interest groups resumed meetings, including the G-29 on delimitation and a smaller group on regime of islands; in both of these the Irish delegation was one of the parties. The EEC members also continued their regular meetings.

PLENARY

On the first day of the session the President proposed a programme of work comprising (i) continuation of the work on four outstanding issues (the preparatory commission, PIP, participation and delimitation) in their appropriate fora and (ii) informal plenary meetings at which the US concerns would be presented and debated (as distinct from private consultations as preferred by the US).

Peru objected to (ii), which it saw as providing for meetings to consider the concerns of one delegation, and was supported by the Soviet Union. Nevertheless, the US made its presentation on 5 August that merely listed areas of concern, all within the ISBA regime, without any indications of desired changes. It evoked an immediate Soviet Union response that accused the US of attempting to subvert the package, as comprised in the Draft Convention, which had been achieved with great difficulty over lengthy negotiations. On 10 August Pakistan, for the G-77 (who had consulted over the weekend), in a lengthy statement, also criticised what it labelled as the cavalier US attitude. It spoke of progressive erosion of the positions of the G-77 over several sessions. It proposed that the Conference pursue the work programme as determined at the end of the Ninth Session, i.e. negotiation of the four outstanding issues followed by formalisation of the Draft Convention. Unlike the G-77, the EE specifically objected to consideration of the US concerns and were supported trenchantly by Norway. Australia was also critical but more conciliatory, and favoured finding a way to discuss the US concerns. Delivery of an EEC common statement was regarded as impossible as it might require last-minute adaptation that would not be practicable. The Irish delegation sought and secured an understanding that, with a view to preserving the possibility of a later common stand, any individual statement would not depart from an agreed position. This position consisted of favouring consideration of the US concerns without associating with them. Four members spoke, including the Federal Republic of Germany (the FRG). Its statement specified provisions of the ISBA regime in which it wished for change. As these were also among the US concerns the statement was hardly consistent with the EEC members' understanding. (Consequently, and not surprisingly, further efforts at a later stage to agree a common statement by the EEC-10, as had been made at the first part of the session, failed.)

The President concluded that many delegations favoured consideration of the US concerns and the G-77 was apparently not opposed to doing so. He would therefore seek a venue for such consideration. He convened meetings of a number of delegations, including a meeting of the members of the G-21 at which, on 13 August, the US elaborated on its presentation. It rejected what it perceived as the absence of unrestricted rights of access for US companies to the ISBA and the more favourable conditions applicable to the Enterprise. It also questioned further fundamental features of the regime in the Draft Convention. The EEC-10 failed to agree a reaction, proposed by some of them, to the effect that certain fundamental provisions of the Draft Convention were not open to re-negotiation. Others of the EEC-10 were unwilling to say so. The G-77 response was one of dismay and a request for an adjournment. It was clear that the Conference was in serious crisis.

Various abortive private consultations were held, including a meeting of the Conference President with a number of Western delegations (among them the Irish delegation). Eventually the G-77 acquiesced in Plenary consultations, while indicating that they would not reply to the US. Three further Plenary exchanges featured more detail from the US, a statement by Pakistan (in an individual capacity) that was both general and critical, and efforts by some Western countries, including the Netherlands and Australia, to distinguish between fundamental and re-negotiable provisions. Pakistan's statement insisted that the US had fared at least as well as any other country in the compromises reached and incorporated in the Draft Convention, giving details to illustrate this premise. On 17 August, while these exchanges were continuing, the US additionally identified difficulties it had with the provisions for future review of the system of exploitation. In a formal meeting of Plenary Pakistan proposed formalisation of the Draft Convention at the end of the session, as originally intended. This direct opposition to the stated US position against enhancement again raised prospects of a serious stalemate threatening the viability of the Conference. The potential for breakdown was relieved by arrangement (by Keith Brennan, head of the Australian delegation) of a secret meeting on 23 August involving the US, some members of the G-77 and some Western countries, including the FRG, France and the UK. Following a full and detailed explanation of US concerns and some G-77 reaction, the US delegation agreed to report to its authorities that there was a willingness to distinguish between fundamental and re-negotiable provisions. The secrecy of this meeting was unusually well preserved, although the Irish delegation quickly became aware of it. The success of the Conference was obviously in the balance, depending on the reaction of the US authorities to their delegation's report.

SECOND COMMITTEE

Delimitation

On the first day of the resumed session the President met with the coordinators of the two interest groups (Irish and Spanish delegates) on delimitation, and exhorted them to resolve the issue at the session. The Spanish coordinator of the opposing group anticipated continued reluctance on their part in view of uncertainty regarding the Conference as a whole. However, after the groups had met separately on 4 August, the prospects were improved when the Spanish delegate indicated, during a meeting with the President the next day, that their group was prepared to conclude the issue. Further encouragement derived from an express Soviet wish to be helpful, and US indication of willingness to deal with this matter immediately and apart from their review. The Irish delegate, in welcoming these developments, explained the wish of the members of the G-29 to reach agreement. He explained, however, that the wish did not extend to accepting a solution that would be a vehicle for changing the existing law to their detriment. Agreement on procedure was reached at a further meeting with the President on 11 August. The coordinators would engage in direct consultations *ad referendum* to the interest groups. Moving to other procedures (but not the previous assembly of 20 delegations that the G-29 regarded as no longer useful) was not excluded. (A G-29 meeting on that date was attended also by the US, the Soviet Union and the FRG.) Three coordinators' meetings were held between 14 and 24 August, with the coordinators reporting to their respective groups after each meeting. The exchanges were devoted entirely to the criteria paragraph of the provision. Prospects were again boosted at the first of these meetings, when the Spanish delegate indicated that the reference to international law in the criteria paragraph, which the members of his group supported, was not intended by them to impose the 1958 convention delimitation provision on states not bound by it. The Irish delegate responded by welcoming this indication, and pointing out that the reference should therefore govern all the criteria and not only the equitable principles criterion.

The coordinators identified three objectives for their consultations, all in regard to the paragraph on criteria—(i) clarification of the reference to international law; (ii) a formulation acceptable to both sides on circumstances to be taken into account; and (iii) an overall construction of the provision acceptable to both sides. The Irish coordinator reported to the G-29 after each meeting and kept the Soviet and US delegations informed of the exchanges. Each coordinator submitted a draft on (i) (reference to international law), neither of which was fully acceptable to either interest group. The Spanish delegate responded fairly positively to an Irish suggestion to include in the reference a link to Article 38 of the Statute of the International Court of Justice (ICJ). That article, in specifying the sources of law to be applied by the ICJ, required its application of international conventions in a manner that would ensure that the 1958 convention rule on delimitation would not be binding on states not bound already by that rule. A formula proposed by the Irish delegate on (ii) (circumstances) was recommended by both coordinators. It was accepted fully by the G-29 and partially by the others. On (iii) (overall construction) each coordinator submitted a draft at their final meeting on 24 August. The

Spanish draft would subject both the equitable principles and median line criteria to similar limitations. This was so obviously unacceptable to the G-29, and so out of character with the preceding exchanges, as to seriously undermine in the Irish delegate's eyes any hope of reaching a settlement at the session (of which only four days were left), if at all.

The Irish delegate responded very positively when, later on the day of the final coordinators' meeting, the President's close collaborator, Satya Nandan, again suggested to the President that he should take an initiative. This change of response was influenced by: the pending revision and enhancement of the status of the Draft Convention at the end of the session (see below); the diminished prospects of an agreement between the interest groups that would enable amendment of the delimitation text to be included in that revision; the increase in difficulty of achieving any change to the existing delimitation text if carried over in the revision; and, finally, awareness of the secret meeting on the ISBA regime that made almost exclusive concentration on that regime likely at the next session. In short, the time for making the final effort had arrived. The fact that a President's initiative would involve taking the matter out of the control of the Second Committee was not sufficient reason to oppose it. The President put the idea of an initiative to the coordinators on 25 August, having listened to their account of their exchanges. Nandan proposed an approach to the criteria paragraph that would require agreement in accordance with international law, as referred to in Article 38 of the Statute of the ICJ, in order to reach an equitable solution. It would omit specific reference to any of the criteria (other than agreement), leaving them and the details of their interrelationship under the umbrella of the reference to international law. He gave an impromptu verbal draft. Both coordinators were personally positive and willing to submit the proposal to their respective groups, although each was also doubtful that dropping specific mention of the criteria would be accepted by his group.

Second Committee Chairman Aguilar also responded positively when informed by the Irish delegate of the proposed initiative. The proposal was approved, virtually unanimously, by the G-29 on 25 August, and approved broadly by the opposing group. When a written draft was put to the coordinators later its language was looser and, in the eyes of the Irish delegate, presentationally less satisfactory than the impromptu verbal draft. Nevertheless, it expressly required an equitable solution and tied the international law reference to Article 38 of the Statute of the ICJ. In a further meeting of the coordinators with the President the Irish delegate sought amendments, some of which were achieved (but not all) and secured that reservations would not be allowed. The Spanish delegate said his group's acceptance was conditional on that of the Soviet Union and the US, and to an understanding that existing provisions on delimitation of territorial seas, on regime of islands and on the conditions attaching to exception of delimitation disputes from settlement procedures would be retained. The Irish delegate, in response, said his delegation would not seek to change these provisions, but indicated that the G-29 was not concerned with the latter two provisions. He would mention the first of the provisions to the group but could not guarantee the reaction. He did not refer to the Soviet Union or the US who had clearly not been kept informed by the President. In the G-29 the written draft evoked considerable opposition and requests for further changes. The understandings sought by the other group were rejected. When the President met the coordinators again the Spanish delegate objected to any further change in the draft. When the Irish delegate put forward the proposals for changes as suggested in the G-29, they were rejected by the President as lacking legal significance. He indicated that he would withdraw his draft rather than re-enter negotiations on it. He also rejected the understandings submitted on the other side as irrelevant. Despite rejection of their proposals both coordinators agreed to urge acceptance of the draft in their respective groups.

The Irish delegation assessment of the text in comparison to that incorporated in informal composite negotiating text (ICNT) Rev. 2 and later carried into Rev. 3 (the Draft Convention) was as follows. The new text had the disadvantage of not having a clear substantive statement of the applicable law. Its advantages were: (i) the reference to international law imported the criteria as well as the priorities and qualifications as identified mainly in the ICJ decision in the North Sea cases; (ii) the tie to Article 38 of the Statute of the ICJ precluded the importation of the 1958 convention provision as between states not bound by it; and (iii) the equitable principles criterion enjoyed an echo, even if limited, through the stated objective of an equitable solution, whereas there was no such echo for the median line.

In each group a minority opposed the draft. In the G-29 Morocco, Romania and Venezuela were dissatisfied, but Romania said it would not object. Outside the groups the Soviet Union accepted the proposal, but the US objected that the substance of the draft was unacceptable. The US delegation lobbied the President not to present the draft and lobbied other delegations, including some in the interest groups, to oppose it. (The delegate of Turkey, in refusing the US request, reminded his interlocutor that the US had refused his request, at the Ninth Session, for assistance in seeking any change to the existing text.) The

US delegation portrayed the proposal as an additional threat to the success of the Conference, and was expressly critical of those involved in supporting it. The President rejected the US approach and was reported to believe (despite earlier US indications of willingness to settle the matter at the session) that the opposition was tactical, as a solution would leave the US concerns in regard to the ISBA regime as the main outstanding issue. The Irish delegation was not lobbied but heard that the US delegation was unhappy with the mention of the Charter Article, whose interpretation it regarded as controversial. China, also a supporter of the G-29 position, consulted with Ireland and was non-committal.

The President introduced the draft in Plenary as his own proposal (A/Conf.62/W.P.11) representing that it enjoyed widespread and substantial support in the two interest groups and in the Conference at large (the criterion for a revision of the Draft Convention text). The two coordinators spoke briefly to endorse this assessment as regards their respective groups. Faint hopes that there would be no further debate were disappointed when the US head of delegation spoke to oppose strongly. He attacked the substance and read to the meeting his delegation's interpretation of conversations with delegations from within both interest groups, implicitly casting doubts on the statements of the coordinators. The Soviet Union strongly supported the draft as a revision. Eight other delegations, including Venezuela from the G-29, some from the opposing group and China, requested deferral for further consideration. Some of these (not including Venezuela or China) were clearly responding to US lobbying. Twelve other delegations, including six from within the interest groups, spoke to support the proposal. Libya (a member of the G-29), without any prior warning, made a statement giving the text an interpretation clearly favourable to the G-29 position. Irish delegation fears that this would evoke a response and lead to a destructive debate were, surprisingly, not realised. In due course the Collegium, facilitated by the acquiescence of Second Committee Chairman Aguilar of Venezuela, despite Venezuela's opposition in Plenary, concluded that the draft had sufficient support to qualify as a revision. It was incorporated in the revised and enhanced Draft Convention.

Regime of islands

Ireland continued to consult with like-minded delegations on the regime of islands. These shared a concern that the basic provision that islands had the same maritime zones as continental territories might be applied in delimitation situations. Although two amendments to ensure prevention of this had been tabled (one by Ireland), these amendments would lapse if (as at the Ninth Session) there were no debate on the topic. The like-minded delegations again considered sending a letter on the topic to the President, and continuously redrafted it in the light of developments. However, it was not sent. As was apparent from the instruction submission, the Irish delegation was not very anxious about the existing provision, in which the exclusion of rocks and uninhabited islands from having an exclusive economic zone (EEZ) or continental shelf was, from the Irish viewpoint, a very important improvement on the corresponding provision in the 1958 convention. The delegation was aware that only a very small number of delegations would support either amendment, and that defeat could detrimentally affect interpretation of the provision. Re-opening could also jeopardise the exclusion. Moreover, the history of delimitation settlements featured treatment of islands in delimitation situations without undue regard to the regime of islands. Accordingly, failure to seek to debate the issue further was not regarded as unacceptable. This attitude was copper-fastened at the end of the session when, in the consultations on delimitation with the President, the Irish delegate undertook not to be involved in efforts to amend the islands provision.

Continental shelf, anadromous species and regime of islands

The Committee did not meet during the resumed session, with the implication that all the other issues (including the outer limits of the continental shelf, anadromous species (salmon) and regime of islands) had been effectively agreed. The texts on these issues were carried through into the revised and enhanced Draft Convention.

THIRD COMMITTEE

No meeting of the Committee was held during the resumed session, re-enforcing the Chairman's undisputed indication in New York that all issues in regard to preservation of the marine environment, marine scientific research, and transfer of technology had been effectively agreed. The existing texts were carried through into the revised and enhanced the Draft Convention.

FIRST COMMITTEE

International seabed area

Parallel to the consultations in informal plenary on the US concerns, the programme of work on ISBA issues continued, particularly on the preparatory commission. This was discussed mainly in the G-21, and on the basis of the draft resolution prepared at the first part of the session by the President and the First Committee Chairman. The G-77 proposed an alternative draft on 13 August that evoked strong opposition from the industrialised countries. At the end of the session progress had been made on organisational issues such as (i) that the preparatory commission would be established by a special Conference resolution; (ii) that it would be convened by the UN Secretary-General, who would also provide its secretariat; and (iii) that it would meet at the seat of the (ISBA) authority. Some of its tasks were also outlined. Membership, decision-making and financing remained controversial. The G-21 reported accordingly to the Committee at its only meeting of the resumed session. The FRG (possibly on behalf of the land-locked and geographically disadvantaged states (LLGDS)) proposed that the preparatory commission tasks should include establishment of the Commission on the Limits of the Continental Shelf. This conflicted with the Margineers position. Following Irish representations to the FRG delegation it did not pursue the proposal but it was nevertheless subsequently maintained by the LLGDS. The President and the First Committee Chairman prepared an amended text on the preparatory commission, including provisions on the issues on which progress had been made. However, as some elements were still controversial the text was not incorporated in the revision.

Efforts by the Committee Chairman to begin discussion of PIP failed in the face of US disinterest, EEC caution and G-77 unwillingness, all stemming from the US general position. The concept reflected a concern that entities that had invested in deep seabed mining exploration prior to entry into force of the convention, with a view to assessing the technical and economic feasibility of exploitation, should be given preference in authorisation of exploitation. No proposal was submitted by the interested industrialised countries. The EE was prepared to engage in discussions, although they claimed that they were not convinced that a provision was needed.

Several African countries proposed that production limitation should be on a combined nickel and cobalt basis instead of just nickel, following the concerns voiced at the Ninth Session. As compared with the provision in the Draft Convention this would have the collateral result of slowing nickel production significantly. A Conference Secretariat study of the impact of seabed production on the economies of developing countries was requested, ensuring that the issue would be live at the Eleventh Session. The Committee Chairman mooted a combination of measures as a solution, including compensation or economic adjustment assistance and commodity agreements.

DRAFTING COMMITTEE

The Committee had met for several weeks between the two parts of the session and continued its work throughout the resumed session. It submitted a large number of recommendations on the provisions on settlement of disputes and some on the provisions on conduct of activities in the ISBA. Many proposals from its language groups were yet to be considered by the Committee as well as some more difficult areas of the text, including most of the provisions on the ISBA regime.

PLENARY

The recommendations submitted by the Drafting Committee were accepted.

Seats of the International Seabed Authority and International Tribunal for the Law of the Sea

Many delegations, including some of the candidates, were not anxious to have a vote at the meeting to decide the seats of, respectively, the International Seabed Authority and the International Tribunal for the Law of the Sea. Nevertheless the President, in accordance with his announcement at the first part of the session, proposed to proceed to a decision by way of a declaratory vote on both seats in informal plenary, on the understanding, accepted by all the candidates, that those losing this vote would withdraw their candidatures. At the informal plenary meeting on 21 August his proposal was opposed and put to a vote. A roll call vote was held in which his proposal was upheld by a not very large majority. There were three candidates for each seat—Fiji, Jamaica and Malta for the authority and the FRG, Portugal and Yugoslavia for the tribunal. Ireland had given commitments to support respectively Jamaica (at an early stage when it was the only declared candidate) and its EEC co-member, the FRG. These were the winners of the votes. Each achieved a majority in the first ballot but not an absolute majority. Thus a second ballot, following elimination of the third-placed candidate, was required in each case to reach a decision. There was some advance concern at the impact of a decision by vote at a critical phase of the Conference, even if not on a substantive issue. However, the effect was to create a positive atmosphere, which was not an insignificant factor in reaching a settlement of the delimitation issue within a few days.

Final clauses—participation

The only aspect of the final clauses considered at the resumed session was that of participation. The President's report from the first part of the session was discussed in the early days. This dealt mainly with technical and legal criteria that would determine whether an entity other than a state would qualify for participation, leaving aside the political aspects. It was supplemented by an informal President's draft. On international organisations this draft differed from the EEC proposal in that (i) participation was not simply stated as a right but was couched in terms of entitlement to sign and become party by subsequent act of approval; (ii) approval was permissible only if a majority of the organisation members were party; (iii) notice of competences transferred to the organisation would be required, not only on request to the organisation or a member state, but also by declaration by the organisation at signature, and again as part of its instrument of approval—and later changes would have to be notified promptly both by the organisation and its member states; (iv) a member state could not exercise rights in an area in respect of which competence had been transferred; (v) a member state not party to the convention could not derive benefits from it through the organisation; and (vi) in case of conflict between the convention and the internal rules of the organisation, the former would prevail. There was little difference between the two texts in provisions prohibiting increase of representation or voting rights. The President's text did not deflect the opposition of the Soviet Union and the G-77. He engaged in more restricted consultations on this part of the topic, following which he circulated a revised draft text in which the conditions were comprised in an annex. There were some slight changes regarding notification of competences and there was more detail in regard to application of peaceful settlement of disputes procedures. It was generally acceptable to the EEC members, who decided to support it, subject to concerns about a few legal points that were subsequently conveyed to the President by letter.

There were also proposals for criteria under which self-governing and associated states and dependent territories could qualify to participate. Discussions on participation of National Liberation Movements (NLMs) were also confined to legal and technical problems. Clearly, the political aspects would have to be addressed shortly and, in that context, NLM participation would undoubtedly be linked by NLM supporters to participation by international organisations.

No drafts on any of these participation issues were incorporated in the revision. However, the final clauses covering other issues, as comprised in the Draft Convention (Informal Text), were carried into the enhanced Draft Convention (see below).

On 24 August it was decided that the session should end on 28 August without availing of a possible fifth week; that the Draft Convention would be revised and its status enhanced, but without ending informal negotiations or the possibility of informal amendment; and that a recommendation should be made to the UN General Assembly that the final and decision-making session (for adoption of the convention) be held in New York for eight weeks from 8 March 1982. Holding of the Signature Session in Caracas in September 1982 was anticipated. These progressive decisions, to which the US did not object, were probably facilitated by the secret meeting organised by Keith Brennan the previous day (see above). The EEC-10 had sought to prepare a common statement on the future of the Conference for delivery by the UK Presidency in Plenary, if appropriate. These efforts failed, in part because the final UK draft was rejected by the Irish delegation as failing to reflect most of the points it wished to have made. These included an assertion that certain provisions of the Draft Convention on fundamental issues were not re-negotiable. In the event an appropriate occasion on which such a statement could have been made did not arise. Revision was carried out by the Collegium and the enhancement took the form of dropping the words '(Informal Text)' from the title, whereby the text became the official Draft Convention at the Conference.

At the final Plenary meeting on 28 August a programme of work for the Eleventh Session was adopted. It provided for five stages comprising

(i) three weeks of consultations and negotiations on the pending issues;

(ii) three days of Plenary discussion of the results of the first stage consultations and negotiations, followed at the end of that fourth week by a further revision of the draft convention by the Collegium in the light of those discussions and the established criteria for revision;

(iii) a fifth week, during which
    (a) the Conference would decide when rule 33 of the Rules of Procedure would become operative, whereby submission of formal amendments would become appropriate;
    (b) the formal decision-making process would come into operation; and
    (c) delegations could consult their authorities on decision-making stages;

(iv) a week and a half for submission of, debate on and, if appropriate, voting on any formal amendments, and during which the President and Committee Chairmen would continue to seek general agreements; and

(v) a final week, during which the Conference would decide on the question of exhaustion of all efforts to reach agreement, adoption of the convention, the final act and other pertinent Conference instruments.

The clear signals that conclusion of the Conference was realistically anticipated were reinforced by a decision to seek authority for extension of the session only if the final decision-making stage had begun and more time was needed to complete the process. In due course the UN General Assembly accepted the recommendation to convene the Eleventh Session.

Chapter XV

ELEVENTH SESSION—FIRST PART

The first part of the Eleventh Session, which proved to be the final negotiating meeting as planned, was held at the United Nations headquarters in New York for eight weeks, from 8 March to 30 April 1982. It developed into an extremely active and eventful meeting.

PREPARATIONS

The preparations followed the usual pattern with meetings of the Inter-Departmental Committee in Dublin, although very few, and EEC coordination and cooperation meetings. The EEC meetings were concentrated mainly on the 'Community clause' and on the international seabed area (ISBA) regime. On the former the President's revised text presented at the Tenth Session, comprising an enabling provision in the convention and an annex setting out the conditions, was the focus of consideration. The Commission in particular felt that the annex provisions were excessively onerous in (a) imposing a condition that the organisation could become a party only if a majority of its members were party, and (b) requiring supply of information on transfer of competences. It also felt that provisions on (c) prevention of accrual of benefits to a member not party to the convention and (d) giving the convention priority in the event of conflict with internal regulations of the organisation posed legal problems for the EEC. The member states' delegations were sceptical of some of these views. Nevertheless, the Presidency sent an agreed letter to the Conference President in February indicating these difficulties, linking (a) and (c), and requiring clarification that information on allocation of competences could not be challenged. It also asserted that participation of international organisations was separate from participation of National Liberation Movements (NLMs) and from the proposed Transitional Provision on non-independent territories.

On the ISBA regime Belgium and Italy as well as the Federal Republic of Germany (the FRG), France and the UK, were supportive of the US stance whereas others, particularly Ireland, Denmark and the Netherlands, were to varying degrees less sympathetic to the US and more concerned about the threat to the success of the Conference. Although sceptical in advance about its prospects, Ireland supported a Danish proposal at a January meeting of the heads of delegations that the EEC members should adopt the role of bridge builders between the US and the Group of 77 (G-77). The proposal was rejected by those sympathising with the US. (The subsequent acceptance of the Danish proposal by the Scandinavians led to the formation of the group of 10/12 during the session—see below.) The FRG raised the ISBA issue in a meeting of the EEC Political Committee (EPC), supporting the US stance and favouring interim agreements between seabed miners. (There was even an ominous reference to the desirability of changes in other parts of the Draft Convention, including provisions on coastal state marine zones.) In December three commissioners presented to the Commission a working paper, ostensibly on supply of minerals from the seabed, but in fact extending into many other aspects of the ISBA regime. It had a paragraph proposing to the Council of Members wide-ranging guidelines for the ISBA negotiation—and even foresaw a role for the authority in definition of the continental shelf. It was briefly discussed at the January heads of delegation meeting, where some (including the Irish head) were more than doubtful about its content and utility, whereas others considered it useful. *En marge* of that meeting the heads were invited to lunch by one of the three commissioners who had presented the working paper, the commissioner having responsibilities for industrial development. Despite the host–guest relationship, the Irish head clashed with him over his persistent reference to the policy of those supporting the US stance as EEC policy. Unsurprisingly, this did not discourage the pursuit of the working paper as the basis of a commission submission to be made to the Council of Ministers, for adoption of EEC policy along those lines. In the commission only the Irish and Danish members opposed this proposal, while the UK members abstained, and it was sent to the council in February. *En marge* of another heads of delegations meeting in February, the heads were invited to attend the meeting of the Committee of Permanent Representatives (COREPER) at which the submission was examined before consideration by the council. The Irish head and some others explained their dissatisfaction with the proposal and COREPER subsequently suggested some changes to it. The council in due course approved an extremely modified version of the original, adopting a rather general policy directive. This was effectively to seek to ensure reasonable access for the EEC to seabed minerals and, to that end, to encourage the Conference to address the difficulties some countries had expressed in regard to some of the ISBA provisions in the Draft Convention.

The US review was completed at official level in December and submitted to President Reagan in January. Following his decision in February the US prepared a document entitled 'General Solutions' comprising a list of concerns and corresponding possible solutions. In an intersessional meeting at the end of February arranged by the Conference President (probably not attended by the Irish delegation) the G-77 rejected the document as a basis for negotiation.

A decision was reached by the International Court of Justice (ICJ) in a delimitation case between Libya and Tunisia. Not surprisingly it largely confirmed the decision in the North Sea cases. It found that in the circumstances of this dispute the prolongation principle was inapplicable to achieve a resolution. It affirmed that delimitation should be effected in accordance with equitable principles, taking account of all relevant circumstances. Application of equitable principles must lead to an equitable result, the result being the dominant element and the principles being subordinate to that objective. In addition, the Court held that the equidistance method of division was not in accordance with equitable principles in the case. These findings were very much in line with the drafts proposed by the G-29 in the negotiations. The Argentinian delegation was particularly impressed with this decision's support for the G-29 position, and called for a meeting of the group early in the session to consider the implications.

INSTRUCTIONS

Following the usual consultations the Minister for Foreign Affairs again made a submission to the Government on instructions for the delegation. As the Draft Convention included provisions on the matters of vital interest to Ireland that reflected acceptable compromises, a general directive to observe existing instructions on these was suggested. That would enable the delegation to oppose re-opening of such issues, unless there was an opportunity to achieve an improvement in circumstances that would not risk detrimental change or threaten the overall package.

The main emphasis of the submission was on the possibility of a stand-off between the G-77 and the industrialised countries on the ISBA regime. The possible consequences included unravelling of the settlements on fundamental issues reached through long and difficult negotiations, a prolongation of the Conference with the attendant risks of unilateral actions undermining these advances, or even collapse of the Conference, immediately or later. A stand-off would be more likely if the US insisted on re-negotiating fundamental issues in the regime. The G-77 reaction to such a stance, whether by acquiescence, rejection or even split, was unpredictable. In this uncertain scenario confirmation was sought that the delegation should support provisions favouring Irish policy, and also support others commanding substantial approval at the Conference and not inimical to Irish interests.

Voting

The question of voting at the Conference, both on particular provisions and on the convention as a whole, was addressed. Voting was described as undesirable but possibly unavoidable. It was suggested that the delegation be authorised to vote in accordance with negotiating instructions, even where that involved voting against the wishes of some Western industrialised countries (including some of the EEC partners and the US). A proviso was added that this authorisation could be departed from if, after consultation with the Minister for Foreign Affairs in the light of developments at the Conference and of the likely voting pattern, an abstention were considered more appropriate. This could be influenced by a situation where abstention was the choice of the bulk of countries with which Ireland normally shared common interests (not principally those industrialised countries).

Delimitation

The submission adverted specifically to a few items. On delimitation, it was indicated that the text incorporated into the Draft Convention in the latest revision was a welcome improvement on the previous text, but not absolutely ideal. It was suggested that, if a realistic opportunity for further improvement arose, which was regarded as very unlikely, it should be availed of, but not at the risk of a detrimental change to the existing text.

International seabed area

On the ISBA regime only a few questions were specifically raised. Regarding the preparatory commission, it was proposed that full membership for all signatories of the final act of the Conference should be supported. However, if this did not seem feasible, the draft resolution provisions granting full membership to signatories of the convention and observer status to signatories of the final act could be accepted. Ireland's full membership would be ensured by the preferred provision and observer status by the less-preferred provision. (Signature of the final act did not involve any commitment, even political, in regard to the Convention and would be routine for a participant in the Conference.) Support for financing of the preparatory commission from the UN budget (as favoured by the G-77) was proposed in preference to financing by a UN loan, repayable by the authority (as favoured by the US). At the behest of the Minister for Industry and Commerce, it was proposed that support should be given to provision for effective liaison between the (ISBA) authority and international commodity organisations, to avoid any unsettling effect on commodity agreements.

Continental shelf

Mention was made of the proposal that the preparatory commission's tasks should include establishment of the boundary commission on the outer limits of continental shelf jurisdiction. This would be somewhat against Ireland's interest as it could shorten the time within which its submission on limits must be made, and should be opposed.

The Government approved the submission's proposals for instructions.

DELEGATION

The attending delegates were again reduced in the light of the reduction of direct interests to be covered, particularly settlement of the delimitation issue. They comprised only the author, as head of delegation, and Geraldine Skinner. The responsibilities for coverage included the proceedings in regard to the ISBA; the Plenary consideration of peaceful settlement of disputes (PSD) and final clauses (including participation and the 'Community clause'); the remaining limited Second and Third Committee deliberations; the examination by Plenary of reports by the President and the Committee Chairmen with proposals for revision of the Draft Convention; the examination by Plenary of the proposals of the Drafting Committee; the servicing of the General Committee (it was Ireland's turn to hold a Vice-Presidency) and the Credentials Committee (of which Ireland was one of the members); dealing with formal amendments and adoption of the Convention in Plenary; and of course activities *en marge*, including EEC meetings.

GENERAL

At the session, EEC meetings continued to discuss both participation of international organisations and, less fruitfully, the ISBA regime. On the latter there was no advance on the general policy directive adopted by the Council of Members. Ireland consulted with several other delegations on the regime of islands. The delegation also became one of a group of 10 (G-10) (later 12) heads of delegations (from Australia, Canada, New Zealand, Ireland, the Netherlands, Denmark and the four other Scandinavian countries) who sought, in their personal capacities, to find a basis for negotiation on the ISBA regime between the US and its allies and the G-77. This initiative followed the Scandinavian acceptance of the Danish proposal (previously made to the EEC members but rejected by some of them, see above) that they should seek to act as bridge builders. Meanwhile, consultations on the ISBA regime between the US and other industrialised countries having seabed mining capacity resulted in the emergence of a new group of five (France, the FRG, the UK, Japan as well as the US) or seven (with the addition of Belgium and Italy).

The newly re-elected Taoiseach, Mr C.J. Haughey, demonstrated his direct interest in the outcome of the Conference when he was in New York as part of the Taoiseach's traditional visit to the US for St Patrick's Day. He sought a briefing from the head of delegation on progress at, and prospects for, the negotiations. The head's briefing included a positive response to the Taoiseach's query whether a convention was likely to be adopted—a response considered by his delegation colleague as rash, having regard to the Conference circumstances. Fortunately events justified it.

PLENARY

The President adhered to the work programme as adopted at the end of the Tenth Session, at least in moving on to the successive stages in fairly close accordance with the agreed schedule. He nevertheless succeeded in preserving flexibility on continuance of consultations and in securing general acceptance that, where these led to consensus, the results could be incorporated into the Draft Convention. Thus, at the beginning of the fourth week, the results of the consultations of the first stage were discussed in Plenary, on the basis of reports from the President and the Committee Chairmen. In the light of these discussions and the prior understanding, the Collegium issued a memorandum, dated 2 April, setting out a list of changes to be incorporated in the Draft Convention. Early in the fifth week the third stage was reached on schedule, and it was decided on 7 April to invoke Rule 33 of the Rules of Procedure of the Conference, thereby enabling the submission of formal amendments. It was agreed that these should be tabled during the period from 8 to 13 April. By the latter date 31 papers of formal amendments had been submitted. At the fourth stage, beginning on 14 April, the President's proposal to defer voting on the amendments for eight days, with a view to facilitating continuation of efforts to reach general agreement, was accepted. While these efforts proceeded the amendments were introduced in Plenary and debated from 15 to 17 April. The President reported on 22 April on continuing efforts to reach general agreement on certain topics. On 23 April, again on schedule, it was decided in Plenary that all efforts at reaching general agreement had been exhausted—a formality that opened the way for decision by voting. Nevertheless, it was again accepted that consultations could still continue and any result reached by general agreement could be adopted. The amendments pressed to a vote (only three) were put to the vote on 26 April. In the final stage the President's report of 22 April (on efforts to reach agreement) was debated on 28 and 29 April and, based on that debate, the President's last report dated 29 April resulted in the final incorporation of texts in the Draft Convention and associated instruments. On 30 April the convention and associated instruments were adopted by vote. The Irish delegation made statements in the Plenary debates on 30 March during the second stage (on results of the first stage consultations), on 17 April during the fourth stage (on formal amendments) and on 28 April during the final stage (on the President's report of 22 April). It also made statements during the first stage in the debates in Plenary (on participation) and in the First and Second Committees (see below). It did not make any statement in Plenary on the final day, either before or after adoption of the convention.

FIRST COMMITTEE

International seabed area

There was little of the negotiation on the ISBA regime that had been envisaged for the first stage. The G-77 maintained their formal position that, other than negotiation on the two outstanding issues, i.e. the preparatory commission and preliminary investment protection (PIP), no further negotiation on fundamental issues in the regime was acceptable, and only adjustments could be considered. The EEC Presidency made a brief statement on behalf of the ten reflecting the substance of the EEC Council guidelines. Two points specifically were (1) that, as adoption of the convention by consensus was desirable, the Conference should consider the changes to the ISBA regime suggested by several delegations, including the points raised by the US and (2) that, in view of the need for a supply of ISBA products to industrialised (including

EEC) countries, it was in the mutual interests of industrialised and developing countries to ensure that the resources were exploited.

The US was persuaded that it should present indications of amendments it required, rather than merely solutions as in its document. On 12 March it presented to the Committee a book of amendments comprising a very large number of proposals, including many related to fundamental provisions, reflecting the US position at its most extreme. It included proposals (i) to ensure that the seven largest contributors to the UN would have permanent seats on the council of the authority, that they would have an effective veto on council decisions, and power in some cases to carry council decisions by themselves; (ii) to exclude from the control of the authority minerals not subject to authority regulations, with a veto for the permanent seven on identifying minerals subject to such regulations; (iii) to deprive the assembly of the authority of its pre-eminent position and residual powers; (iv) to remove the mandatory element from provisions on technology transfer to the enterprise and drop the 'Brazil clause'; (v) to substitute a restricted system of compensation to developing land-based producers in place of limitation of production; (vi) to take from the council its role of approval of exploitation contracts; and (vii) to drop the anti-monopoly clause. On 12 March also, four of the G-5 tabled a draft resolution on PIP. This draft was supported also by the fifth member of the group, France, and by the Netherlands.

On 16 March the G-77, not surprisingly, refused to negotiate on the US book of amendments, maintaining that many of the amendments were inconsistent with the UN General Assembly Declaration of Principles. They indicated willingness to consider adjustments to the text but not fundamental changes. The US accepted that negotiations could continue other than on the basis of its amendments. In the absence of agreement among the EEC-10 on a common statement going further than the council guidelines, eight of them, including the Irish delegate, made statements, thus revealing differences among them. The Irish statement reaffirmed the objective of a convention adopted by consensus, and hoped for identification of proposals not inconsistent with the fundamentals of the Draft Convention as a basis for negotiation. This hope was obviously connected to the current activities in the G-10.

Anticipating the subsequent impasse and anxious to prevent collapse, the G-10 (see above) engaged from an early stage in the drafting of an alternative document in regard to the ISBA regime. This contained compromise provisions on several of the areas of concern to the US, for example membership of the council (effectively guaranteeing permanent US membership), voting in the council, transfer of technology (TOT) (a slight softening of obligations but retention of the 'Brazil clause'), procedures for allocating mining licences and the review conference. The document essayed the difficult task of devising provisions that would go some way towards meeting US demands without being unacceptable to the G-77. On 18 March the Irish head of delegation, on behalf of the G-10 (then in fact eleven with the addition of Austria), presented this document to the Conference President to be used at his discretion. To the satisfaction of the group, he decided to hold consultations with the opposing sides (involving also the four drafters from the group of 11 (G-11)) with a view to acceptance of the document as a basis for negotiation. In that context the Irish head, on behalf of the eleven, also approached a Peruvian delegate, one of the most prominent G-77 spokesman on the ISBA, to urge that the G-77 give serious consideration to the eleven's document. The response was positive.

Although the G-10/G-11 had sought to keep their efforts confidential to avoid lobbying, or worse, from either of the opposing sides, news of their activities had inevitably leaked. The Irish head of delegation was quizzed by an EEC Commission delegate as to the membership, Chairmanship (in fact rotating), and objective of the group, and refused to divulge information affecting other delegations. Although the ten/eleven were, in fact, pursuing the agreed EEC objective of seeking consideration of the proposals for change, the Commission delegate expressed doubts about the compatibility of the group's activities with a search for a common EEC position. This was a somewhat unrealistic proposition, in view both of the Commission's failure to get the council to direct a substantial common position, and of the activities of several of the EEC members in the G-5/G-7. The Irish head of delegation nevertheless responded that the Irish delegation would continue to seek a common position, however unlikely the prospects of success. The news of the presentation of the document to the President by the Irish head became known at an EEC heads of delegations meeting held at the same time. The Irish head being absent from the meeting, it fell to the deputy head to speak for the delegation. She was subjected to a very strong attack by the Belgian Presidency about engaging in the exercise without informing EEC partners, and failing to give them a copy of the document. She defended the Irish (and other EEC members') actions effectively, even without countering, as she might justifiably have done, with questions about activities of other EEC members (*inter alios* the Presidency) in the G-5/G-7, and documents prepared in that group that they had, similarly, not brought to attention of other EEC member states.

The G-77 indicated willingness to discuss the G-11's document, but only as the exclusive basis for negotiation, whereas the US insisted on a wider agenda. Hence a stalemate on a basis for negotiation continued. At the President's behest, the G-11 met with the G-7 for exchanges that were not very productive. The US was virtually sole speaker among the seven and not forthcoming. During the third stage, in the fifth week, following a further review in Washington, the US reduced its demands for re-negotiation. These were the subject of consultations between the two opposing groups on 6 and 7 April. However, they still covered a much wider field than the G-11's document. Some minor modifications were on offer from the G-77 but these were insufficient to encourage the G-5/G-7. Again at the President's behest, Australia, Canada, Denmark and Norway (the drafters among the group of then twelve (G-12), Switzerland having joined), submitted the group's paper as formal amendments on behalf of eleven of its members (the Netherlands being unwilling to co-sponsor an official amendment). It was introduced in Plenary on 15 April by Jens Evensen of Norway, who described it as an attempt to achieve progress, within the limits of proposals for adjustment that would not alter the fundamental balance of the consensus already reached. The Irish statement in the debate supported the eleven's amendment; echoed the indication that adjustments, not fundamental changes, would promote consensus; and specifically refuted an allegation that some of the changes in the amendment were for the benefit of the co-sponsors. The G-5/G-7 also submitted amendments representing a substantial reduction of previous demands, and adopting some suggestions from the original G-11 document, where they considered these adequate. The demands were still extensive, including many clearly unlikely to be accepted by the G-77. The latter in its statements did not welcome the amendments of the eleven, opposed the G-7 amendments, and claimed that their acceptance of PIP was a major concession. They seemed to have decided to make no concessions on the ISBA regime. Early in the seventh week the G-12, concerned at this situation, decided to make a further effort to persuade the G-77. On 20 April the Irish head of delegation, on behalf of the G-12 and with the prior approval of President Koh, again approached the Peruvian G-77 spokesman to urge G-77 participation in consultations. The Irish head explained the group were not making any suggestion regarding the positions of the G-77, only that consultations should take place. This was met with an assurance that the G-77 would enter consultations, but had not decided on an agenda or even if an agenda would be necessary. The Irish head suggested that consultations could start with whatever item seemed easiest for the G-77, but expressed the hope that none of the issues dealt with in the eleven's amendment paper would be omitted. In that seventh week open discussions on the ISBA regime began at last. By then the fourth stage (dealing with formal amendments, including those on the ISBA regime) had almost been completed and draft resolutions on the preparatory commission and PIP had been incorporated in the text (although still subject to consultation), together with some revisions in other parts of the Draft Convention, as the stages moved on. The President's report of 22 April, following these discussions, proposed a few minor changes to the Draft Convention provisions. The eleven proposers (from the G-12) withdrew their amendments at the request of the President and, in response to his plea, the G-7 amendments were not pressed to a vote. The amendments were dealt with on 26 April. The discussions on the ISBA continued in the final week but without significant results. Another approach to the G-77 by the G-12 requesting greater flexibility was to no avail. The President's report of 22 April was debated in Plenary on 28 and 29 April, following which he issued his final report of 29 April. This again proposed some more minor changes to the ISBA provisions. The changes proposed in the two reports were incorporated in the Draft Convention. The President paid handsome tribute in his final report to the eleven co-sponsors (from the G-12) for their efforts.

Preparatory investment protection

The draft resolution on PIP presented by four of the G-5 on 12 March was quickly transmitted to the group of 21 (G-21). It was attacked strongly by the G-77, which submitted an alternative on 19 March, in the form of a resolution *inter alia* requiring signature of the convention by a country if its exploring entity were to benefit from the PIP resolution as a 'pioneer investor'. The President identified twelve differences between the proposals that provided a basis for discussion in the G-21. Probably feeling that meeting US concerns on this matter would facilitate negotiations on the ISBA regime, the President later requested the group of (then) 11 to prepare a draft. This, when prepared, sought to propose appropriate solutions to the twelve differences identified by the President, but it was given only cursory consideration in the G-21. The President and the First Committee Chairman prepared a compromise proposal, based on this draft, for consideration in the context of suggestions for revision. Although subject to some criticisms from both sides in Plenary, it had broad support and was included in the Collegium's list of revisions of 2 April. The G-77 countries felt that their acceptance of PIP in principle was a major concession on their part. Nevertheless, the President (probably influenced by the scaling down of US demands in regard to the ISBA regime) continued consultations with members of the G-21 and the four drafting members of the group of (then) 12. The G-5/G-7 was dismayed when the G-77, on 12 April, proposed thirteen changes to the revised text. These changes were later submitted as formal amendments, as were radical amendments in the opposite direction by five of the G-7. On 20 April the President presented an informal paper that evoked strong resistance from the G-77. In addition a new problem emerged in the form of a complaint by the Soviet Union that, as a result of a change in the method of definition of 'pioneer investors', this latest draft discriminated in favour of Western industries as compared with the rival Soviet Union enterprise. A revelation at the same time of Soviet Union unilateral legislation on deep seabed mining drew the usual objections from the G-77. The President's report on 22 April suggested some limited changes to the revised text and, in response to his plea, neither set of amendments was pressed to a vote. The report was debated in Plenary on 28 and 29 April, coinciding with continuing consultations. In his final report of 29 April the President suggested some further slight changes to the draft that were generally agreed (despite continued Soviet Union dissatisfaction). They were incorporated in the draft of the resolution submitted to the final vote. The President rejected the Soviet Union objections. This was apparently why the Soviet Union and most of the other EE members abstained in the final vote.

Preparatory commission

The draft on a preparatory commission, in the form of a resolution of the Conference, submitted and subsequently amended by the President and the Chairman of the First Committee at the Tenth Session, was examined in the G-21. The main substantive issues were membership and financing. At the end of these discussions the authors amended the draft, mostly for purposes of clarification of procedural questions and to accommodate more easily some commission functions (including functions in regard to PIP and a study of the problems of land-based producers). There was no provision for a commission function regarding establishment of the Commission on the Limits of the Continental Shelf. No change was made to membership or financing provisions. They remained, respectively, that its members should be states that had signed or acceded to the convention and that states signatory to the final act could participate as observers (not as members as the industrialised countries proposed and Ireland preferred); and that its initial expenses should be met from the UN budget if the UN General

Assembly approved. Thus the position of the G-77 prevailed over that of the industrialised countries in both instances. In the plenary revision debate of 29 to 31 March the amended draft attracted considerable support, but was criticised by the industrialised countries, in particular in regard to the provisions on membership and to a link they saw with decision-making in the council of the authority. It was included in the list of revisions in the Collegium's memorandum of 2 April. Although consultations continued few further changes were adopted. The most significant related to participation in the commission. Namibia was expressly added to states eligible for participation (see below) and it was clarified that international organisations that had signed the final act would be entitled to participation as observers (an EEC preoccupation). The resolution was among the associated instruments adopted by vote with the convention.

SECOND COMMITTEE

The Committee met only during the first stage, for three days altogether. The Chairman's appeal that issues should not be re-opened did not prevent many questions being raised, but most were inconsequential.

Delimitation

Despite the recent ICJ decision (see above) the general feeling among members of the G-29 was that it would not be advisable to seek amendment to the delimitation provisions. The Irish delegation felt there would be no sympathy from the President, or among the vast majority of delegations, for an effort, regardless of its merits, to re-open this most intractable issue shortly after agreement had been achieved with great difficulty. Moreover, the effect of the recent decision would influence the interpretation of the criteria provision through the reference in that provision to international law. Even Venezuela was not enthusiastic about re-opening, despite its dissatisfaction with the provisions. Its problem was addressed in private consultations with the Irish delegate, and subsequently with some other members of the G-29 under Irish chairmanship. The dissatisfaction was based broadly on a fear that the Draft Convention provision (Article 15) on delimitation of territorial seas (re-enacting the 1958 convention provision giving median line priority, on which Venezuela had entered a reservation) could be imported into the other delimitation provisions through the reference to international law—a fear not shared to any significant degree by the other members of the G-29. Moderation of the scope of Venezuela's apparently inevitable efforts to seek a remedy was urged. In the plenary debate in the fourth week on the Collegium's proposals for revision, Venezuela set out the legal grounds for its concerns—unhelpfully from the Irish point of view, although the argument was clearly strained. The possibility of permissibility of reservation was raised and was supported by a few others, notably Turkey. Among a few other mentions of the topic only that of Columbia, in direct response to Venezuela, was significant. The Irish statement made no direct reference to the issue but covered it in a general acceptance of the Draft Convention. No change resulted.

Regime of islands

Likewise the existing diametrically opposed proposals respectively by the UK and Romania on the regime of islands were not raised in the Committee—but were mentioned by a few speakers in the plenary debate. The Irish and other like-minded delegations (including Romania) had consulted on the topic, and had decided that they would not collectively propose substantive amendments. The Venezuelan statement in plenary also criticised this provision.

Territorial seas

Among matters that were discussed in the Committee was the existing proposal for an amendment affecting the exercise of right of innocent passage by warships in the territorial seas. It had many supporters, mainly small coastal states, but was vehemently resisted by the major powers (see below).

Straddle stocks and exclusive economic zone

Co-sponsors led by Australia and Canada again advocated their proposal on straddle stocks. This was the source of a slight *contretemps* in EEC consultations. When it was originally raised at the Tenth Session only Ireland and the UK of the EEC members favoured it. Most of the others rejected it as extending coastal state fisheries jurisdiction beyond the EEZ, which they regarded as a further example of what they called creeping coastal state jurisdiction. As it was potentially inconsistent with the EEC common position previously put forward, Ireland and the UK then agreed that it would be opposed. Later in that session, the EEC opponents relented in the face of a modification of the proposal, and it was agreed that the sponsors could be told that the EEC would not oppose the modified version. The Irish and UK delegations duly conveyed this message. In the course of heated EEC exchanges during the Eleventh Session, this agreement was denied by some members, and vehemently by the Commission representatives. Only production by the council secretariat of a record of the decision resolved that difference. Nevertheless, the opposing members maintained their opposition, and the Commission submitted the issue to Brussels. The formal amendment actually submitted by Australia and Canada was in the original unmodified form opposed by the EEC, and was later withdrawn without being replaced by the more modified version.

Continental shelf

China mentioned the continental shelf definition provisions, suggesting slight amendments to its first two paragraphs, which were supported by a few delegations. The UK-proposed amendment regarding the obligation to dismantle abandoned installations on the shelf was also raised and adjusted in the light of the exchanges. Another UK amendment, to substitute 'taking account of' in place of 'on the basis of', in regard to the coastal state's response to the report of the Commission on the Limits of the Continental Shelf, received little support, even from among the Margineers.

The Irish delegation in a very brief statement on 18 March supported the Chairman's appeal not to jeopardise the balance of what been achieved (impliedly including the provisions on delimitation, regime of islands, the continental shelf and anadromous species (salmon)) and also confirmed its support for the UK amendment on artificial islands only, as not being a threat to the balance. Only this amendment was recommended by the Committee Chairman for incorporation into the Draft Convention, and it was included in the list of changes on in the Collegium's memorandum of 2 April.

THIRD COMMITTEE

The Chairman's suggestion that the negotiations had been completed was generally accepted and no proposals for change emerged.

DRAFTING COMMITTEE

The Committee met mainly to consider proposals for language concordance on some provisions that were prepared for reference to plenary. It also later made recommendations on some of the provisions of the ISBA regime, including provisions on activities in the area, system of exploitation and the authority.

PLENARY

Most of the Drafting Committee proposals on language coordination were accepted in meetings of plenary (chaired by the Irish Vice-Presidency in the person of the head of delegation) on 12 March, 15 March and 16 April. The last meeting also dealt with recommendations on provisions of the ISBA regime. It was decided that the Committee should meet in July and August to complete its work, including consideration of the provisions not yet examined, particularly provisions on the ISBA regime.

There was no further discussion of the PSD provisions or the preamble. In regard to the final clauses only the number of ratifications/accessions required for entry into force of the convention (60 was easily agreed) and the provisions on participation were addressed. Discussion of provisions on participation of international organisations and of NLMs began in the first week.

Participation

The President's treatment of participation of international organisations as presented at the Tenth Session was debated and delegations again raised such questions as (i) a requirement of prior participation by a number of members of the organisation (all/a majority/some); (ii) avoidance of double representation; (iii) methodology for provision of information on division of competences between the organisation and its members; and (iv) prevention of convention benefits accruing through a participating organisation to a member that was not itself a party. The Belgian EEC Presidency reiterated the concerns expressed in the pre-session letter to the President, emphasising in particular the provision on non-accrual of benefits, seen internally as requiring EEC discrimination between its members, contrary to EEC law. The EEC suggested (a) a redrafting of this provision (delayed pending clearance by COREPER in Brussels at the insistence of the Commission delegation, which was not fully satisfied with it) to provide for non-accrual through absence of obligation of third parties, rather than through an obligation of the organisation to prevent accrual; and (b) addition of a provision requiring third states to accept EEC declarations of transfer of competences. The President held consultations with *inter alios* EEC representatives and on 23 March produced a new paper that was in some respects an improvement from the EEC viewpoint (including a useful clarification of the application of PSD procedures and a slight modification of the nature of information on transfer of competences). However, a condition regarding the signature by the organisation was added that a majority of its member states must have signed (corresponding to the previously provided similar prior condition to becoming a party); the drafting of the non-accrual of benefits provision, although improved, remained unsatisfactory; and circumstances in which the organisation could denounce the convention were strictly circumscribed. The EEC made further representations to the President, and learned with satisfaction that the non-accrual clause would be redrafted in an acceptable form (expressing it in terms of the convention not conferring rights on non-parties) on the basis of a Soviet Union proposal. The President's report of 26 March had a new text including this latest redraft, and a new provision that was helpful in reducing EEC difficulties with some of the other provisions. However, the provision designed to permit the organisation to have special treatment arrangements between its members had become dangerous, with the evolution of the texts and, particularly, linkage to the non-accrual of benefits clause. This was ironic, as the special treatment provision had been the forerunner of the clause in EEC deliberations, and had been included in the EEC draft of the clause. The EEC heads of delegations considered this new text and concluded, despite Commission misgivings, that it should be accepted on condition only of omission of the special treatment clause. (The Commission delegation again sought, unsuccessfully, to have this conclusion overruled in Brussels.) A Commission concern that the provisions would prevent the EEC from participating in the preparatory commission was taken on board by the Conference President and subsequently clarified. In the plenary debate on revision, the Belgian Presidency sought omission of the special treatment clause as the only change to the President's text and was supported by other EEC members, including the Irish delegate in his statement on 30 March. Nevertheless, the Collegium's list of revisions to the Draft Convention, which appeared on 2 April, incorporated the President's text with the special treatment clause still in place. The President's response to private EEC protests was that any change would have to be balanced by a change in the draft on NLM participation that would not be welcome to Western countries. He subsequently indicated privately to the Belgian Presidency that the desired amendment would be incorporated in his next report (as well as a change to the NLM text). That report was expected after the time for tabling of formal amendments (in fact appearing on 22 April). The EEC members, strongly pressed by the Commission and after some days of hesitating in fear of implying lack of faith in the President's goodwill, on 13 April proposed an appropriate formal amendment to guard against any unexpected hitch. (Iraq did likewise on the NLM text.) In the debate on the amendments the President described the EEC amendment (and the Iraqi amendment) as qualifying for incorporation in revision. This indication was welcomed by the Belgian Presidency and scarcely questioned otherwise. When he so listed the amendment in his report of 22 April it was not necessary to pursue it further, and it was included in the final revision of the Draft Convention on 29 April.

On participation of NLMs the President sought to avoid repetition of previous arguments by summarising them at the beginning. On one side the argument was that, since the convention should benefit all peoples, NLMs must be permitted to be parties to it, and that there were precedents for such participation, as well as parallels with the situation in regard to international organisations (for example, irrelevance of territoriality). On the other side the argument was that a party must be able to undertake the obligations (a capacity lacking in NLMs) as well as enjoy the benefits of the convention. The debate did not indicate progress and the President undertook informal consultations. His paper presented at the Tenth Session had provisions on both international organisations and NLMs and he clearly hoped to resolve both issues together, contrary to EEC urgings. His new drafts of 23 March covered both. They also included the Transitional Provision in regard to resource rights of a territory whose people were not fully independent, that was perceived to be linked to the NLM provision. These drafts gave a general indication of the provisions on NLMs, leaving open their form and location. They provided that NLMs participating in the Conference would be permitted to sign the final act, and that such signature would give them the status of observers at the preparatory commission. It would also entitle them to attend meetings of parties to the convention as observers, and to receive any communications sent to the parties by the depositary (the UN Secretary-General). There was no provision for NLMs to become party to the convention. The Transitional Provision became the subject of exchanges between the countries directly concerned, including the UK. The President's report of 26 March contained: (i) a draft in the form of a Conference Decision on NLMs largely unchanged in substance from that of 23 March; and (ii) a draft, in the form of a resolution of the Conference, on the resources of non-independent territories, invoking particularly Article 73 of the UN Charter (which established criteria for treatment of non-self-governing territories and their peoples). This draft omitted previous reference to territories under foreign occupation, as well as softening the language. In the plenary revision debate the G-77 emphasised that participation was a package. They welcomed the President's proposals as achieving progress on which improvements could be made, particularly in regard to NLMs—the Arabs especially seeking to enhance their status. There was general support for the compromise. The Collegium's memorandum of 2 April listing revisions to the Draft Convention included the President's proposals. Iraq later proposed a formal amendment to the texts referring to the NLMs that would enable them to be observers at the assembly of the (ISBA) authority. During the formal amendments debate the President described it (as well as the EEC amendment in regard to international organisations) as qualifying for incorporation in revision. It was supported by the G-77 and the EE and opposed by the US and others. The President included his participation proposals (as so amended) in his report of 22 April. They were included in the collegium memorandum of 29 April and were incorporated in the final revision on that date. Thus they formed part of the Draft Convention and associated documents put to the vote on the last day of the session.

The UN Council for Namibia submitted a formal amendment that would specifically include Namibia (represented by the council) as a state in the relevant sub-paragraph of the signature provision. Apart from opposition by the five members of the UN Contact Group on Namibia (Canada, France, the FRG, the UK and the Soviet Union), as well as Belgium and New Zealand, there was generally support for the amendment. The President convened a small consultative group, under the chairmanship of the Irish head of delegation, comprising representatives of the five Contact Group members, Belgium, New Zealand, Brazil, Bulgaria, Tunisia, United Arab Emirates, the US and the Council for Namibia, to consider the question. After an exchange of views the consultative group chairman proposed addition of a separate sub-paragraph in the signature provision to include Namibia among the entities entitled to sign (and ratify or accede). This solution was accepted by the council but rejected by the Contact Group members. An informal UK proposal that would permit signature by the council on behalf of Namibia but preclude Namibia from becoming a party until it had attained independence, was rejected by the council. Following separate consultations with the two sides, the Chairman concluded that the substance of the council's proposal should be met. He therefore again proposed a new sub-paragraph to enable Namibia, represented by the council, to sign the convention (and ratify or accede), together with an amendment to the preparatory commission draft resolution admitting Namibia to membership of the commission upon such signature. This was accepted by most of the consultative group members, and the others agreed not to oppose it. It was submitted by the President to the plenary as part of his final report on 29 April. It was unopposed although some members of the Contact Group indicated reluctance in acquiescing. It was incorporated in the final revision of the Draft Convention.

Formal amendments comprised in 31 papers were proposed, including those on the ISBA regime. Most were withdrawn or not put to a vote, including: (i) those on the ISBA regime; (ii) those by the UK and Romania on a regime of islands; (iii) that by Australia, Canada and others on straddle stocks; and (iv) on condition of a relevant Presidential Statement in Plenary, that on exercise of innocent passage of warships in territorial seas. The President's statement was to the effect that, in the context of that amendment, certain states had indicated that they would rely on Articles 19 and 25 to safeguard their security interests. Only three of the formal amendments were put to a vote, including one by Turkey proposing deletion of the prohibition on reservations (reflecting some dissatisfaction with *inter alia* the provisions on regime of islands and on extension of the territorial sea). Its heavy defeat (with Ireland among those voting against it), presumably due to a widely held view that the convention was a package, was followed by withdrawal of a Venezuela amendment to permit reservation to the delimitation provisions. The two other amendments put to a vote, those proposed by Spain regarding straits, were also lost. One of these amendments achieved a two-thirds majority in the vote, but not half of the Conference participants, as was also required for adoption. Ireland abstained on both. Thus the Draft Convention that came before plenary for adoption comprised the text that emanated from the Tenth Session, as amended by the revisions carried out at the session by the Collegium. These revisions were based on the plenary debates on the reports of consultations by the President and Committee Chairman at the end of the first stage, and by the President subsequently.

The President appealed to delegations to accept the Draft Convention and the related instruments as a package and adopt it without a vote. However, the US, by letter addressed to him, requested a vote, and the Convention and Instruments were put to a recorded vote. At the last minute Canada proposed deferment of a decision to facilitate further consideration of the changes to the ISBA regime submitted by the G-10/G-12, and was supported by the US. The G-77 rejected this proposal as coming too late, and the President deplored the rejection by the US of this proposal when made by him some time earlier. The vote proceeded. The result was 130 for (including Ireland, Denmark, Greece, France, the four other Scandinavian countries, Argentina, Australia, Austria, Canada, China, New Zealand, Japan and virtually all of the G-77); four against (the US, Israel, Turkey and

Venezuela); seventeen abstentions (including Belgium, the FRG, Italy, Luxembourg, the Netherlands, the UK, Portugal, Spain, Switzerland, the Soviet Union and the other EE countries, except Romania and Yugoslavia). The recorded vote, conducted electronically, emerged progressively on an electronic screen. The audible reaction as the numbers progressed was a clear indication of both the surprise and satisfaction of the vast majority of the delegations. A general debate followed the vote, presided over by the Irish head of delegation while the President completed preparation of his finishing statement.

The plenary decided that the Drafting Committee would meet to examine the provisions it had not yet considered, and recommended that there would be a three-day resumption of the session in New York in September, mainly to consider the final Drafting Committee proposals and to deal with a few outstanding matters. These included the arrangements for the Signature Session that was planned for Caracas in early December.

The G-12 decided that they should maintain contact and, for this purpose, the Irish head of delegation was nominated as coordinator through whom they would share any significant information that came to hand.

Chapter XVI

ELEVENTH SESSION—RESUMED

As arranged, a resumption of the Eleventh Session was held at the United Nations headquarters in New York for three days, from 22 to 24 September 1982.

The agenda was mainly to deal with the proposals of the Drafting Committee (following its meeting during July and August to examine the convention provisions, the consideration of which it had not previously undertaken or completed), to finalise the drafting of the final act of the Conference and to determine the venue and dates of the Signature Session. Tidying up of some other details was also required. In the event it also became an occasion for further off-stage exchanges relative to the international seabed area regime.

PREPARATIONS

The Inter-Departmental Committee met in Dublin to assess the results of the Conference. The Minister for Foreign Affairs submitted a report on the session to the Government on 28 May. On consideration of the report the Government decided on 4 June that Ireland should sign the convention.

Off-stage efforts continued to explore the feasibility of persuading, in particular, those Western industrialised countries that had abstained in the vote on the convention to accept it, and to explore also, in this context, the possibility of amendment. The International Law Commission (ILC) annual session was held as usual in Geneva in the summer, its membership including several prominent delegates to UNCLOS III. Taking advantage of this situation Jens Evensen, head of the Norwegian delegation and one of the group of 12 (G-12) at the Eleventh Session, with the assistance of the Irish head of delegation (serving in Geneva as Permanent Representative to the United Nations Office since November 1981) invited an influential group of delegates to an informal lunch meeting on May 26. These included seven members of the ILC who were also UNCLOS III delegates, five of them from G-77 countries, the other two being Professor Willem Riphagen, leader of the Netherlands delegation and also one of the G-12, and Professor Ogiso of Japan, whose country was one of the G-5 at the Eleventh Session. The other participants included a Danish delegate (also from the G-12). The objective was to examine whether some limited amendments to the ISBA regime would be both tolerable to the G-77 and sufficient to win the acceptance of the convention by at least some of the reluctant industrialised countries. Evensen mentioned a limited number of topics he had in mind. It was considered that if consensus on changes emerged they could be incorporated in the convention at the resumed session. There were, however, serious doubts of the possibility of achieving consensus, not least because of the position of the EE. Nevertheless, there was unanimous encouragement among those at the meeting for such an effort. The Irish head of delegation informed the other members of the G-12 of the meeting and of other items of information as they came to hand. Evensen offered to prepare some drafts, but these did not emerge before the resumed session, where this drafting was subsumed into the latest G-12 efforts—see below. Other members from the G-12 were also active. The Australian delegation was apparently also thinking of an initiative, and joined with Canada and New Zealand in making representations in Washington and London. Reports in regard to the Washington representations were pessimistic about the possibility of US engagement in light of post-adoption developments there and particularly because of the apparent dominance of the hardliners in the administration, including the head of delegation. In London the benefits of the convention seemed to have a counterbalance to the dissatisfaction with (only) a few parts of the ISBA regime and solidarity with the US (possibly influenced by its support in the current Falklands/Malvinas war). There was another Geneva meeting with participants including representatives of France, the UK and other Western states having seabed mining capacity that, however, had no obvious result, largely due to the continued absence of any commitment from these countries to signature in the event of amendment.

The G-12 became aware, through diverse sources, that the US, in communications with France, the FRG and the UK, had proposed establishment of an alternative regime for seabed mining founded on a mini-treaty between them. This was apparently met with a lack of enthusiasm, particularly from France and the FRG. They did, however, agree, if reluctantly, to attend a meeting suggested by the US. The approach and unenthusiastic reaction were acknowledged by these three European states at an EEC heads of delegations meeting in late June. An associated suggestion for a reciprocating states agreement to resolve overlapping claims to potential mining sites was more favourably considered by the three European states, although they were anxious that any such agreement should be in line with the preparatory investment protection (PIP) resolution, so as not to foreclose their convention options. Canada, one of the G-12 that was also among the countries listed in the PIP resolution, separately proposed a meeting of all the countries named in that resolution. The purpose of the proposed meeting was to explore the possibility of conclusion of a memorandum of understanding on potentially conflicting site claims, in a form compatible with the convention and the PIP resolution. This proposal was not encouraged, particularly by the US. On 10 July the US, as expected, announced that it had decided not to sign the convention. In late July a reciprocating states agreement on sites, as proposed, was negotiated between France, the FRG, the UK and the US *en marge* of a North Atlantic Treaty Organization (NATO) meeting. It was concluded in early September. It dealt only with resolution of overlapping sites and not recognition of claims, and thus the European parties claimed that it was not incompatible with the convention. There were also reports that a second stage negotiation was planned for 1983 on the possibility of a mini-treaty. Canada also maintained its initiative for a more widely negotiated memorandum of understanding, and held a meeting in Geneva in early August, to which four of the G-12, including the Irish head of delegation, were also invited.

EEC meetings were held to consider the implications of the adoption of the convention, including preparations for possible signature by the EEC. The Commission undertook preparation of a draft communication to the Council of Ministers.

From contacts, mainly in Geneva, the Irish head of delegation became convinced that there would be at least 50 signatures at the Signature Session, which would trigger the convening of the preparatory commission in the following March.

DELEGATION

In the light of severe budgetary constraints, the Department of Foreign Affairs was doubtful about arranging for attendance at the resumed session, otherwise than by an officer from the Mission to the UN. In the event, it was decided that there were developments that required the attendance of one of the regular delegates, and the head of delegation was nominated. Patrick O'Connor, counsellor in the New York Mission, was also accredited, and he covered the belated final stages of the last meeting, following the unavoidable departure of the head of delegation from New York.

GENERAL

The Irish head of delegation reached New York in time to attend a lunch in honour of President Koh on 20 September, two days before resumption of the session. He thus also had prior opportunity both to seek details of the arrangements for the Signature Session and engage in consultations. Two prominent Latin American delegates, one of them a participant in the May Geneva discussions, immediately conveyed privately to him that any possibility of G-77 acceptance of changes in the convention had passed. Various informal meetings were attended before and during the resumed session, including meetings of the G-12.

On 20 September President Koh was approached by representatives of France, the FRG and the UK (possibly encouraged by the Geneva exchanges) to urge a total of nineteen changes to the ISBA convention provisions—on TOT, the review conference and the Authority budget—and to the PIP resolution. The changes were described as helpful towards a decision by these three countries to sign but no responding commitment to do so was on offer. Apparently when the President floated this idea to the Soviet Union representative it was met with a flat rejection that was expressed to apply even if the changes were combined with a firm commitment to signature. Nevertheless, the President arranged a consultation on 21 September with the G-77 spokesman (Peru), the EE spokesman (the Soviet Union) and four of the G-12 (the Canadian, Danish, Irish and Norwegian delegates). The Peruvian delegate, although anxious for a consensus convention, anticipated G-77 negative reaction in the light of the obstacles. The Soviet Union was implacably opposed to any attempt at amendment. The other four (including the Irish delegate) described the timing, the number of changes suggested and the absence of a signature commitment in response as unrealistic. To avoid the impression of a summary rebuff, a meeting of these four with the requesting states was mooted, but was deferred, at an Irish suggestion, pending the G-77 reaction. The position and approach of its four members participating in these exchanges were endorsed in a subsequent meeting of the G-12. The President's resumed consultation later on the same day included also the three requesting states. Peru reported G-77 total rejection of any re-opening, and doubts about the seriousness of the suggestion in the absence of any offer of commitment to signature. The Soviet Union reiterated its opposition. The Irish delegate, for the G-12, mentioned willingness to help towards consensus, but only in the context of a realistic approach. The group saw such an approach as comprising three elements: (i) a limited number of suggested changes; (ii) consensus on the changes; and (iii) commitment to signature in return for adoption of the changes. The Canadian delegate suggested that a contingency amending instrument be drafted, with a view to incorporation in the convention by consensus only if the three requesting states decided to sign. This was welcomed by the three requesting states, opposed by the Soviet Union and not commented on by Peru. The Irish delegate reserved the position of the G-12, and the President proposed reflection. Next day, before the resumed session began, the idea gained support in the G-12. Ireland and Australia were, however, concerned that such a move would delay generally national decisions on signature. The group, although recognising both the enormous difficulties and the need for further thought, decided its drafting group should prepare amendments, in case the procedure might get under way. These were amendments to provisions on the review conference and TOT (identified by the FRG to the Irish delegate as their most important concerns). The offstage efforts at seeking an accommodation with the abstaining Western industrialised countries continued during the resumed session, albeit with no greater success (see below).

Canada convened a meeting on 20 September on its proposal for a memorandum of understanding among the PIP countries to resolve possible overlapping of sites. Participants were the states named in the PIP resolution (Belgium, Canada, France, the FRG, India, Italy, Japan, the Netherlands, the Soviet Union, the UK and the US), Brazil, Chile, and four others of the G-12 (Australia, Denmark, Ireland and Norway). The prior agreement on the topic between France, the FRG, the UK and the US was a significant source of friction. It was criticised by Japan as inconsistent with both the convention and the PIP resolution, and more trenchantly by the Soviet Union as a contravention of both. Of the four parties to the agreement only the UK sought to defend it. Despite Soviet Union insistence that any memorandum of understanding must be confined to convention signatories, Canada and Japan pushed for consideration of the substance of such a memorandum. France, the FRG and the UK reluctantly agreed to participate in drafting a blueprint for further discussion, but the US and other Western industrialised countries remained silent.

A question by the Danish Presidency in an EEC meeting on 21 September regarding the four-state agreement drew the reading by the UK delegate of a carefully worded statement to the effect that the agreement did not prejudice decisions on signature. At the same meeting it emerged that, so far, Ireland alone among the members had decided to sign the convention. All intended to sign the final act. There was preliminary discussion of a Commission paper for a submission to the Council of Ministers. This harked back to the February submission in assuming that certain parts of that submission were EEC objectives. Thus the paper ignored the fact that the February submission had been rejected by several delegations, including the Irish delegation, because of these suggestions that had not been adopted in the subsequent council decision. The paper also proposed a common position on signature, and claimed that the first member state to sign would have to make a declaration of EEC competences. At the meeting several delegations were not in a position to comment and most of those that did described their comments as preliminary. Only the FRG supported the proposal for a common position on signature. The Irish delegate was generally critical of the paper, and was supported by Denmark in rejecting the assumed objectives. He joined Denmark, France and the UK in opposition to a common position on signature, as well as the need for a declaration of EEC competences by the first member state to sign. The Commission in reply claimed that signature by less than a majority of member states (which would not be sufficient to enable EEC signature) without a declaration of transferred competences would be illegal in the EEC context, as such signature would be in respect of the whole convention, including parts covered by EEC competences. The Irish head denied the claims of illegality, on the grounds that signature did not involve acceptance of any binding obligation. On a separate matter the FRG head mentioned the possibility of the FRG making interpretative declarations, but not before signature. Despite the clear limitation by the relevant convention provision of the effect of a declaration, Ireland was not comfortable with this idea, bearing in mind the possibility of an escalation of the procedure.

Doubts had arisen after the first part of the session as to Venezuela's willingness to host the Signature Session as presumed, a matter still not clarified two days before commencement of the resumed session. The UN Secretary-General's special representative, Under-Secretary-General Zuleta, conveyed to the Irish head of delegation his expectation of a withdrawal of the invitation, but also his fears that, alternatively, a delay might be requested. He felt that the Conference would not accept a deferral. He mentioned other possible venues, including Manila and Jamaica. The costs to be borne might be a deterrent, and he thought that Geneva or New York might be most likely, with some of the Latin American and Caribbean Group (LAC) preferring Geneva in view of the US attitude. Zuleta anticipated the Signature Session would last five days, with statements for four days followed by signature at the last meeting. He listed states that had already decided to sign, others on the point of doing so and yet others most likely to do so shortly. He had no doubt that there would be at least 50 signatures at the session and that, therefore, the preparatory commission would convene by mid-March 1983. He foresaw no difficulties in regard to signature of the final act by international organisations, unless those with transferred competences (effectively only the EEC) sought to be in a separate category. (The Irish delegate mentioned to the Danish EEC Presidency the danger in such a situation of a pre-condition that a list of competences transferred be furnished.) Venezuela withdrew its invitation on 21 September.

PLENARY

Opening statements for the G-77 and the EE supported the convention and condemned alternative arrangements or actions as illegal. The G-77 maintained that only parties to the convention could claim rights under it, and would have no obligations to non-parties (contrary to the claim by some of their members in the post-adoption debate in April that the convention comprised generally applicable law binding on all). The Soviet Union specifically criticised the four-party reciprocating states agreement. The FRG, one of the four parties to that agreement, responded cautiously along the lines of the UK statement earlier at the EEC meeting, and reserved the right to reply fully later. The US claimed many convention provisions reflected existing international law, and were thus binding regardless of participation in the convention.

Processing of the Drafting Committee recommendations was commenced in plenary, with the Irish head of delegation as Chairman for some of the meetings. The recommendations included amendments to the French language version of the delimitation provisions, but the G-29 were satisfied that these were not prejudicial to the group's interests. None of the other recommendations posed any problem for Ireland. The few that gave rise to controversy were resolved following discussions with the concerned parties. These deliberations were concluded on the second day, and the task was completed on the third day with adoption of the final paper, including consequential amendments. This last stage also featured consideration of two slight amendments from the floor, which were adopted. They included a slight change in the wording and the placement of the paragraph dealing with entities, other than states, that could become parties to the convention. The EEC Commission was concerned about the change, but the member states concluded that it was not significant and decided not to oppose it. The other amendment was not of concern to Ireland.

In a similar context, and not unrelated to the earlier EEC deliberations about signature and its consequences, the Conference Secretariat raised with the Danish EEC Presidency questions about the modalities of EEC signature. This was inspired, apparently, by an anxiety to avoid signature by international organisations not having competences, which ran counter to what Zuleta had said to the Irish head of delegation. Denmark was inclined to try to meet the concerns expressed. However, the EEC heads of delegations, prompted by the Irish head, required the Presidency to take the line that it was for the secretariat to find a way of implementing the guarantee of EEC right to sign, and to solve any collateral problems that might arise.

The Conference President initiated private consultations on the question of a venue and dates for the Signature Session. Jamaica, Manila and Lisbon seemed to be the main candidates. Jamaica was reluctant to accept that it should bear all the additional expense (arising from holding the session outside a UN office). The G-77 approved the Jamaican candidature, including the position of no responsibility for additional expense. The G-12 was concerned at the possibility of a necessary UN General Assembly decision causing delay. In the event date and venue were decided by consensus as 6 to 10 December in Jamaica, despite continued ambivalence by Jamaica on the additional expenses.

The draft final act was adopted with a number of not very significant amendments, and it was decided that the convention would be entitled 'United Nations Convention on the Law of the Sea', without addition of a reference to the signature venue.

One of Ireland's closest allies at the Conference, Argentina, indicated it had intended to vote against Resolution III (the previously entitled 'Transitional Provision', on resources accruing to non-independent territories—shades of the current Falklands/Malvinas conflict) but was prevented from doing so by the package deal approach. Accordingly, it could not sign the final act with Resolution III attached, or (surprisingly) the convention. The UK responded moderately that it too was less than happy with the resolution, but accepted it as a compromise.

GENERAL

Meanwhile, as arranged, the G-12 drafters produced amendments to the provisions on (ISBA) TOT and the review conference, which were considered in the full group on 23 September. Opinions differed as to whether they were inadequate or the maximum possible. Another approach (inspired by the FRG without attribution) was considered, i.e. to enable the preparatory commission to recommend changes to these provisions. Reactions among the twelve were widely divided. At an Irish suggestion it was decided to convey both the amendments and the alternative approach to the President, while indicating that the group was divided in assessing both. The President responded very cautiously, and asked the group to consult Peru and France on the prospects. The Irish delegate, engaged as acting Chairman of the Plenary, was unable to accompany the Danish and Norwegian delegates in these consultations. Peru was interested in the preparatory commission approach. However, when it was mentioned at a G-77 meeting it was met by resistance to any change. Nevertheless, on the last day, the President and Peru favoured a statement by the G-12 urging further efforts. However, the group demurred, considering such action unwise in the light of the G-77 position. Consultations continued without any result. The Danish and Norwegian delegates, acting for the G-12, privately gave to the delegations of France, the FRG and the UK, for their later reaction, copies of alternative drafts prepared (as part of the aborted proposal) in regard to the preparatory commission approach.

On the last day also the Irish delegate was among a widely representative group of guests at a lunch hosted by Elliot Richardson, former head of the US delegation. Richardson explored the possibility of those present achieving changes in the convention that might alter the US attitude, while ruling out any US response at that time. Several G-77 delegates flatly dismissed the possibility of re-negotiation, whereas others were less trenchant although substantively similar in their views. The Irish delegate gave a summary of his understanding of the situation. Political realities in Washington and other Western capitals precluded a *quid pro quo* at this stage, while political realities in Moscow and Third World capitals precluded changes in the absence of at least a commitment to signature in return. Thus the challenge was to invent a method of devising proposals for amendment, without their being conceded before a commitment and, more importantly, without undermining the convention in the meantime. The summary was accepted by all but, not surprisingly, no one had a solution to the dilemma.

The Irish delegation was not involved in any further developments on the Canadian initiative for a memorandum of understanding in regard to potential overlapping mining site claims.

Chapter XVII

SIGNATURE SESSION

The Signature Session was held in Montego Bay, Jamaica, for one week, from 6 to 10 December 1982.

PREPARATIONS

European Economic Community meetings became more active after the resumed Eleventh Session. They undertook a general assessment of the situation, and particularly the question of participation. The details addressed included (a) the positions of the members on signature; (b) in the context of eventual EEC signature, the implications of signature by some but not all of the members; and (c) preparation of a declaration of the relevant competences that had been transferred to the EEC. At the beginning of these meetings Ireland was the only member to have decided to sign and the Irish rationale was explained as (i) concern for certainty of applicable law and consequent reduction of potential for international conflict; (ii) a view that the convention represented as fair a balance between varied interests as was realistically achievable; and (iii) satisfaction that a number of national interests were adequately, even if not totally, met by the convention. Among the other members the question of signature was still under consideration. The Danish, French, Greek and Netherlands delegations anticipated, with varying degrees of confidence, positive decisions before the session. Luxembourg, with little direct national interest at stake, expected to follow the example of other members, but not merely one or two. Among others an 'at least not yet' decision before the Signature Session was regarded as a possibility. For these the international seabed area (ISBA) regime was a negative factor, while for the FRG (one of their number) the establishment of the seat of the International Tribunal in Hamburg was a positive counter factor. In the event, in accordance with anticipations, five members (including Ireland) had decided to sign before the session.

The EEC Commission still insisted that there should be a common position of the members on signature. (The commissioner who had been the prime promoter of the February Commission paper was reported to have told US officials that the EEC would seek a common position on signature, and Denmark reported the US appointment of a special emissary to urge negative decisions in regard to signature on industrialised countries, including France, the FRG and the UK as well as Japan.) In parallel, intensive work on a declaration on relevant competences transferred to the EEC was undertaken in meetings of legal experts, on the basis of a Commission draft. The revised draft prepared in these meetings was subsequently considered by a meeting of the heads of delegation. The Irish delegation was concerned that the Commission draft seemed to overstate some EEC competences. It also felt that the language should be more clearly linked to the convention, particularly the provision enabling participation of international organisations. Some other members shared these concerns generally and the draft was revised accordingly. In addition an over-elaborate reference to ongoing transfers of competences was simplified. The idea of a common position on signature not having been accepted, the Commission representative maintained its position that, where a member state signed before the EEC, it must make a declaration on signature of the relevant competences transferred to the EEC. A combination of moves, by the Danish (Presidency) and Irish heads of delegation and a senior EEC Council official, secured a compromise. This consisted of (i) an agreed draft of an EEC Council of Ministers decision on EEC participation that provided for a declaration of relevant transferred competences by the EEC on signature and by members on ratification and (ii) acceptance that each member would make a declaration, on signature, that it was a member of the EEC to which relevant competences had been transferred, without specifying them. These meetings also prepared a common statement to be delivered at the Signature Session by the Danish delegation as EEC Presidency.

It was apparent as the session was about to begin that five EEC members would sign the convention at the session. The Luxembourg delegation realised that, if Luxembourg also signed, a majority of members would be signatories, thus enabling the EEC also to sign. Encouraged by the Commission representatives, the Luxembourg delegation communicated from Jamaica with its capital suggesting that a decision to sign at the session be again considered. In the event, probably because there was insufficient time to comply with the necessary procedures, the effort was dropped.

En marge of an EEC meeting on 8 October, the heads of the French, FRG and UK delegations conveyed to the heads of the Irish and Danish delegations their reaction to the paper given to them by the Danish and Norwegian delegations at the end of the resumed Eleventh Session. This paper was a draft of a proposed G-12 statement at that resumed session, never actually delivered, suggesting that the preparatory commission's mandate might be expanded to enable it to recommend amendments to the convention provisions in regard to the review conference and regarding TOT in the ISBA context. On behalf of the three, the UK head suggested an alternative draft differing from the original in two respects: (i) in proposing preparatory commission recommendations on modalities for application of convention provisions rather than on amendments to them and (ii) in applying this procedure to all of the ISBA regime rather than just to the provisions in regard to the two topics covered by the G-12 draft. The three hoped that the G-12 would promote the idea of a statement by the Conference President on the lines of their draft, together with a prior arrangement that his statement would not be challenged. The three were not in a position to give a commitment to signature in response. The Irish head of delegation, in reply, anticipated that the G-12 would be willing to convey the new draft to the President as one that would be helpful to the three, and probably to others, and to leave it to him, if willing, to seek to secure the acquiescence of the G-77 and the EE. If he made such an effort a result would hardly emerge until the Signature Session, when decisions on signature would already have been made by the three. Hence the Danish head of delegation urged the FRG and the UK to give 'not yet' as their worst decision rather than give a negative decision.

The Danish head of delegation reported the development to the other members of the G-12 and conveyed the draft to them, suggesting contacts in regard to further steps. Canada informed President Koh who reacted positively. Netherlands contacted the Peruvian head of delegation who undertook to forcefully recommend acceptance of the proposal by the G-77. Canada and Denmark both gave the draft to the Soviet Union. The G-12 decided not to launch a campaign in support of the move, but to speak individually to sympathetic delegations and to respond to queries. The writer has a recollection, unsupported by any available record, of an informal meeting hosted by President Koh in Geneva at about that time. The recollection places representatives of France, the FRG and the UK as present, as well as the Irish head of delegation and probably other Western representatives. At this meeting the lack of a commitment to signature in return for concessions again emerged as a significant obstacle to further action. In due course the effort petered out in the face of obstacles on both sides of the divide, and no such initiative was undertaken at the session.

DELEGATION

The delegation comprised the Minister for Foreign Affairs, Mr Gerald Collins, and the author.

PLENARY

The opening meeting was addressed by the Prime Minister of Jamaica, Mr Edward Seaga, who welcomed the UNCLOS III to his country and lauded its achievements. The special representative of the United Nations Secretary-General replied. Four days of the session were devoted to statements by 121 delegations, following an opening statement by President Koh.

The President posed, and answered in the positive, the question whether the Conference had achieved its fundamental objective of producing a comprehensive constitution for the oceans that would stand the test of time. He listed eight features of the convention as reasons for this conclusion. These included promotion and maintenance of international peace and security through replacement of a plethora of conflicting coastal state claims with agreed limits on the four zones of jurisdiction; preservation of high seas freedom of navigation through several varied provisions; and translating the principle that the resources of the deep seabed constituted the common heritage of mankind into a regime on the ISBA. He asserted that the convention's series of compromises and packages formed an integral whole, and that it was, therefore, not legally permissible to claim rights under it without being willing to assume corollary duties.

The Irish statement, delivered by the Minister for Foreign Affairs on the afternoon of the first day, was wide ranging. It recalled that Ireland was a member of the EEC and had, together with the other EEC members, transferred competences to it in certain matters covered by the convention. The statement endorsed that already made by the Danish delegation on behalf of the EEC and its member states (see below). The Minister referred to the convention as a most significant advance in the rule of international law. This was an enormous achievement of negotiation and diplomacy, over a long period of work and based on many sacrifices and compromises. Ireland had hoped that the convention would be adopted by consensus and, in due course, universally accepted. While this hope had been disappointed in regard to adoption, it still survived in regard to universal acceptance. The Minister characterised the framing of a regime for the international seabed area, an entirely new development of international law, as UNCLOS III's most historic achievement, even if it was at the root of most misgivings about the convention. He went on to make general observations about that regime, describing it as tentative. He urged joint efforts to put it into practice, bearing in mind that shortcomings could be identified and met by adaptation and by the results of the review conference.

The Minister mentioned the main issues dealt with by the convention that engaged major Irish national concerns—the EEZ, the continental shelf, MSR, preservation of the marine environment, delimitation, participation and peaceful settlement of disputes. He surveyed approvingly the compromises reached on each of these. Reflecting on the manner of resolution of the stalemate on criteria for delimitation, he expressed satisfaction that the relevant principles of international law, referred to in the convention provision, were those identified by the International Courts of Justice in the North Sea cases and confirmed in subsequent judicial and arbitral decisions.

In conclusion the Minister recalled the Irish statement during the opening general debate of the Conference. It had urged participants to pursue their legitimate interests in an enlightened manner. It had identified as the objective of the Conference the establishment of rules of law that would be binding, just and reasonable, and the setting up of machinery to secure their implementation. Adoption of the convention was a major step towards that objective. It was essential that it should enter into force as soon as possible and that all countries should become parties to it in due course.

The part of the Danish statement made on behalf of the EEC and its member states referred to the transfer of competences to the EEC by the member states in matters falling within the scope of the convention. The statement, therefore, welcomed the provisions allowing for participation by international organisations like the EEC in the convention, and also that the EEC had been expressly admitted as a signatory of the final act. He indicated EEC satisfaction with results obtained in matters within its competence, particularly in regard to fisheries and preservation of the marine environment. The part of his statement made solely on behalf of Denmark welcomed the convention. It attached great importance to achievement of universal acceptance, and in this context mentioned the efforts of the G-12, albeit unsuccessful. It emphasised the view that there was no satisfactory alternative to the convention.

The delegate of Peru, in the part of his statement made as Chairman of the G-77, paid tribute particularly to the role of the delegations of developing countries through their constructive, instructive and exemplary work in the negotiations. He described the convention as a cornerstone of the task of establishing a new international economic order, a UN goal. The basic achievement was establishment of the ISBA regime in accordance with the principle that the ISBA was the common heritage of mankind, a principle that had already become customary international law. The convention was an indivisible package, excluding the possibility of selective implementation or claims to rights under it by a non-party.

The US statement was made on the afternoon of the fourth day by a delegate who had been one of the Vice-Chairmen of the delegation throughout the Conference. He regretted that US hopes that the delegation would do more than sign the final act had been disappointed despite its efforts at the Eleventh Session. The US welcomed most provisions of the convention as reflecting prevailing international practice and serving the interests of the international community. However, the ISBA regime as in the convention would not serve those interests. Consensus on that regime had not been achieved and alternative ways of preserving national access to ISBA resources were necessary, just and permitted by international law. On future developments the statement was conciliatory in tone, but vague on how an accommodation between US and opposing interests might be reached.

On 10 December the final act and the convention were opened for signature. The convention was signed by 119 countries (including Ireland) and one country, Fiji, deposited its instrument of ratification. Statements were then made by the Jamaican Deputy Prime Minister and Foreign Minister and the UN Secretary-General. The President of the Conference made a closing statement.

The President described the number of first day signatures as a record in judicial history, enhanced by the fact that the signatories came from every region of the world and included both coastal states and land-locked and geographically disadvantaged states (LLGDS). From the 121 delegation statements he extrapolated five major themes. Firstly, the convention did not fully satisfy the interests of any state. Secondly, the convention was an integral package, thus precluding selective implementation. Thirdly, claims that it was a codification convention other than in the part in regard to the ISBA regime were incorrect. He instanced the provisions on passage through straits and archipelagos, as well as expansion of the concept of continental shelf jurisdiction, as examples, among many, of new concepts. He believed that a non-party could not invoke the continental shelf provisions. Fourthly, the doctrine of freedom of the high seas did not provide a legal basis for the grant by any state of exclusive title to a specific mine site in the ISBA—and he pleaded with the US to reconsider its position. Fifthly, there was emphasis on the vital importance of the forthcoming work of the preparatory commission.

Thus UNCLOS III closed.

Chapter XVIII

CONCLUSION

UNCLOS III was a conference of huge consequence to all states, not only because of the very important national interests involved, but also as a world forum for international cooperation, implementing one of the main functions of its parent body, the UN. While the Conference was proceeding it was described by US Secretary of State Kissinger as 'one of the most significant negotiations in diplomatic history'. At the Signature Session, Conference President Koh asserted that the objective of producing a comprehensive constitution for the oceans had been achieved. At that session also, Mr Gerald Collins, the Irish Minister for Foreign Affairs, described the convention as a most significant advancement in the rule of international law and an enormous achievement of negotiation and diplomacy.

UNCLOS III achieved a reform of the law of the sea that would otherwise have taken many decades to achieve, if indeed it were achieved at all. The most significant innovations it realised were probably (1) the establishment of an international regime covering the international seabed area (ISBA) outside national jurisdiction (a radical measure that placed a significant part of the planet's natural resources under the control of an international organisation whose membership is open to all states); (2) establishment of the exclusive economic zone (EEZ) of coastal state jurisdiction; and (3) clarification and development of jurisdictional rules in regard to protection of the marine environment. A significant factor that contributed to the success of UNCLOS III was the employment of some unprecedented procedural devices, particularly those designed to overcome the absence of a preparatory negotiating text as a principal working document. The obstacle was surmounted by conferring on the Committee Chairmen the authority to prepare single negotiating texts; by the acceptance of those texts by the participants as the basis for negotiations; and by the subsequent successive revisions of each of the seven texts. Each of the chairman's texts were revised initially by himself, with the whole text being revised by the Collegium afterwards. Each Collegium revision derived from debates in the plenary on proposals for revision, with steps along the way to formalising the text into a draft convention before the final revisions and submission to formal adoption. That this ambitious innovation succeeded was a tribute to the Conference participants, especially its officers, as was the fact that the Conference objective of decision-making, as far as possible, by consensus was achieved in regard to most of the issues.

The US dissatisfaction with Part XI of the convention on the ISBA regime was shared, at least partially, by some other industrialised countries, particularly those having deep seabed mining capacity. This meant realistically that the convention would not be accepted universally until some adaptations in respect of this part were made. That this came about in later years, fortunately without threatening the agreements reached in the other parts, is another story. In the meantime a large number of states, including Ireland, had signed the convention and quite a few had ratified it. Many others also accepted its provisions and implemented them. As to Part XI, the preparatory commission to prepare for the establishment of the International Sea Bed Authority and also for establishment of the International Tribunal for the Law of the Sea was set up, and went about its preparatory work. This work was eventually fully accepted when Part XI was subsequently adapted.

The convention entered into force on 14 November 1994 and its provisions are widely observed. Thus the main objective of UNCLOS III, a generally accepted law of the sea, was realised. This was so virtually immediately in regard to a large part of the convention (other than Part XI), to the advantage of the international community as a whole. Ireland warmly subscribed to this objective and shared in the advantage of its achievement.

The convention also saw significant advancement of Ireland's interests in regard to an extended coastal state fishery zone; measures in regard to anadromous species (salmon) recognising the special interest of the state of origin; a wide area of continental shelf jurisdiction; provisions on delimitation of areas of continental shelf jurisdiction, and also of the EEZ, between neighbouring states, which preserved the advantages Ireland derived from the ICJ decision in the North Sea cases; improvements in control, including enhancement of coastal state powers, in regard to marine scientific research, environmental protection and conservation; and all without unduly restricting freedom of navigation. A comparison with the pre-Conference summarisation of

Ireland's interests, seven in number (see Chapter III above), confirmed that all had fared well. A further considerable achievement was the adoption of the 'Community clause', a provision enabling the EEC to become a party to the convention. This was a very significant break-through for the EEC, not only in the immediate context but also in establishing its worldwide international legal status for all time. In this context the 'Community clause' served as a most useful precedent in many international negotiations in the following years. It was an achievement in which the Irish delegation played no small part. Apart from fulfilling its EEC Presidency role in this respect during the Third and Eighth Sessions of managing the preparations and pursuing the objective at the Conference, it was active in other sessions in helping to adapt the draft clause, in making supporting statements in the dis-cussions and in lobbying delegations.

The Conference made relatively little impact on Irish national public consciousness, due at least partly to the technicality and complexity of many of the issues involved and the length of the nego-tiations. Nevertheless, it ranks among the most important and successful negotiations undertaken up to then by the comparatively young Irish state. In brief, the Irish delegation had the considerable sat-isfaction of having achieved most of what it sought, including all that was essential. The convention formally entered into force for Ireland on 21 July 1996 following ratification on 21 June 1996.

ANNEX 1

GUIDE TO THE CONFERENCE SESSIONS

FIRST SESSION

Two weeks from 3 to 15 December 1973, in New York

The first session dealt exclusively, in plenary, with organisational and procedural matters, including establishment of a General Committee, three Main Committees and a Drafting Committee, and allocation of responsibilities among them; election of Conference officers; establishment of decision-making procedures. (This work was not fully completed until early in the Second Session.)

SECOND SESSION

Ten weeks from 20 June to 29 August 1974, in Caracas

A general debate in plenary was followed by commencement of negotiations in the three Main Committees, firstly in formal meetings and afterwards in informal meetings. The work was based mainly on the report of the Preparatory Committee, the numerous documents appended to it, and many further documents tabled by delegations at the session. In due course the Second and Third Committee Chairmen prepared main trend documents. These were a set of informal working papers based on the documents before, and discussions in, each Committee. Their purpose was to reflect the main trends, often multiple, among the proposals on each issue.

THIRD SESSION

Eight weeks from 17 March to 9 May 1975, in Geneva

Discussion proceeded in the three Main Committees. In the Second and Third Committees these were based on the main trends documents, and working groups were set up with a view to seeking agreement or at least a reduction of the alternative texts. After five weeks' discussions the Conference mandated the three Committee Chairmen to each prepare a single text on the topics in his Committee, as an informal negotiating aid. The text so prepared was dubbed the informal single negotiating text—the ISNT.

FOURTH SESSION

Eight weeks, from 15 March to 7 May 1976, in New York

The work was conducted mainly through examination of the ISNT at informal meetings of the three Committees. Each Committee Chairman was directed by the Conference to revise the ISNT on the basis of his assessment, in the light of the discussions in his Committee, that the revision on each topic would facilitate efforts to reach consensus. The new text so prepared was dubbed the revised single negotiating text—the RSNT. Separately a draft on peaceful settlement of disputes (PSD), prepared by the President, was examined in informal meetings of Plenary. It was revised by the President in the light of those discussions, but not included in the RSNT.

FIFTH SESSION

Seven weeks, from 2 August to 17 September 1976, in New York

The conference decided that the Main Committees should concentrate on key issues, on the understanding that further revision of the RSNT would not be undertaken at the session. Key issues identified in the Second and Third Committees included several involving important Irish interests. Plenary, in informal meetings, considered the texts on PSD as revised by the President following the Fourth Session. The President again revised these texts in the light of the discussions, and they were added to the RSNT as a fourth part.

SIXTH SESSION

Eight weeks, from 23 May to 15 July 1977, in New York

Negotiations continued mainly in the Main Committees as at the Fifth Session and (on PSD) in Plenary. The conference decided that these discussions should be a platform for preparation of a comprehensive text dealing in single document with all the topics covered by all four parts of the RSNT. The task of preparing this document was entrusted to a group comprising the President, the three Main Committee Chairmen, the Drafting Committee Chairman and the Special Rapporteur, which became known as the Collegium in respect of this function. The text so prepared was dubbed the informal composite negotiating text—ICNT. It also included drafts of a preamble and final clauses (prepared by the Conference Secretariat) although these had not been considered by the conference.

SEVENTH SESSION

A first part of eight weeks, from 28 March to 19 May 1978 in Geneva; a second part of four weeks, from 21 August to 15 September 1978, in New York

The Conference decided that the main concentration should be on seven identified core issues. Of these, three were within the mandate of the First Committee and four within the mandate of the Second Committee. A separate negotiating group was set up for each core issue. Irish interests were involved in all four Second Committee core issues, including vital interests in two of them. Only one (First Committee) negotiating group was fully successful at the session. Progress was made also in some of the others and on some issues during continuing work in the Third Committee. Progress was minimal in the two (Second Committee) negotiating groups involving vital Irish interests. Revision of the ICNT was not undertaken.

EIGHTH SESSION

A first part of six weeks, from 19 March to 27 April 1979, in Geneva; a second part of six weeks, from 19 July to 24 August 1979, in New York

Work proceeded in the negotiating groups and in the Third Committee. Some issues in the Second and Third Committees were effectively settled and considerable progress was made on some First Committee issues. A partial revision of the ICNT was effected at the end of the first part of the session, resulting in the ICNT Rev. 1. One of the two Second Committee core issues involving a vital Irish interest was covered in the revision, but there was no progress on the other. There were continuing efforts to review a Third Committee issue also involving an Irish interest. Despite indications of continuing progress at the second part, no further revision was undertaken. In Plenary the draft final clauses were examined for the first time, and Ireland, as EEC Presidency, introduced a proposal for a text to provide for EEC participation in the future convention.

Ninth session

*A first part of five weeks, from 3 March to 4 April 1980, in
New York; a second part of five weeks, from 28 July to
29 August 1980 in Geneva*

Work continued in those negotiating groups that had not completed
their tasks, including the two under the Second Committee dealing
with issues involving vital Irish interests. The Third Committee
reviewed an issue also involving an Irish interest and other issues were
raised briefly in the Committees. A further partial revision of the text
was effected at the end of each part of the session resulting in ICNT
Rev. 2 and Rev. 3 (Draft Convention) respectively. These revisions featured, *inter alia,* significant advances on First Committee matters and
incorporation of agreed texts on two issues of special interest for
Ireland, one each in the Second and Third Committee. Incorporation
of a text (not agreed) on the other issue in the Second Committee
involving a vital Irish interest was a set-back to that interest. Neither
revision incorporated a provision to enable EEC participation in the
future convention.

Tenth session

*A first part of seven weeks, from 9 March to 24 April 1981,
in New York; a second part of four weeks, from 3 to
28 August 1981 in Geneva*

Optimistic expectations were disappointed by the new US
Administration's conclusion that it was dissatisfied with the Draft
Convention, and its decision to conduct a review, which would take
some time, to identify what changes, if any, would make it acceptable.
Pending the review the US was not prepared to complete negotiations.
The Conference President having died, a new President was elected. At
his suggestion the Conference continued to work on the few outstanding issues, pending US return to negotiation. In the face of US
reluctance it was decided to hold a second part to the session. As the
US was still not ready to negotiate at the second part, work on the outstanding issues again continued. An informal procedure was devised to
enable the US to explain its concerns, which related exclusively to First
Committee issues (the regime for the ISBA). Attempts to have exchanges
on these concerns between the US and the developing countries proved
abortive until a secret caucus meeting was arranged near the end of the
session. Meanwhile, on the basis of the continuing work on the outstanding issues, a partial revision of the Draft Convention was effected

at the end of the session, resulting in Draft Convention Rev. 1. The main element of the revision was a new (and agreed) text on the outstanding Second Committee issue in which Ireland had a vital interest. Again the revision did not incorporate any text on participation in the future Convention by the EEC or any other non-state entity.

ELEVENTH SESSION

A first part of eight weeks, from 6 March to 30 April 1982, in New York; a second part of 3 days, from 22 to 24 September 1982, in New York

The session proceeded through a pre-planned series of stages, involving, firstly, partial revisions of the Draft Convention reflecting general agreements reached in consultations and approved in Plenary; secondly, formalisation of the Draft Convention, and submission of, and decision on, formal amendments to it; and, finally, decision on adoption of the Convention. Meanwhile, there was a stand-off between the US and some other industrialised countries on one side, and the developing countries on the other, regarding the regime for the ISBA. The latter refused to negotiate on successive documents submitted by the US based on its review findings reached before the session. Various attempts to create a basis for negotiation between the two sides failed. A group of Western delegates (including Ireland) presented an alternative compromise document to no avail. The revisions of the Draft Convention included incorporation of an adequate clause on EEC participation in the future Convention. None of the few formal amendments put to a vote was adopted. Finally the Convention was adopted by vote on the last day of the first part of the session. The second part was concerned only with formal matters, for example processing the Drafting Committee's recommendations on the Convention texts, preparation of the final act of the Conference and deciding on the venue and dates for the Signature Session.

SIGNATURE SESSION

One week, from 6 to 10 December 1982, in Montego Bay

Following a formal opening, a statement by the Conference President set the proceedings in motion. Statements by 121 delegations were made over the first four days. These included a statement by the Minister for Foreign Affairs on behalf of Ireland, and one on behalf of the EEC and its member states by the Danish delegation, as current holder of the EEC Presidency. On the fifth day the Convention was opened for signature. It was signed on behalf of 119 states, including Ireland.

ANNEX 2

GUIDE TO THE GROUPS

Several groups of states met regularly *en marge* of the Conference mainly, but not exclusively, to identify common objectives and to seek to pursue them collectively.

The groups included the long established regional groups traditional in the UN context as follows:

- The African Group
- The Asian Group
- The Eastern European Group (EE)
- The Latin American and Caribbean Group (LAC)
- The Western European and Others Group (WEOG)

The membership of these groups is largely self-explanatory, except for WEOG, where the 'Others' comprise Australia, Canada and New Zealand and, for some purposes, the US. In the context of UN institutions and bodies under UN auspices these groups were particularly used for distribution of electoral offices and seats. They were also fora for consideration of procedural matters. There was a certain element of political purpose in each of these groups when formed, a factor in their establishment, but by the time of UNCLOS III some were significantly more cohesive in this respect than others—the EE being the most cohesive and the WEOG least so. An unofficial Arab Group emerged in the UN General Assembly in the early 1970s, crossing but not taking from, the African and Asian Groups, and cooperating on common Arab interests. It became active at UNCLOS III from about the Seventh Session, particularly in seeking curtailment of the area of coastal state continental shelf jurisdiction.

Also established in the UN system, although much later than, and not unrelated to, the regional groups was the Group of 77 (G-77).

Membership of this group comprises the Third World (developing and underdeveloped) states that combine in the group to pursue their common purpose of adoption of measures in the UN context to help their economic development. Almost all of the African, Asian and LAC regional groups are also members of this group. While its original membership was 77, the expansion of UN membership carried into the group so that by the commencement of UNCLOS III it had comfortably more than 100 members. At the conference it was most active in regard to the emerging regime for the (ISBA).

Most of the other groups were specific to UNCLOS III and based on particular shared interests.

THE COASTAL STATES GROUP (CSG)

The CSG was composed of coastal states seeking to maximise in the future convention the advantages for coastal states, particularly in the extent of coastal state zones and the rights and jurisdiction accruing to coastal states in such zones. This group had come together at the (preparatory) Seabed Committee where its membership was confined largely to Third World states. It continued to be active from the beginning of the Conference and was gradually joined by countries other than Third World states, including Ireland at the Fifth Session. Being very numerous, the members of the group inevitably had a wide range of variations on the basic position. Nevertheless, it achieved sufficient cohesion to figure as a very significant force.

THE GROUP OF MARITIME STATES (G-17)

This group was active at least from the Third Session and comprised the main major maritime powers that shared the common purpose of protecting rights, mainly traditional high seas rights and freedoms, against erosion through expansion of coastal state jurisdiction and rights. Composed of a number of globally important states, including major powers, it was clearly influential.

THE GROUP OF LAND-LOCKED AND GEOGRAPHICALLY DISADVANTAGED STATES (LLGDS)

This group was also active from the beginning of the Conference. It evolved from the group of land-locked states formed at UNCLOS I. These were joined at UNCLOS III by states with short coastlines or situate in confined seas, whose benefits from expanded coastal state jurisdiction would be negligible. Their common purpose was to achieve in the future convention confirmation of access to the sea (for land-locked states) and to natural resources of the sea, whether through restricting coastal state jurisdiction or acquiring special rights for themselves in coastal state zones.

THE MARGINEERS GROUP

This group was formed at the Third Session by states having broad continental margins off their coasts. At first it comprised ten states, including Ireland, and was later enlarged to include two more. Its purpose was to secure acceptance of coastal state continental shelf jurisdiction throughout the margin. It was led at first by Australia, but later Ireland and Canada became joint coordinators and chief spokesmen. The Irish delegation acted alone in that capacity in the final stages.

THE GROUP OF 29 (G-29)

The G-29 was formed at the Seventh Session by states already more loosely aligned in pursuit of a particular solution on delimitation of areas of marine jurisdiction between neighbouring states. Its membership subsequently enlarged to about 35. The group's position was based on the decision of the International Court of Justice in the North Sea cases, which identified equitable principles as the overriding criterion for agreement to resolve differences in delimitation situations. Ireland acted as the group's coordinator and chief spokesman.

THE GROUP OF 5/ GROUP OF 7 (G-5/G-7);

This group was formed at the Eleventh Session in support of US suggestions for amendment of the provisions for the regime of the ISBA. In addition to the US it comprised France, the FRG, the UK and Japan as well as Belgium and Italy. These were among the countries having deep seabed mining capacity.

THE EVENSEN GROUP

Unlike the groups previously mentioned, the Evensen group was not an interest group. It emerged at the Second Session when Minister Jens Evensen, head of the Norwegian delegation, invited heads of delegations and legal experts from a limited number of delegations, mainly from Western countries, to engage in informal exchanges on some topics within the mandate of the Second Committee (i.e. most of the hitherto traditional law of the sea topics). The group subsequently enlarged, at first to include some delegations from all regions and later, to become open to all. It also widened its agenda to cover topics from the other Committees and the Plenary. The Irish first attended the group at intersessional meetings between the Third and Fourth Sessions, when environmental and continental shelf issues were discussed. Evensen adopted the *modus operandi* of sending to the relevant Chairman, on his own responsibility, drafts based on the discussions in his group.

GROUP OF 10/ GROUP OF 12 (G-10/G-12)

Likewise, G-10/G-12 was not an interest group. It was formed at the Eleventh Session, comprising at first ten, and later twelve, delegates from Western states, including Ireland. It sought to bridge the gap between the G-5/G-7 and the G-77 on the regime for the ISBA. It spontaneously prepared, for the assistance of the Conference President, compromise draft texts on some of the controversial issues designed to be acceptable to both sides. The members also engaged, both spontaneously and at the President's request, in informal exchanges with the two sides.

THE EUROPEAN ECONOMIC COMMUNITY (EEC)

The EEC and its member states were not a group specific to UNCLOS III. It was in fact both established practice and necessary for this group to consult regularly, both generally and *en marge* at international meetings to arrange for safeguarding of EEC interests and pursuit of common objectives. At UNCLOS III, EEC interests arose specifically from the fact that competences in some fields covered in the Conference rested in the EEC rather than in the member states, thus requiring an EEC position in the negotiation (reached through a coordination process, in EEC parlance). In addition the practice extended to seeking common positions among the member states on foreign policy matters as far as possible (reached through a cooperation process). Both management of coordination and cooperation and spokesmanship fell to the member state holding the EEC Presidency at the time, which changed every six months. (Ireland held the Presidency twice during the conference, covering the Third Session and the second part of the Eighth Session).

This guide does not list various informal negotiating and consultative groups set up from time to time under the auspices of the institutions of the conference with a view to facilitating progress in negotiation. These were *ad hoc* and are explained in the narrative.

FURTHER READING

The Official Records of the Third United Nations Conference on the Law of the Sea Vols I to XVII

The United Nations Conference on the Law of the Sea 1982: A Commentary, Vols I to VII Center for Oceans Law and Policy, University of Virginia

United Nations, *Treaty Series*, vol. 516, p. 205.
United Nations, *Treaty Series*, vol. 450, p. 82.
United Nations, *Treaty Series*, vol. 559, p. 285.
United Nations, *Treaty Series*, vol. 499, p. 311.

Anglo-Norwegian Fisheries Case (UK v Norway) 1951 International Court of Justice Report 116.
North Sea Continental Shelf 1969 International Court of Justice Report 3.
Continental Shelf (Tunisia/Libyan Arab Jamahiriya) 1982 International Court of Justice Report 18.
Anglo-French Continental Shelf Case 1977 International Law Report 54, p. 6

UN Vienna Convention on the Law of Treaties 1969

ABBREVIATIONS

ASEAN	Association of South Eastern Asian States
COREPER	Committee of Permanent Representatives of the EEC
CSG	Coastal States Group*
EE	Eastern European Group
EEC	European Economic Community
EEC-9	EEC Group of 9
EEC-10	EEC Group of 10
EEZ	Exclusive Economic Zone
FRG	Federal Republic of Germany
G-5	Group of 5*
G-7	Group of 7*
G-10	Group of 10*
G-11	Group of 11
G-12	Group of 12*
G-17	Group of 17*
G-29	Group of 29*
G-77	Group of 77
GSI	Geological Survey of Ireland
ICJ	International Court of Justice
ICNT	Informal Composite Negotiating Text (UNCLOS III)
IDC	Inter-Departmental Committee (Irish Government)
ILC	International Law Commission
IMCO	International Maritime Consultative Organisation
IOC	Intergovernmental Oceanographic Commission (UNESCO)
ISBA	International Seabed Area
ISNT	Informal Single Negotiating Text (UNCLOS III)
LAC	Latin Americal and Carribean regional group
LLGDS	Land-locked and Geographically Disadvantaged States*
MSR	Marine Scientific Research
NATO	North Atlantic Treaty Organisation
NBST	National Board of Science and Technology
OAU	Organisation of African Unity
PIP	Preparatory Investment Protection
PLO	Palestinian Liberation Organization
PR	Permanent Representative (UN)
PSD	Peaceful Settlement of Disputes

RSNT	Revised Single Negotiating Text (UNCLOS III)
TAC	Total Allowable Catch
TOT	Transfer of Technology
UN	United Nations
UNESCO	United Nations Educational, Scientific Cultural Organization
UNCITRAL	United Nations Commission on International Trade Law
UNCTAD	UN Conference on Trade and Development

* see Annex 2 for Guide to UNCLOS III groups

INDEX

A

African Group, 31, 156
  membership, 269
African states
  delimitation, 37
  ISBA, 107, 111, 214
  support for EEZs, 3
Agriculture and Fisheries, Department
  of, 7, 17
Aguilar, Andres
  candidate for Presidency, 196
  Chairman of Second Committee, 29,
    35, 76, 156, 174–7, 182
  meeting with Brian Lenihan, 172
  negotiations on delimitation, 210, 212
Aiken, Frank, 5
Algeria
  delimitation, 180
  regime of islands, 61
Amerasinghe, Shirley H., 27, 76, 172
  death, 194, 196
  debate on Presidency, 131–2
  organisational proposals, 77
  proposes ISNT (informal single nego-
    tiating text), 58
Amoco Cadiz, 141
anadromous species
  Second Session, 39–40
  Sixth Session, 117
  Seventh Session, 140
  Eighth Session, 148, 152
  Ninth Session, 173–7
  Tenth Session (II), 213
  Attorney General's statement, 33
  see also fisheries
Anglo-Norwegian fisheries case, 4
Arab Group, 32, 100
  continental shelf jurisdiction, 103,
    135, 174, 176–7
  NLM participation, 237
archipelagos

Third Session, 65
Fourth Session, 78
Argentina
  continental shelf jurisdiction, 80, 153,
    176, 221
  decision not to sign convention, 248
  fishing rights, 174
  Margineers Group, 57–8
  MSR, 183
  PSD, 138
  regime of islands, 38
  revenue sharing, 154
  vote on Draft Convention, 238
Article 38 of the Statute of the
  International Court of Justice, 209,
  210, 211
Asian Group, 31
  appointment of new Conference
    President, 195
  membership, 269
Attorney General: addresses to conference, 33–4, 38, 41, 55, 91–2
Attorney General, Office of the, 7
  instructions to delegates, 18, 53, 74
Australia
  continental shelf jurisdiction, 80, 103,
    153, 175, 176, 177
  environment, 84
  final negotiations, 245
  ISBA, 207, 208
  Margineers Group, 58
  MSR, 44, 183
  peaceful settlement of disputes, 48
  PIP, 245
  PSD, 107–8
  revenue sharing, 154, 155
  seabed mining, 146
  straddle stocks, 200, 232–3, 238
  vote on Draft Convention, 238
Austria
  continental shelf jurisdiction, 81, 82, 135
  vote on Draft Convention, 238

W

Waldheim, Kurt, 27, 29
WEOG (Western European and Others
    Group), 10, 31, 100
  membership, 269
  PSD, 107
West Germany *see* FRG
Western European and Others Group
    see WEOG
Western Samoa: regime of islands, 38
Wuensche, Harry, 163

Y

Yankov, Alexander, 29
Yugoslavia, 215
  delimitation, 180
  vote on Draft Convention, 239

Z

Zaire, 201
Zambia, 201
Zimbabwe, 201
Zuleta, Bernardo, 29, 172, 198–9
  Signature Session, 246, 247